The Bloomsbury Introduction to Adaptation Studies

Adapting the Canon in Film, TV, Novels and Popular Culture

Yvonne Griggs

BLOOMSBURY ACADEMIC
LONDON • NEW YORK • OXFORD • NEW DELHI • SYDNEY

BLOOMSBURY ACADEMIC
Bloomsbury Publishing Plc
50 Bedford Square, London, WC1B 3DP, UK
1385 Broadway, New York, NY 10018, USA

BLOOMSBURY, BLOOMSBURY ACADEMIC and the Diana logo are trademarks
of Bloomsbury Publishing Plc

First published 2016
Reprinted by Bloomsbury Academic 2019, 2020

A catalogue record for this book is available from the British Library.

A catalog record for this book is available from the Library of Congress.

ISBN: HB: 978-1-4411-3848-4
         PB: 978-1-4411-6614-2
       ePDF: 978-1-4411-6702-6
      eBook: 978-1-4411-6769-9

Typeset by Integra Software Services Pvt. Ltd.
Printed and bound in Great Britain

To find out more about our authors and books visit www.bloomsbury.com
and sign up for our newsletters.

The Bloomsbury Introduction to Adaptation Studies

Permissions

The author and Bloomsbury Publishing Plc are grateful to the following for granting permission to use noted images and works:

- 'Havisham' from *Meantime* (© Carol Ann Duffy 1993, reproduced by permission of the author c/o Rogers, Cleridge & White Ltd, 20 Powis Mews, London, W11 1JN)
- 'A Fine Pickle', Salman Rushdie c/o The Wylie Agency, Inc and The Wylie Agency UK, Ltd.
- *Jane Eyre* (2006) screen grabs, courtesy of the BBC and with agreement of Sandy Welch, Ruth Wilson and Georgie Henley
- 'In Defence of Literary Adaptation as Cultural Production', in *M/C-a Journal of Media & Culture* 10.2 (2007), creative commons licence http://creativecommons.org/licenses/by-nc-nd/3.0/legalcode
- Whip Grafting image (licensed by The Florida Center for Instructional Technology)

Disclaimer: Every effort has been made to contact copyright holders for their permission to use material. The publishers would be grateful to hear from any copyright holder who is not here acknowledged and will undertake to rectify any omissions in future editions of this title.

For Rob, my Duderino

Contents

Drawing Conclusions

Preface

What exactly do we mean when we refer to something as an adaptation? How, if at all, does the term adaptation differ from the process of adaptation? What are we adapting and why? Writing in *The Guardian* about the stage adaptation of his Booker-prize winning novel, *Midnight's Children*, Salman Rushdie defines 'adaptation' in its broadest sense as 'translation, migration and metamorphosis, all the means by which one thing becomes another' – a process that 'goes beyond the realm of art into the rest of life'. It is, notes Rushdie, all-encompassing – a natural and ongoing process that permeates our lives as well as our literature. However, the terms we apply to texts seen to adapt existing narratives are more problematic and less easy to define. Academic interest in the study of textual adaptation continues to grow and, like the texts themselves, to evolve. There are a number of acclaimed and highly complex publications, both theoretical and case study based, that explore the current status of Adaptation Studies. And yet, there is a conspicuous absence of publications aimed at providing readers with a comprehensive and accessible route to the study of literary adaptation in its widest sense. This study guide provides a clear overview of debates past and present and equips readers with an all-round introduction to the history and theory of Adaptation Studies. It offers a series of practical ways in to critiquing the processes which underpin literary adaptation and a range of creative approaches to the application of theory. While the majority of current publications take the adaptation of literature to screen as the focus for debate, we deal here with a number of canonical core texts and their adaptive 'journeys' not only into other media platforms like film but into other prose and performance-based forms. The text outlines the various approaches adaptations theorists have adopted over time and maps the emergence of adaptations scholarship, but it is by engaging with these theories via their practical application to prescribed texts in each section that we shall come to a better understanding of what adaptation studies entails and why it is an increasingly popular field of academic enquiry.

Acknowledgements

I would like to express my thanks to three people whose tireless support for this project has ensured its journey to completion: my editor, David Avital, for his endless patience and timely advice; my current head of school, Alan Davison (University of New England), for his guidance and encouragement throughout the writing process; and finally my partner, Rob Griggs, for putting up with all of those long nights and lost weekends.

1

An Introduction to Adaptation Studies and the Canon

A theoretical overview

Despite its increasing popularity as an intriguing and accessible means to the exploration of literature and the moving image, adaptation studies is a field of academic theorizing that forever finds itself in defence of its own existence; it is often viewed as an interloper in literature departments and film departments alike, and as a 'catch-all' in the area of cultural studies. As a consequence, it is constantly preoccupied with theoretical 'models' generated to validate its position as a contender for scholarly debate. These models provide meaningful frameworks within which to couch discussion of the relationship between a body of texts rather than definitive answers as to the nature of that relationship, and if we trace the evolution of adaptation studies as an academic mode of enquiry we find that, like the texts they aim to explore, the models generated to examine these texts, are themselves recycled, revisited and revised ideas, originating from a range of academic disciplines. The interdisciplinary nature of adaptation studies ensures a certain inclusivity, offering a dynamic convergence of diverse academic disciplines, from film, literature, history, languages, creative writing, media, music, drama, performance art, visual art, and new media; but its inherently fractured nature can also herald division and competing interest. Reductive preoccupation with disputes about value systems can dominate discussion to its detriment, and questions of fidelity or the so-called 'faithfulness' of one text to another can result in hierarchical positioning of texts according to 'type' and presumed seniority. But in recent years, adaptations theorists have forged frameworks for discussion that take us away from such loaded lines of enquiry, and during the course of our studies we shall apply a number of theories that help us to explore the relationship between a body of prescribed texts, from the canonical to the populist, and operating within a wide range of media platforms. 'Models' abound and none are perfect but all lead to productive debate.

The series of analytical and creative exercises found in this study are designed to fine tune our understanding of theory. However, it is useful at this stage to outline the evolution of theories that surround the field of adaptation studies. Prior to the 1957 publication of George Bluestone's highly influential text, *Novels into Film*, discussion of adaptations to screen in particular, revolved around issues of fidelity; but Bluestone notes that 'changes are *inevitable* the moment one abandons the linguistic for the visual medium' and argues that 'it is insufficiently recognized that the end products of novel and film represent different aesthetic genera, as different from each other as ballet is from architecture'. It is, he contends, 'fruitless to say that film A is better or worse than novel B' as there is no medium-specific equivalency between the two (5). Since the seventies, classification systems supporting this viewpoint have been generated by a number of theorists in order to challenge the primacy of the fidelity debate and its inherent assumption that there is an identifiable and transferrable 'essence' or 'spirit' embodied in each text. Geoffrey Wagner, for example, offers us three types of 'adaptation': transposition (where the text is 'given directly on screen with a minimum of interference'); commentary (where an original is 'taken and either purposely or inadvertently altered in some respect'); and analogy ('which must represent a fairly considerable departure for the sake of making another work of art') (222–223). Here adaptations are measured in degrees, according to their 'faithfulness' (or lack of) to the 'original' text being adapted. Writing back in the eighties, Andrew observes that 'the most frequent and most tiresome discussion of adaptation concerns fidelity and transformation', and the pursuit of 'something essential about an original text' (28–32). And yet, the taxonomies generated by theorists like Andrew return us inevitably to *some* consideration of fidelity, even if only via a *denial* of its significance. From the early seventies to the late nineties, the comparative approach to the study of adaptations prevails, and as a result adaptations are constantly critiqued in relation to a so-called 'source' text, placed at the centre of discussion and thus given a privileged position within adaptations discourse. Attempts by theorists to generate ways of moving discussion away from the fidelity debate continue, however, to yield meaningful discussion of the relationship between text and adaptation: Michael Klein and Gillian Parker (9), Dudley Andrew (28–37), Kamilla Elliott (133–183), and Thomas Leitch ('Jekyll, Hyde': 28–50) have all posited similarly effective taxonomies that aid our understanding, and some of these systems will be explored in closer detail through our analysis of texts found in each section.

Other theorists take a more narratological approach to the study of adaptations, foregrounding the significance of identifying codes and signifiers that translate across different media, but again, such models inevitably return us to a comparative mode of engagement with 'source' texts and their adaptive offspring. Though not writing directly to the practice of adaptation, some of the vocabulary and systems identified by French literary theorist Gerard Genette help to inform our understanding of the processes at work in the reconfiguration of one text to another medium. Genette couches the discussion of such transmutations in the accessible language of horticulture, naming the 'source' text as 'hypotext' onto which the adapted narrative (or 'hypertext' as Genette labels it) grafts itself (5). The work of fellow literary structuralists like Claude Levi-Strauss and Roland Barthes (whose ideas are influenced by the earlier work of Soviet Formalist Vladimir Propp) has also added, if indirectly, to the adaptations debate; in his ground-breaking text *Novel to Film: An Introduction to the Theory of Adaptation*, Brian McFarlane builds upon the ideas of Barthes as a means to steering the adaptation debate towards a closer consideration of the mechanics of the processes at the heart of adaptation. He asks, *what* are the essential, identifiable and transferable elements of a narrative, and *how* do we transfer them to a different medium? Similarly, in *Coming to Terms: the Rhetoric of Narrative in Fiction and Film*, narratologist Seymour Chatman separates the 'story' from the 'discourse' (or in lay terms, the 'what' from the 'how') of adaptations practice, and we shall be applying the findings of both McFarlane and Chatman in a number of the practical exercises in sections two to four.

Sarah Cardwell builds upon Genette's horticultural metaphor by comparing cultural adaptation with biological adaptation and finds perceptions of the latter far more positive than those associated with the former. She observes that the assumption of betterment and evolution that characterizes our study of genetics does not, regrettably, transfer to our assumptions about cultural adaptation. In cultural adaptation (which we may read here as the adaptation of narratives), she argues, the newly formed adaptation is seen not as a product of evolution and/or betterment but as an 'aid to the survival of the original' – a means merely to 'revitalize the source'

(13). Many of the models generated by theorists are inherently geared towards the centralized positioning of what is deemed the 'source' text, with the adaptive offspring circulating that 'primary' text, and this inevitably leads to the kind of hierarchical value judgements that have haunted the adaptations discipline for many years. Robert Stam notes that discourse surrounding the study of adaptations is 'profoundly moralistic, awash in terms such as *infidelity, betrayal, defamation, violation, vulgarization*, and *desecration*, each accusation carrying its specific charge of outraged negativity' (54). In order to avoid a reductive, values-based engagement with the study of adaptations, Cardwell advocates an approach that sees the adaptation as 'the gradual development of a "meta-text"' that has a relationship with prior adaptations as well as a so-called originary text (25); rather than defining the source text/ hypotext as the 'major part of the adaptation's identity' (19–20), she sees the adaptation as a new thing that takes its place within a different set of cultural referents that relate to its *own* era of production, its *own* industry structures, its *own* issues-based agenda, its *own* cluster of narratives.

Critical debate has, since the late nineties, moved towards a more conscious consideration of the socio-cultural and industrial influences at work in the translation of texts. In their *Pulping Fictions* series and *Adaptations: From Text to Screen, Screen to Text*, Deborah Cartmell and Imelda Whelehan consciously shift the boundaries of our engagement with adaptations by widening the field of debate through inclusion of a different type of case study (explored first and foremost in its own right rather than as an appendage to its so-called 'source' text) and a closer examination of the cultural context surrounding the reception and consumption of adapted texts. Leitch also continues to probe the boundaries of adaptation studies; film adaptations are, according to Leitch, a discrete cinematic genre, and though film theorists may dispute such claims, his genre-based framework for the discussion of adaptations can lead to intriguing debate ('Adaptation, the Genre'). Simone Murray similarly widens the parameters of discussion by refocusing the critical lens, from matters of 'aesthetic evaluation' to matters of economic and industrial significance. Linda Hutcheon (*Theory*), Julie Sanders, and Stam have in recent years further reinvigorated debates concerning intertextuality, bringing us back to the notion that all narratives are part of 'an endless process of recycling, transformation and mutation with no clear point of origin' (66). Work undertaken in the field has blossomed to such an extent in the last decade that to name and identify the approaches of all scholars involved would be exhaustive and counter-productive, but through engaging with ideas of key theorists (and through referencing the work of many other scholars) we shall come to a clearer understanding of this popular field of academic enquiry.

Adaptation as 'creative process' rather than as 'academic critique' has been around for as long as stories have been told. The medium used to *tell* these recycled narratives that permeate our culture varies: but the tale and its place within our culture remains a constant in one form or another. The specific origin of its birth may not always be clear, and it may be reshaped by a wide range of influences at work in its textual transformation (by the adapter's authorial intent, its mode of delivery and reception, the socio-cultural climate of its era of production, and so on), yet the tale itself continues to thrive. The adaptive process works to ensure a story's on-going rebirth within other communication platforms, other political and cultural contexts; the various taxonomies generated by adaptations theorists give us a framework for discussion of these revised narratives and the array of influences at work in their textual re-visions. They promote discussion that takes us away from the tired fidelity debate that has particularly dominated consideration of the adaptation of literature to film, where issues related to hierarchy and the albatross fidelity remain prominent (if only at times in denial thereof) despite attempts to refocus the critical lens. The question 'Yes, but is it as good as the book?' continues to haunt matters relating to screen adaptations: even if it is merely a ghostly presence, shadowing but not dominating debate in academic circles, it remains a concrete manifestation for reviewers in the twenty-first century, especially when we are dealing with the screen adaptation of works revered as part of the canon. Can the adaptation of a text be as good or better than the canonical text that it is supposedly adapting? Who determines that? How and why is it an issue? Debates, regardless of the theory we are dealing with, still tend to revolve around case studies to the dismay of scholars like Robert Ray who bewail the textual analytical approach that this entails as a natural by-product (39); however, it is an approach that theorists inevitably return to, and one that is consciously embraced in this study as a means of examining both the canonical texts that provide the springboard for our exploration and their relationship with the varied texts they engage with.

Though not the one and only source of an adaptation's identity, the canonical text that an adaptation is in dialogue with nevertheless plays a vital part in that adaptation's 'identity': each adaptation is a new thing in and of itself, but it evolves from a complex web of adaptive processes related to existing narratives, cultural mores, industrial practices, and to the agenda of those engaging in its construction. The relationship between canonical texts and their filmic reincarnations has been central to debate since the birth of cinema, and interest in this specific adaptive platform has proved to be the mainstay of adaptations scholars' theorizing for the past fifty years, sometimes to the exclusion of debate concerning other forms of 'adaptation', and without due consideration of the fact that the recycling of stories has been a cultural practice for such a very long time. This study traces the rich and varied adaptive journeys of a number of canonical texts from the Anglo-American canon; however, while most studies with an adaptations focus tend to cluster around adaptation to screen, here, we explore the canonical text's relationship with *all* types of adaptation produced across a variety of media platforms. During the course of our examination of adaptations related to four core canonical novels, we engage in close analysis of the processes involved in the transition of narrative from page to screen and stage space, looking at the very different storytelling techniques employed by adapters working in a performative, audio-visual medium. But the study of adaptations that move from novel to novel yields a similarly fertile and intriguing line of enquiry; how and why do such adapters work with the narrative to reposition its textual politics and/or its target audience within the same prose medium? To what end is narrative appropriated in these novels as, for example, Young Adult literature, soft-porn erotica, graphic novel?

Defining the canon and its relationship with adaptation studies

One of the first questions to address in a study of this nature is who defines the canon and what are the identifiable markers of works seen fit for the label canonical text. In traditional readings of the canon, texts given canonical status are viewed as works of individual creative genius: they are an individual expression from a specific writer's imagination – one which 'speaks to' universal and timeless values and that enshrines a certain way of thinking that is, supposedly, readily perceived and received by all readers. When viewed from this traditional standpoint, it is inevitable that adapters and their resultant adaptations are held to account and found lacking. To revise and reinscribe a work of 'individual creative genius' with impunity seems an impossible task. However, such a traditional stance is difficult to defend, especially in today's theory-conscious climate: for many reasons, academics have generated a whole host of theories (based on issues of race, class, gender, sexual choice) that challenge this traditional view of the relationship between writer and audience, and as a consequence of that, between canonical text and adapted text. How, we may ask, can beliefs be universally applied to or received by people from diverse ethnic backgrounds, class systems, or gender positions? In a traditional sense, the 'universal values' supposedly espoused by canonical texts serve to 'enshrine' the beliefs of specific groups and as such will inevitably serve their own often elitist agenda. Film theorist André Bazin notes that the 'individualistic conception of the "author" and of the "work"' is a relatively recent concern (23). Such a concept would, for example, have had no validity in Elizabethan and Jacobean times when writers like William Shakespeare were adept in the art of 'borrowing' the ideas of other writers; the very notion of a stable 'work' by the 'author', Shakespeare, would have been alien to thought in this age and 'borrowing' seen as an age-old accepted means of creating. Such 'borrowing' is clearly a practice which would, by traditional definitions, lead us to question the place of Shakespeare's plays – and works by many other writers – within the canon of great literature. The 'romantic' view of literature as the end product of an individual's creative genius is itself a cultural by-product of a specific literary era dating back to the end of the eighteenth century. Notions of authorship in a postmodernist post-millennial context are inherently problematic. Stories are, as Stam notes, constantly engaged in 'an endless process of recycling, transformation and mutation with no clear point of origin' (66). Whether texts engage with the ideas and narratives of earlier texts in a conscious manner or in a less overt and more tentative way, there remains little room for doubt that canonical texts both feed into and off of the thematic and narratological ideas of other texts: they are neither conceived nor consumed in a cultural vacuum.

The creative practice of layering as a way of enriching narrative whilst also paying homage to the literature and ideas that precede it is one that writers have engaged in for centuries. For some, such layering has a more political bent: feminist critic Adrienne Rich, writing during the height of feminist thought in the seventies, argues that this referencing of earlier texts functions as a means to countering the ideas and the status of precursor texts. The act of 're-vision', of 'looking back, of seeing with fresh eyes' enables the writer to 'ent[er] an old text from a new critical direction' (18) and thus to challenge the ideas embedded within it. Sanders notes, however, that by engaging with works from the canon, such 'counter-discourses' inevitably 're-inscribe the canon': writerly acts of 're-vision' *may* challenge the canon but they also serve to acknowledge its status, even if they do so in 'new and critical ways' (105). As we shall see when we explore texts that take, for example, a very different narrative viewpoint or place the narrative within another socio-cultural context or media platform, adapters prompt us not only to engage with ideas embedded in their own text but to question those found in its literary forerunner. Susana Onega and Christian Gutleben argue that what is at work in textual transitions that set themselves up in relation to canonical texts from the Victorian era, is a 'double process' termed 'refraction' – a process 'involving the ways in which a text exploits and integrates both the reflections of a previous text and the new light shed on the original work by its rewriting' (7). Rather than focusing on textual interactions in general and intertextuality in particular, 'refraction involves the assumption of a dialectic relation between the canonical and the postmodernist texts' they inspire (8). Instead of exploring the intertextuality of such writings in an attempt to understand the relationship between the 'new products and the old codes' embedded in the canonical text, Onega and Gutleben urge us to view neither as the 'source' text, placing the emphasis on the way in which *each* text 'sheds light on the other' and thus 'obliterat[ing] hierarchical or evaluative distinction between the two related texts – however canonical one of them might be' (9). If we adopt a similar approach to the study of adaptation in general, viewing one text as a 'reading prism' for another, tired debates of an evaluative nature dissipate. Moreover, as Leitch astutely observes, 'every text', whether canonical or populist, 'offers itself as an invitation to be rewritten' (*Film Adaptation* 16).

Such re-visionist adaptations become part of the ongoing debate surrounding the canonical texts that engender their creation but they can also attain their own place within that canon: they are neither consumed by nor solely defined by it but rather present us with other manifestations of the cultural anxieties that circulate around the initiating canonical text *and* its various adaptations. The canonization of texts is, like adaptation itself, an ongoing process that reacts to and interacts with the cultural and critical preoccupations of its time of production. Cora Kaplan maintains that the mythic status of Greek and Roman classics, and of biblical narratives, have now been 'displaced' by novels like *Jane Eyre, Moby Dick, David Copperfield,* and *The Scarlet Letter*: they provide a fertile site for further exploration of ongoing cultural anxieties related to sexuality, identity, scientific progress, religious belief, and urban growth (133). Brian A. Rose concurs, referring to the canonical texts of the nineteenth century as 'cultural text[s]' – texts that evolve as they are adapted, 'permit[ting] a redefinition of anxiety-provoking issues' (2) of the kind noted by Kaplan. However, the mythical and culturally loaded qualities of canonical texts from the nineteenth century are not the sole provenance of works from the nineteenth century. Though a product of the 1920s, F. Scott Fitzgerald's *The Great Gatsby* may also be seen as a 'cultural text' invested with a similarly mythical weight: his study of 1920s America has become synonymous with the culturally loaded pursuit of the all-pervading American dream and the adaptations that connect with it continue to redefine the 'anxiety-provoking issues' explored in Fitzgerald's canonical text. Adaptations reconfigure the cultural anxieties of these 'mythic' texts within different geographical, temporal, medial frameworks, but the cultural anxieties that they address connect them to the canonical text, even when reconfigured in a very different guise.

The study of adaptations continues to revolve around canonical authors to a marked extent, despite a growing interest in other forms of the type foregrounded by Hutcheon in *A Theory of Adaptation*, and this study is no exception; however, the canonical text serves here as a springboard for exploration of texts that move between the realms of literary high art and the populist mainstream. Some texts openly declare their affiliation with a canonical precursor, while others have a much less explicit relationship with the canon or any specific text; Sandra Goldbacher's film, *The Governess*, serves as a prime example of a text that operates at the unconscious margins of adaptation: at no point does it declare its affiliation with Charlotte Brontë's *Jane Eyre*, though to viewers familiar with the latter, its narrative structure and its themes effortlessly mirror those of Brontë's novel. Sanders defines this kind of textual re-vision as an act of 'appropriation' rather than 'adaptation' – one that embodies an 'intertextual relationship' that is 'less explicit, more embedded' and yet capable of 'encourag[ing] the ongoing, evolving production of meaning, and an ever-expanding network of textual relations' (2–3). Similarly, Hutcheon argues that 'Adaptation as *adaptation* involves, for its knowing audience, a conceptual flipping back and forth between the work we know and the work we are experiencing', inferring a level of mutual dependency; moreover, Hutcheon claims, our experience of a particular narrative may focus first and foremost on the narrative as told in its adaptive form ('Theory' 139). Perception of a text like Mary Shelley's *Frankenstein*, for example, may be coloured retrospectively by our viewing of its 1931 film 'adaptation', but for some the tale is negotiated first and foremost via its realization as 1930s cinematic horror, and for those viewers it may be *this* film text that is experienced as the 'primary' text.

Establishing a direction

We are now more likely to view canonical texts not as works of individual genius but as cultural artefacts that are reliant for their construction and consumption on more than the writer's imaginative outpourings. We may ask what processes are involved in the construction of such a product; how and why it may attain canonical status; and how its canonical status may influence our relationship (and *its* relationship) with other related texts. During the course of our studies, we will engage with these questions through a number of critical exercises, looking closely at the prescribed canonical texts and at the adaptations that engage with it. What should become apparent is the notion that the body of works deemed canonical is not static, that our readings of and our relationships with texts seen as canonical evolve, as does the canonical text's relationship with adaptations that set up a dialogue with it. Some critics object to the way in which adaptations discourse may be utilized as a means to providing accessible routes into the study of canonical texts; such an approach can lead to further valorization of the canon, and this study has no intention of presenting adaptation as the educator's bridge to the accessible study of literature. It is the complex, interdependent *relationship* between the canonical text and those adaptive works that engage with it that remains the focus of debate.

In recent years theorists have endeavoured to move the study of adaptations away from the kind of traditional organizational patterns usually employed in studies of this type, whereby canonical texts form the hub for further discussion. However, the canonical focus of this study dictates a traditional sectional division. Here, we focus on four key works from the Anglo-American canon, each selected because of its relationship with a rich and varied body of adaptations. In order to generate a model that provides a workable framework for discussion, sections are organized around three classifications, though as with all such classification systems, the placement of an adaptation into one category does not preclude the possibility that it may also work within the parameters of another.[1] The 'classic treatment' foregrounds the quest for fidelity, whereas (using Rich's observations as a starting point) adaptations identified as a 're-visioning the text' reconfigure the canonical text's thematic and ideological preoccupations, and those termed 'radical rethink' entail a definitive move (conscious or subconscious) away from source. In each section, the texts under review will be considered in light of the socio/cultural/political/industry-based climate of their individual production and within the context of existing critical scholarship.

This study also widens the parameters by encouraging a creative, process-driven approach to the exploration of adaptation studies. Building on the ideas of Thomas Leitch, who challenges the 'readerly' emphasis of existing debate and advocates instead the importance of a more 'writerly' interaction with texts under review (*Film Adaptation* 18–19), our studies here focus in part on the mechanics of adaptation via a series of creative exercises. Such an approach invites us to experience the various opportunities and constraints of textual transformation from one medium to another, one 'voice' to another, one set of ideological preoccupations to another and asks us to consider the socio/cultural/political/critical and industrial influences at work in the creation of an adaptation in ways that an analytical dissection of an existing adaptation cannot. It offers a different kind of bridge to the canonical text and a different way of perceiving the relationship between source text and resultant adaptation: it demystifies the process and changes our relationship with the canonical text in ways that theory alone cannot.

> The need to incorporate both activities [reading and writing] into what we might call the discipline of textual studies – the study of how texts are produced, consumed, canonized, transformed, resisted, and denied – offers a unique opportunity to adaptation studies, which can serve not as an avatar of literacy over literature but as a sorely needed bridge between the two (*Film Adaptation* 17–18).

The study aims to build these bridges by engaging its readers in *writerly* activities that will inevitably aid critical understanding of both the canonical text and the adaptations that continue to revolve and evolve around it. We engage with theories and critical reading of text through practical application, and to this end, each section takes a particular approach to the study of the selected adaptations through inclusion of a series of related exercises. The first chapter (Adapting *Jane Eyre*: an Analytical Approach) employs an analytical methodology; in the second chapter (Adapting *Great Expectations*: a Creative Practice-based Approach), the emphasis shifts to matters of process; chapter three (Adapting 'The Turn of the Screw':

Drawing Parallels Across Texts) focuses on the inter-connectivity of texts working with a particular narrative; and the final chapter (*The Great Gatsby*: Contesting the Boundaries of Classification) tests the limits and uses of taxonomies employed in the field of adaptation studies, including those generated as part of this study.

While it may be argued that *any* foregrounding of the so-called source text inevitably positions the adaptation as secondary and thus in some way inferior, the study of adaptation as a *process* envisages prior knowledge of the source text/s being adapted: though not arguing in favour of a centre-based model for the study of adaptation, knowledge of the canonical texts we engage with is a prerequisite if we are to explore the relationship between adaptations and the texts with which they choose to enter into a dialogue. An awareness of the originary text's ideological concerns, and of its contemporaneous cultural/socio-political scene enables us to explore, in an informed and more meaningful manner, the ways in which it is translated to other adaptive media; it does not preclude consideration of the adaptation in its own right. As such, for practical reasons, each chapter begins with an overview of the canonical text and a survey of the range of adaptations it has generated thus far. The focus then shifts to various representative types of adaptation, using what is inevitably a useful taxonomical framework (Classic/Re-vision/Radical Rethink) as a means to grouping together adaptations of a particular type. In order to ensure a comparative component to our studies, each classification is explored in relation to two or three adaptations of the specified canonical text and, where appropriate, comparisons are drawn not only between adaptations across classifications within each chapter but across the four canonical texts that are the portals for the study as a whole, further illustrating the complexity of adaptive relationships.

Opening up the debate: Exercises related to the study of adaptation

What is 'Adaptation'?

Step one

Read the following excerpts from Salman Rushdie's a 'A Fine Pickle' (*The Guardian*, 28 February 2009):

The question raised by the adaptive excesses of Adaptation is the question at the heart of the entire subject of adaptation – that is to say, the question of essence. 'Poetry is what gets lost in translation,' said Robert Frost, but Joseph Brodsky retorted: 'Poetry is what is gained in translation,' and the battle-lines could not be more clearly drawn. My own view has always been that whether we are talking about a poem moving across a language border to become another poem in another tongue, a book crossing the frontier between the world of print and celluloid, or human beings migrating from one world to another, both Frost and Brodsky are right. Something is always lost in translation; and yet something can also be gained. I am defining adaptation very broadly, to include translation, migration and metamorphosis, all the means by which one thing becomes another. In my novel *Midnight's Children* the narrator Saleem discusses the making of pickles as this sort of adaptive process: 'I reconcile myself,' he says, 'to the inevitable distortions of the pickling process. To pickle is to give immortality, after all: fish, vegetables, fruit hang embalmed in spice-and-vinegar; a certain alteration, a slight intensification of taste, is a small matter, surely? The art is to change the flavour in degree, but not in kind; and above all (in my thirty jars and a jar) to give it shape and form – that is to say, meaning.'

The question of essences remains at the heart of the adaptive act: how to make a second version of a first thing, of a book or film or poem or vegetable, or of yourself, that is successfully its own, new thing and yet carries with it the essence, the spirit, the soul of the first thing, the thing that you yourself, or your book or poem or film or your pre-pickle mango or lime, originally were.

Is it impossible? Is the intangible in our arts and our natures, the space between our words, the things seen in between the things shown, inevitably discarded in the remaking process, and if so can it be filled up with other spaces, other visions, that satisfy or even enrich us enough so that we do not mind the loss? To look at adaptation in this broad-spectrum way, to take it beyond the realm of art into the rest of life, is to see that all the meanings of the word deal with the question of what is essential – in a work adapted to another form, in an individual adapting to a new home, in a society adapting to a new age. What do you preserve? What do you jettison? What is changeable, and where must you draw the line? The questions are always the same, and the way we answer them determines the quality of the adaptation, of the book, the poem, or of our own lives.

As individuals, as communities, as nations, we are the constant adapters of ourselves, and must constantly ask ourselves the question wherein does our richness lie: what are the things we cannot ever give up unless we wish to cease to be ourselves?

We can learn this much from the poets who translate the poetry of others, from the screenwriters and film-makers who turn words on the page into images on a screen, from all those who carry across one thing into another state: an adaptation works best when it is a genuine transaction between the old and the new, carried out by persons who understand and care for both, who can help the thing adapted to leap the gulf and shine again in a different light. In other words, the process of social, cultural and individual adaptation, just like artistic adaptation, needs to be free, not rigid, if it is to succeed. Those who cling too fiercely to the old text, the thing to be adapted, the old ways, the past, are doomed to produce something that does not work, an unhappiness, an alienation, a quarrel, a failure, a loss.

Step two

Using Rushdie's observations as a writer engaged in the process of adaptation as a starting point, try to formulate your own response to these questions:

- How do we define such terms as 'essence' and 'spirit'?
- Does the 'essence'/'spirit' of a text necessarily constitute the same thing to all readers/viewers? Why/why not?
- *Should* the adapter's aim be to create a 'second version' of the text being adapted? Why? Why not?
- What should we make of texts that have a subconscious connection to other texts rather than a declared association with a literary forerunner?
- What other words are used by Rushdie to describe 'adaptation'? Consider each of these words: do they have positive or negative connotations?
- What other words could we substitute for the term 'adaptation'? Draw up a list of alternative words. What connotations do we associate with such words? Are they positive or negative? Why?

The language of adaptation

Robert Stam argues against what he sees as the 'moralistic approach' to discussion of the relationships between adaptation and source. Read the following extract from Stam's 'Beyond Fidelity: The Dialogics of Adaptation':

> The language of criticism dealing with film adaptation of novels has often been profoundly moralistic, awash in terms such as *infidelity, betrayal, deformation, violation, vulgarization,* and *desecration. Infidelity* resonates with overtones of Victorian prudishness; *betrayal* evokes ethical perfidy; *deformation* implies aesthetic disgust; *violation* calls to mind sexual violence; *vulgarization* conjures up class degradation; and *desecration* intimates a kind of religious sacrilege toward the 'sacred word' [74].

Step one

- Draw up a list of the negative words Stam identifies as commonly used by some critics to describe the act of 'adaptation'; now place alongside each word the connotations of that word as noted by Stam – e.g. '*violation* calls to mind sexual violence'.
- Now go back to *your* list generated in response to Rushdie's article, and select six words that describe adaptation in a *positive* light. What are the connotations surrounding each of these words? (Try to sum up in a word/short phrase as Stam does and place them side by side).

Step two

- What can we *infer* about the study of adaptation when we think about the language that colours our discussion of adaptations? How may this help and/or hinder our scholarly examination of adaptations and the adaptation process?

The canon as cultural artefact

Step one

In traditional readings of the canon, texts given canonical status are viewed as the work of individual creative genius – an individual expression from a specific writer's imagination, one which 'speaks to' universal and timeless values. The relationship between writer and reader may be mapped as follows:

Author has idea > Author expresses idea in a text > text reaches reader > reader finds author's meaning.

How does this 'position' us as receivers of the text? What assumptions does it make about us? Are such assumptions valid/supportable? Why/why not? Who decides whether or not the piece is worthy of canonical status and for what reasons?

Step two

If instead we view texts given canonical status as cultural artefacts, we may ask ourselves what processes are part of the construction of such a product:

- Where do the raw materials for such a 'product' come from?
- What is the role of the writer in the construction of this 'product'?
- What is the role of the reader in construction of this product?
- Where do the meanings of the text come from?
- What beliefs/value systems inform it?

Choose a canonical text that you are already familiar with from earlier studies (e.g. a play by Shakespeare, a novel by Thomas Hardy, Nathaniel Hawthorne, Virginia Woolf); answer each of the above questions in relation to that text.

What do we learn about the construction of the canon/canonical text, and the way in which texts become part of the canon by taking this wider cultural view?

Using secondary material: Synthesizing ideas

Sometimes, it can be difficult to extract the *salient points* from articles relating to the study of adaptation, and even more difficult to *synthesize these points* into your own discussion whilst ensuring that you *credit the ideas* to their author. This exercise is designed to help you think about meaningful ways to engage with secondary sources.

Step one

Read Linda Hutcheon's online article, 'In Defence of Literary Adaptation as Cultural Production', in *M/C Journal* 10.2 (2007) by accessing it online at: http://journal.media-culture.org.au/0705/01-hutcheon.php

Step two

Asking the right questions:

- Pick out key phrases found in the introduction: try to identify four to five major points.
- What is the line of argument established in this introduction? Using the above, summarize Hutcheon's 'position'/line of argument in two sentences.
- Are the discussion points raised of relevance only to the examples Hutcheon uses in this introduction and the article or can you extract the argument and apply it to other texts that YOU are studying? Why? Why not?
- What is meant by the reference to 'a one-stage art form' (see paragraph 5)? Why, according to Hutcheon, is this concept flawed (see paragraphs 6–9)? Find lines from the text to support this.
- What, claims Hutcheon, leads us to 'prioritize' literature as an art form? What points does she raise to help us question such prioritizing (see paragraph 10–11)?
- How, according to Hutcheon, is the relationship between reader/viewer/adaptation affected by the order in which we 'experience' a given text (see paragraphs 13–25)? Extract 4–5 key lines and then summarize her point in your own words in one or two sentences.
- Look at Hutcheon's closing analogy – 'In biology as in culture, adaptations reign.' In one sentence, outline how it sums up her 'position'.

Step three

Revisiting the ideas of others:

- After reading this article, which academics can we assume share a similar 'theoretical position' to Hutcheon? (Look back through the article and the opening chapter of this study text to identify these academics). What 'positions' do they share? List them.

- Go back through your notes: have you used quotation marks around all words taken directly from Hutcheon's article? Have you, when summarizing her ideas (or those of others that *she* credits in her writing), made sure that you credit them to her? How have you done so?
- If you plan to make reference, what details must you note in order to reference it appropriately?

Note

1. See final exercise ('Taxonomies: Strengths and Limitations': Conclusion), designed to engage readers in ongoing debates related to the efficacy of classification systems.

References

Andrew, Dudley. 'Adaptation'. *Film Adaptation*. Ed. James Naremore. New Brunswick, NJ: Rutgers University Press, 2000. 28–37. Print.

Bazin, Andre. 'Adaptation, or the Cinema as Digest'. *Film Adaptation*. Ed. James Naremore. New Brunswick: Rutgers University Press, 2000. 19–27. Print.

Bluestone, George. *Novels into Film*. Baltimore and London: John Hopkins University Press, 1957. Print.

Cardwell, Sarah. *Adaptation Revisited: Television and the Classic Novel*. Manchester: Manchester University Press, 2002. Print.

Cartmell, Deborah and Imelda Whelehan, eds. *Adaptations: From Text to Screen, Screen to Text*. London: Routledge, 1999. Print.

Cartmell, Deborah, I.Q. Hunter, Heidi Kaye, and Imelda Whelehan, eds. *Pulping Fictions: Consuming Culture Across the Literature/Media Divide*. London: Pluto Press, 1996. Print.

Cartmell, Deborah, I.Q. Hunter, Heidi Kaye, and Imelda Whelehan, eds. *Trash Aesthetics: Popular Culture and Its Audience*. London: Pluto Press, 1997. Print.

Cartmell, Deborah, I.Q. Hunter, Heidi Kaye, and Imelda Whelehan, eds. *Sisterhoods Across the Literature/Media Divide*. London: Pluto Press, 1998. Print.

Cartmell, Deborah, I.Q. Hunter, Heidi Kaye, and Imelda Whelehan, eds. *Alien Identities*. London: Pluto Press, 1999. Print.

Cartmell, Deborah, I.Q. Hunter, Heidi Kaye, and Imelda Whelehan, eds. *Classics in Film and Fiction*. London: Pluto Press, 2000. Print.

Cartmell, Deborah, I.Q. Hunter, Heidi Kaye, and Imelda Whelehan, eds. *Retrovisions: Reinventing the Past in Film and Fiction*. London: Pluto Press, 2001. Print.

Chatman, Seymour. *Coming to Terms: The Rhetoric of Narrative in Fiction and Film*. Ithaca, New York and London: Cornell University Press, 1990. Print.

Elliott, Kamilla. *Rethinking the Novel/Film Debate*. Cambridge: Cambridge University Press, 2003. Print.

Genette, Gérard. *Palimpsests: Literature in the Second Degree*. Trans. Channa Newman, and Claude Doubinsky. Lincoln: University of Nebraska Press, 1997 [1982]. Print.

Hutcheon, Linda. *A Theory of Adaptation*. London: Routledge, 2006. Print.

Hutcheon, Linda. 'In Defence of Literary Adaptation as Cultural Production'. *M/C Journal* 10.2 (2007) n. pag. Web. 12 Jan. 2008.

Kaplan, Cora. *Victoriana: Histories, Fictions, Criticism*. Edinburgh: Edinburgh University Press, 2007. Print.

Klein, Michael and Gillian Parker. *The English Novel and the Movies*. New York: Ungar, 1981. Print.

Leitch, Thomas. *Film Adaptation and Its Discontents: From Gone with the Wind to the Passion of the Christ*. Baltimore: John Hopkins Press, 2007. Print.

Leitch, Thomas. 'Adaptation, the Genre'. *Adaptation* 1.2 (2008): 106–120. Print.

Leitch, Thomas. 'Jekyll, Hyde, Jekyll, Hyde, Jekyll Hyde, Jekyll, Hyde: Four Models of Intertextuality'. *Victorian Literature & Film Adaptation*. Ed. Abigail Burnham Bloom, and Mary Sanders Pollock. New York: Cambria, 2011. 28–50. Print.

McFarlane, Brian. *Novel to Film: An Introduction to the Theory of Adaptation*. Oxford: Oxford University Press, 1996. Print.

Murray, Simone. *The Adaptation Industry: The Cultural Economy of Contemporary Literary Adaptation*. New York: Routledge, 2012. Print.

Onega, Susana and Christian Gutleben, eds. *Refracting the Canon in Contemporary British Literature and Film*. Amsterdam and New York: Rodopi, 2004. Print.

Ray, Robert. 'The Field of Literature and Film'. *Film Adaptation*. Ed. James Naremore. New Brunswick, NJ: Rutgers University Press, 2000. 38–53. Print.

Rich, Adrienne. 'When We Dead Awaken: Writing as Re-Vision'. *College English* 34.1 (1972) 18–30. Print.

Rose, Brian A. *Jekyll and Hyde Adapted: Dramatizations of Cultural Anxiety*. Westport, CT: Greenwood, 1996. Print.

Rushdie, Salman. 'A Fine Pickle'. *The Guardian*. 28 Feb. 2009. Web. 1 Mar. 2009.

Sanders, Julie. *Adaptation and Appropriation*. Abingdon: Routledge, 2006. Print.

Stam, Robert. 'Beyond Fidelity: The Dialogics of Adaptation'. *Film Adaptation*. Ed. James Naremore. New Brunswick, NJ: Rutgers University Press, 2000. 54–78. Print.

Wagner, Geoffrey. *The Novel and the Cinema*. Rutherford, NJ: Fairleigh Dickinson University Press, 1975. Print.

2

Adapting *Jane Eyre*: An Analytical Approach

Charlotte Brontë's *Jane Eyre* remains a fascinating part of the adaptive landscape; it has sustained the interest of adapters working in a variety of media since its initial publication in 1847 and continues to find a twenty-first-century audience in both its original form and its various adapted reincarnations. The novel's capacity to retain its relevance is a sure sign that, in addition to its narrative energy, its thematic preoccupations are still part of contemporary debate. It has a complex relationship with the texts that circulate it, and connects with them in a number of ways, whether via an exploration of its sexual politics and its construction of gendered identity, or through its compelling storytelling and dense characterization. For some adapters it remains at its core a love story – a dark, gothic romance with a strong-willed heroine and a brooding hero – but for others, it represents a site for further feminist or postcolonial discourse and interrogation of the more sinister elements embedded within the tale. This opening discussion of the canonical text is informed by both feminist and postcolonial debates that continue to circulate Brontë's *Jane Eyre*.

Brontë's stories are concerned with what she deems the controlled lives of 'genteel English people', and her thematic preoccupations push the boundaries of what is seen as acceptable in contemporaneous Victorian society. Her heroines in general, and Jane Eyre in particular, refuse to operate within the conventions of Victorian society: they do not fulfil the 'angel in the house' stereotype upheld as the model of femininity, and the restrictions placed upon the Victorian woman are constantly questioned in Brontë's novels. Though Coventry Patmore's very popular poem, 'The Angel in the House', was published seven years after *Jane Eyre*, its sentiments encapsulate the prevailing attitude towards women in Brontë's contemporary society: a *good* woman knows that 'Man must be pleased; but him to please/Is woman's pleasure'. Brontë writes against this value system, and the reception of her work by her contemporaries was understandably conflicted. Though some reviewers welcomed her self-willed, intelligent heroines, the majority were perturbed by them; but whatever the critical response, her influence on the construction of the Victorian heroine 'was felt to have been revolutionary', resulting in the creation of a female protagonist who was not only 'rebellious and passionate ... more intellectual and self-defining than the sweet and submissive heroines' of fellow novelists like Charles Dickens, or William Thackeray, but also in charge of her own story' (Showalter 122–123). It may be argued that *Jane Eyre* is itself an appropriation of sorts since it certainly borrows tropes from the nineteenth century's already established governess genre; however, whilst Brontë's Jane Eyre shares with these former protagonists her status as marginalized social victim journeying towards maturity, she is far more proactive and assertive than the conventional governess prototype.

Brontë's *Jane Eyre* led to the increased popularity of the Governess novel, some appropriating elements of the *Eyre* narrative in more direct ways than others. Like many post-*Eyre* stories involving the governess figure, Henry James' 'The Turn of the Screw', first published in 1898, borrows from this text in a number of ways, and our fascination with the tale stretches from the early days of its release to the present day, over 165 years later. During that time, there have been six silent black and white film renditions, from 1910 to 1918; two black and white talkies in 1934 and 1944; six televised mini-series from 1956 to 2006; and two contemporary films, in 1996 and 2011. Other performative adaptations include seven stage musicals, an opera and numerous radio plays. However, adapters attracted to this narrative have, in the main, chosen to adapt or expand upon the narrative in novel form. The most famous novel adaptations of *Jane Eyre* have become 'classics' in their own right – *Rebecca* and *Wide Sargasso Sea*, like 'The Turn of the Screw', have a place within the modern literary canon – but there are a staggering number of prose adaptations, particularly from 2000 onwards. Some of these adaptations choose, in the vein of *Wide Sargasso Sea*, to explore the story from the narrative perspective of others found in Brontë's text; novels like *Adele: Jane Eyre's Hidden Story* (2000), *Adele, Grace, and Celine: The Other Women of Jane Eyre* (2009) or *Rochester* (2010) abound. Adapters also seem preoccupied with extending the narrative's life via the writing of sequels – from D. M. Thomas's *Charlotte* (2000) to an unfinished manuscript by Angela Carter to *Jane Rochester* (2000) and *Jane Eyre's Daughter* (2008), the obsession with Jane Eyre's story continues and moves into such unexpected territory as vampire parody (*Jane Slayre* 2010), science fiction (*Jenna Starborn* 2002) and genre-bending spin-offs like Jasper Fforde's *The Eyre Affair* (2001). *Jane Eyre* has also become the gothic prototype for the twentieth and twenty-first centuries' populist gothic courtship/romance novel, with writers like Victoria Holt and Phyllis Whitney owing a narrative debt to Brontë's seminal text.

However, to read *Jane Eyre* as nothing more than a Gothic Romance is to deny both its significance as one of the most influential bildungsroman stories of the nineteenth century and its contribution to our understanding of the sexual politics of Brontë's contemporary scene. It is a text that connects with gothic tales from the early eighteenth century, with their 'over-abundance of imaginative frenzy' (Botting 3), but it also turns to what Botting sees as the nineteenth century's 'internalisation of gothic forms', whereby the 'gloom and darkness of the sublime landscapes be[come] external markers of inner mental and emotional states' (91–92). Brontë's tale employs an abundance of gothic tropes: we have the imposing castle-like mansion situated in a gloomy, untamed, weather-beaten landscape; we have the pre-requisite brooding male lead with a dark secret, mysterious events, a demonized spectre associated with insanity and a curious heroine. But, Jane Eyre is not the stereo-typical fainting heroine of gothic convention: the emotive excess characteristic of such female leads is tempered by her capacity to rationalize and increasingly to rein in her passionate nature as she journeys towards the novel's close. The supernatural elements of the gothic become highly charged moments of spiritual epiphany of a very different kind. In true gothic mode, both Jane Eyre and Edward Rochester are figures who are isolated from society – the former ostensibly as a consequence of her social position, the latter as a consequence of past transgression – and despite the romantic implications of the narrative's close, they continue to exist on the margins of society. The nineteenth-century gothic's preoccupation with interiority and alter egos, with mirror images and doubles is also central to our understanding of this novel, and such facets of the text have generated a body of critical scholarship that continues to explore the relationship between the protagonist and Rochester's first wife, Bertha Mason, from both a feminist and a postcolonial perspective. Contemplation of this relationship forms one of the many strands teased out by adapters too, Jean Rhys's *Wide Sargasso Sea* being the most prominent of all, but in its more populist mainstream reincarnations, it is the dark romance element of the *Jane Eyre* narrative that is appropriated over and over, leading to what may be deemed a hijacking of the novel's sexual politics. Following the vogue for vampire rewrites of canonical texts, Total-E-Bound's publication of Clandestine Classic's *Jane Eyre*, a sexually explicit rewrite of the novel prompted by the popularity and success of E. L. James's *Fifty Shades of Grey* trilogy, heralds the arrival of 'mummy porn' classics that, by the addition of detailed, erotic sex scenes give a very different and somewhat disturbing 'spin' to the novel's thematic concerns, despite the publisher's avowed intention to stay as 'close to the original classics as possible' for all of the erotic 'makeovers' they have planned (Emily Andrews). Eve Sinclair's *Jane Eyre Laid Bare* (2012) presents us with a further erotic rendition of the novel, its opening chapter describing the protagonist's thoughts as she masturbates and recalls the delights of her lesbian tristes with a fellow Lowood inmate. Though tempting to dismiss such adaptations, they serve to illustrate the ways in which canonical texts engage with mainstream culture and to this end provide us with interesting lines of postfeminist debate.

Whether amplifying, diluting, or realigning the novel's gothic identity in accordance with their own subsequent agenda, production era and/ or chosen medium, adapters continue to appropriate Brontë's carefully constructed narrative template. *Jane Eyre*'s bildungsroman format provides clear narrative momentum: linear plot development and character growth are inherent within the chosen form, making it particularly well-suited to cinematic or televisual adaptation. It is in essence a quest story that, within the confines of a defined social order, maps the spiritual development of the protagonist from childhood to a moment of adult realization. The narrative builds around a series of clashes between what the protagonist desires and what society expects, traditionally culminating in the protagonist's self-assessment and capacity to find a new place within that society. Jane Eyre's spiritual journey is described by Gilbert and Gubar as:

> a story of enclosure and escape, a distinctively female Bildungsroman in which the problems encountered by the protagonist as she struggles from the imprisonment of her childhood toward an almost unthinkable goal of mature freedom are symptomatic of difficulties Everywoman in a patriarchal society must meet and overcome: oppression (Gateshead), starvation (Lowood), madness (Thornfield), and coldness (Marsh End). (339)

Her everywoman status is aligned here with the feminist politics that inform Gilbert and Gubar's reading of the text, but regardless of whether we see the journey as one related to gender politics *or* religious spiritual awakening, the stages of Eyre's growth and the clashes she encounters along the way mirror the established narrative patterns of the bildungsroman protagonist, taking us with her on the journey towards a moment of self-realization and closure. Our relationship with this protagonist is even more intimately ingrained due to the first person narration employed. Jane Eyre is placed in a privileged position within the narrative as she voices her own story, placing her according to Chih-Ping Chen, 'into the masculine positions of the host and the gazer' as she leads her readers through her 'gallery of memory' (382). Once again, such a narrative device can be seen as gift or a problem for the adapter: it poses problems of narrative voice for the screenwriter/film or TV adapter when translating to a medium that frames events through the third person vehicle of a camera lens, yet it lends itself to the internalized thought processes of prose adaptations like *Rebecca* or *Wide Sargasso Sea*.

The sustained appeal of Charlotte Brontë's *Jane Eyre* as a narrative of gothic romance cannot be denied. However, it is the sexual politics of this canonical text that continues to attract certain adapters. The substantial body of critical feminist discourse that circulates the novel has become part of its adaptive landscape and its significance as a text that foregrounds feminist issues is indisputable. Matters relating to the politics of class also remain central to our understanding of the relationship between Eyre and Rochester in this novel, and within a Victorian context the potential union of lowly governess and wealthy upper class employer represents an act of subversive transgression. As readers we are acquainted with the protagonist's beliefs, voiced through the filter of her first person narration; from her early beginnings as a rebellious and forthright child to her emergence as a calmer, more restrained woman shaped by the lessons of her Lowood experiences, she is constructed as an individual who constantly questions the constraints placed upon her by her gender, and it is this engagement with and questioning of society's marginalization of women that draws the attention of feminist critics:

> Women are supposed to be very calm generally: but women feel just as men feel; they need exercise for their faculties, and a field for their efforts, as much as their brothers do; they suffer from too rigid a restraint, too absolute a stagnation, precisely as men would suffer; and it is narrow-minded in their more privileged fellow-creatures to say that they ought to confine themselves to making puddings and knitting stockings, to playing on the piano and embroidering bags. It is thoughtless to condemn them, or laugh at them, if they seek to do more or learn more than custom has pronounced necessary for their sex. (Brontë 140–141)

Although couched in the voice of calm, rational thought, this persuasive appeal for universal suffrage foregrounds Eyre's (and by inference Brontë's) frustrations; as a woman constrained by the expectations of Victorian society, her choices are limited.

Feminist discourse surrounding the text also focuses on the significance of the relationship between Jane Eyre and Rochester's first wife, Bertha Mason. In adaptations that seek to engage with the novel's exploration of sexual politics, Jane's relationship with Bertha becomes an integral part of any subsequent reconfiguration of the tale, and such re-visions are further influenced by a body of feminist scholarship that builds upon the gothic genre's trope of 'doubling'. Chaste, virginal Jane, repeatedly referred to by Rochester as 'elf', 'fairy', 'sprite', 'angel' stands in stark contrast to promiscuous bestial Bertha, who is constantly referred to in terms that dehumanize her: she is 'the foul German spectre – the vampire' (311), a 'clothed hyena' rising up on 'its hind-feet' (321). But feminist critics like Barbara Rigney argue that Bertha Mason becomes Eyre's alter ego, a 'doppelganger for Jane', creating a 'distorted mirror image of Jane's own dangerous propensities toward "passion"', (16) – a passion that equates with loss of self and of sanity as evidenced by the insane, unchaste and incarcerated Bertha. Since the arrival of second wave feminism, the figure of the madwoman as 'feminist rebel' in literature has been afforded a privileged position in feminist discourse; she offers what Elizabeth Donaldson terms a 'sustained cultural currency' (99). If the madwoman Bertha Mason serves as Jane Eyre's alter ego, then Jane Eyre functions as 'feminist rebel': she refuses to be dominated by patriarchal figures within the text – from John Reed and Mr Brocklehurst to Rochester and St John Rivers – and she values her independence and spiritual freedoms above all else, but through her association with Bertha, she constantly reminds us of the dangers of being consumed by men, whether through our own desires and 'passion' for them or through their positions of power over us. And yet, postcolonial theorists continue to question the implications of feminist interpretations of the relationship between Jane Eyre and the madwoman in the attic; critics like Carl Plasa argue that by turning Bertha Mason into a 'psycho-feminist' and a 'metaphorical expression of Jane's own unconscious desires and discontents', she is 'erase[d]' from the text as a character in her own right, affording her relevance only as a facet of the protagonist's psyche; to view Jane Eyre as 'universally normative' is to suggest says Plasa, 'a certain blindness with regard to female histories which are racially and culturally "other"' (80–83). It may also be argued that Jane Eyre colludes in the de-humanization of Bertha within this text; she does little to find out more about her and speaks of her in the same kind of bestial terms as Rochester. Chih-Ping Chen points out that her 'feminist individualism' does not equip her with the capacity to see the humanity of 'sister' Bertha, despite their similar position as powerless women (369).

Adapters choose to negotiate these readings by excising them or engaging with them to varying degrees. Some adaptations, like Robert Stevenson's *Jane Eyre* (1943), employ Bertha Mason as little more than plot device; she becomes the reason for a disturbance of the narrative's equilibrium and her ultimate removal serves to restore narrative harmony and order. Others, like Rhys's *Wide Sargasso Sea* which places Antoinette/Bertha Mason at the centre of the story, give us a very different narrative viewpoint or signify the connection between Bertha and Jane Eyre throughout via visual means as in the 2006 BBC serialization. In *Rebecca*, the presence of the first wife colonizes the narrative, even *as* the tale is related to us from the first person perspective of the second Mrs De Winter who shares Jane Eyre's inferior social standing and her romantic union with the older, wealthy man but has little of the independence of spirit we associate with the protagonist of Brontë's tale. In Val Lewton's *I Walked with a Zombie* (1943), Bertha is a physical yet dehumanized presence, her incarcerated zombie existence being constructed as a consequence of her sexual transgressions. However, in *The Governess* (1998), a postmodern feminist appropriation of *Jane Eyre*, the sexualized protagonist, Rosina, becomes the physical embodiment of both Jane Eyre and Bertha Mason. Adaptations intertextualize other adaptations within their own narrative too, enriching and reinventing the tale for new audiences by adding layer upon layer of meaning to what is already a complex narrative template. In this section we explore a cross-section of adaptive types, dividing our studies into those which offer seemingly 'classic' interpretations of the text, those that 're-vision' it and lastly those that present us with a 'radical rethink' of Brontë's narrative. Our focus in this chapter is upon analytical responses to the adaptation of *Jane Eyre*, but an understanding of the creative processes at work in the reconfiguration of this canonical text into various adaptive guises will inevitably inform our analytical readings of each.

Jane Eyre: The 'classic' treatment (screen adaptations of *Jane Eyre*: 1944, 2006 and 2011)

How do so-called 'classic' adaptations engage with the canonical texts they are seen to translate? That they are regarded as 'faithful' adaptations seems to be the common belief; but is there an overriding concern with textual fidelity or are such adaptations more concerned with the 'faithful' replication of the narrative's contemporaneous moment in all of its period detail? The term 'classic adaptation' has become synonymous with a particular type of cinematic and televisual reconfiguration of canonical texts – a type often labelled conservative in its ideology, overtly concerned with its own visual splendour and period detail rather than with the thematic preoccupations of the source text it is translating to screen. As twentieth- and twenty-first-century readers and viewers, we approach the narratives of the nineteenth-century realist novel from an historical perspective: the writer of the novel deals in contemporary matters but for us such matters become details from the past, freighted with our knowledge of history.

Such films and TV products become defined by their classification as 'heritage cinema' or 'costume drama'; they are, according to film scholar Richard Dyer, 'characterised by use of a canonical source from the national literature, generally set within the past 150 years'; employ a 'conventional filmic narrative style, with the pace and tone of "(European) art cinema"; a museum aesthetic, period costumes, decor and locations carefully recreated, presented in pristine condition, brightly and artfully lit; a performance style based on nuance and social observation' (204). Higson argues that in these costume dramas, the past is 'displayed as visually spectacular pastiche, inviting a nostalgic gaze that resists the ironies and social critiques so often suggested by these films'; we have access to the touched up image of the moment but, seduced by the visual splendour, we are denied access to the politics of the period and the novelist's ideological agenda (109–129). Higson's comments suggest by inference that adaptations of this type are in some way inferior to the canonical texts they engage with but such a view is abhorred by theorists like Stam who see it is a 'profoundly moralistic' and elitist approach to adaptation (54). These film and television products are also seen to have a specific appeal to a specific viewing audience. What we initially perceive as film and TV products that seek fidelity to a source text often, though not always, attain fidelity to the novel's surface details rather than its politics for reasons related to the adaptation's own contemporary positioning, its adapter's specific agenda, and the industrial as well as the aesthetic parameters of its medium, but it does not necessarily follow that the adaptation is thus in some way inferior. Recent research by Claire Monk suggests that there is no 'cohesive audience for period films'; instead, 'audiences who enjoy period films consist of overlapping, dynamic groups, positioned in varied relationships to both commercial and art cinema, who make sense of the films from a variety of cultural-political perspectives' (167). Her findings suggest that the elitism of critics is not shared by consumers of the film as product and enjoyment of them 'is fully compatible with critical and progressive viewing positions' (176). The same may be true of audiences attracted to televised adaptations of works from the nineteenth-century literary canon, though similar views as to the *type* of viewer they attract continue to dominate the critical landscape.

The televised costume drama that dominated from the fifties through to the late eighties was historically scheduled for serialized Sunday night viewing or as Christmas event special and was seen to appeal to a conservative, discerning audience seeking the comfort of fidelity driven reproductions of the literary canon. From the fifties onwards, the BBC became the main purveyor of the 'classic' serialization; it produced what Sergio Angelini disparagingly terms 'discretely embalm[ed] celebrated literary properties, with an emphasis on textual fidelity and handsome decor', producing 'homogenized versions' of the works of Jane Austen, Charles Dickens and the Brontës in particular. Serializations of *Jane Eyre* produced by the BBC made a regular appearance through the decades: in 1956 (dir. Campbell Logan); in 1963 (dir. Rex Tucker); in 1973 (dir. Joan Craft); in 1983 (dir. Julian Amyes); and though no production was forthcoming from the BBC in the nineties, a similarly faithful costume drama *Jane Eyre* was produced by London Weekend Television (1997, dir. Robert Young). It is not until 2006 that the BBC returns to adaptations of *Jane Eyre* (dir. Susanna White) and by this time, its treatment of classic texts has changed considerably. Since the nineties, TV serializations have become less reverential in their treatment, pushing the boundaries of canonical texts in a number of ways. Andrew Davies' *Pride and Prejudice* (1995) marks a turning point in the treatment of classic serialization. Post Davies' *Pride and Prejudice*, we have a subtle shift in treatment and production values. Not only is the source material given a more contemporary 'spin' but the way it is shot becomes more 'filmic'; Sarah Cardwell notes that the classic serial in the nineties is given 'superior status' by reviewers *because* of its conscious desire to 'distinguish' itself from 'televisual modes of representation' (34). Rather than employing 'the most common modes of televisual expression – relatively fast editing, a reliance upon rapidly developed emotional drama (melodrama) and so forth', it employs the use of 'long, slow shots and smooth, "invisible" editing', an 'attention to detail in costume and setting, and to the understated, reserved and "naturalistic" style of acting' more readily associated with cinema (34). The characteristically static shooting style of earlier televised adaptations of the canon, framed by confined period sets, gives way to a much more self-consciously artistic treatment of these narratives within screen space.

Production values emulate those of cinema in many contemporary televised serializations of canonical nineteenth-century novels, and there is a hitherto unprecedented intertextualization at play between cinematic adaptations and their televisual counterparts. White's *Jane Eyre*, produced in 2006, continues this trend.

Televised serializations of nineteenth-century novels are afforded the time and screen space to develop many aspects of the canonical text, whilst film production dictates a more concise rendition of the narrative and its thematics. The most recent TV serialization of *Jane Eyre*, adapted by Sandy Welch and directed by Susanna White, was broadcast on the BBC as a four part series with a running time of 202 minutes, affording it the luxury of relating the tale without undertaking edits of major plot-lines. It offers a 'faithful' rendition of the text in terms of narrative momentum but unlike former adapters working with *Jane Eyre* for TV serialization, Welch and White also inscribe the text's social and sexual politics from the outset. The text's first person narration is translated to screen via our 'positioning' as audience: from her first introduction to us, Jane's outsider status is visually inscribed. Instead of the anticipated costume drama setting, we open with a desert landscape into which a diminutive figure appears swathed in red silk; the figure – revealed at this point as a child – turns to camera, and we close in on her eyes, entering the narrative through her gaze as the scene shifts to the expected period setting. The very English images from Bewick's *History of British Birds* are replaced by exotic images related to the text this Jane Eyre is reading. White also employs visual means to align the 'Otherness' of child Jane not only with her adult self but with her doppelganger, Bertha Mason. Her initial construction of child Jane as exotic Other, cloaked in red silk and placed in a desert landscape that is alien to the society she lives in, becomes synonymous with adult Jane and the incarcerated Bertha. The connotative power of the colour red and its loaded association with the Red Room (and later Bertha's flame-filled tower) becomes a visual signifier for the innate danger of desire and sexual awakening. Adult Jane's only decorative flourish to her plain attire is a red neckerchief (of the kind worn by Brontë in J. H. Thompson's portrait of the author, 1850) but through this simple addition to costuming, White reminds us of Jane's now controlled yet persistently wilful, passionate nature; similarly, Bertha Mason's red silk scarf, seen floating from her tower at Thornfield Hall at various points in this screen adaptation, serves to remind us of both Bertha's haunting presence at the margins of the narrative and of her function as Jane's 'distorted mirror image' (Rigney 16).

Figure 2.1 Screenshot of child Jane from the opening moments of *Jane Eyre*, Dir. Susanna White (BBC 2006), courtesy of BBC

Figure 2.2 Screenshot of the tower of Thornfield Hall and Bertha's red scarf from *Jane Eyre*, Dir. Susanna White (BBC 2006), courtesy of BBC

Figure 2.3 Screenshot of adult Jane in red neckerchief from *Jane Eyre*, Dir. Susanna White (BBC 2006), courtesy of BBC

This televised *Jane Eyre* follows the bildungsroman journeying of the protagonist, from Gateshead to Lowood, Thornfield to Marsh End and Ferndean, and it successfully reinscribes the dangers of female sexual desire and surrender by foregrounding at a visual level the figures of an independent Jane and an incarcerated Bertha. Jane's reunion with the physically reduced Rochester, at a point in the narrative when she has a level of financial as well as spiritual equality, provides the bildungsroman's anticipated moment of self-realization, and to a certain extent, Jane finds her place in society. However, Brontë's Jane Eyre and Rochester find romantic closure within the solitary confines of Ferndean; their reintegration into society is neither attained nor sought. White takes Brontë's understated happy ending and gives to Jane Rochester all that Jane Eyre has been denied thus far. The closing moments present us with a picture-perfect image of the Rochester 'family' that she now presides over; in an echo of and in contrast to the earlier moment of family portraiture that child Jane is purposely excluded from by her Aunt Reed, adult Jane orchestrates the closing portrait, ensuring inclusion of all members of her household. The 'insalubrious' Ferndean of the novel (455) is replaced by a well-maintained country house, and the edges of this portrait of domestic bliss are neatly framed by bright flowers. Whether such a sugar-coated closing frame is meant as a postfeminist parody or a celebration of romance and domestic harmony remains open to interpretation, but this serialization is arguably the most politicized of all moving image adaptations of Brontë's novel to date.

Figure 2.4 Screenshot of Reed family photo scene from *Jane Eyre*, Dir. Susanna White (BBC 2006), courtesy of BBC

Figure 2.5 Screenshot of Rochester family photo scene from *Jane Eyre*, Dir. Susanna White (BBC 2006), courtesy of BBC

On-screen treatments of the opening and closing moments of Brontë's tale continue to present us with different interpretations, and though they inevitably offer us the anticipated romantic union, the trajectory of Eyre's journey to this point varies considerably and the bildungsroman structure of the canonical text is reshaped accordingly. Our perception of Jane Eyre as the central character who embarks on a journey of individual growth is often constructed as secondary to the novel's romance plot. Cinematic adaptations, like the majority of TV serializations of *Jane Eyre*, seek varying degrees of 'fidelity': they are conditioned by the socio-cultural preoccupations of their time of production, by financial and industrial considerations and by the expectations of the medium. What they share, though to a greater or lesser extent, is an overriding concern with the romance at the centre of the story, and this has numerous implications at the level of casting and genre. Whether adapted to TV or cinema, Jane Eyre's Rochester is consistently cast as the dark, brooding yet incredibly handsome male lead, despite Jane's initial assessment of him when they first meet: she states that 'had he been a handsome, heroic-looking young gentleman, [she] should not have dared to stand thus questioning him against his will, and offering [her] services unasked' (Brontë 145). From Orson Welles (1944) to Timothy Dalton (BBC 1983), from William Hurt (1996) and Toby Stephens (BBC 2006) to Michael Fassbender (2011), Rochester has physically fulfilled the role of masculine heart-throb whilst actors cast as Jane Eyre have, on the whole, retained Brontë's image of the diminutive, plain Jane. The exceptions to this come in the earliest cinematic adaptations of the text, during Hollywood's Golden Age, when the romance genre demanded a certain type of female lead; in the 1934 version, Jane Eyre is played by a tall, buxom blonde, Virginia Bruce, and in the 1944 film, rising star Joan Fontaine plays Jane as the typical romantic heroine, submissive in all things to her commanding romantic hero, Orson Welles. Such casting ensures a more romantic Hollywood 'spin' on what is still seen by many as, first and foremost, a passionate romance narrative; however, Jane's appeal as the everywoman who is able to attain love against the odds is diluted by this move, and the sexual politics of the narrative become secondary, but for their intended Hollywood audience these genre-driven romances deliver anticipated outcomes.

Director Robert Stevenson's 1944 film is ostensibly a romance, with taglines such as 'A love story every woman would die a thousand deaths to live', and marketing posters with the lines 'Their lips knew the ecstasy of first love! Their hearts knew the terror of frustration! Their arms knew the thrill of triumph!' placed alongside a colour image of a physically dominant Rochester and a passive inert Jane (dressed in a revealing ball gown) in a romantic clinch. The romance-focused marketing strategy consciously avoids any hint of either Stevenson's very gothic treatment of the narrative or the screenplay's emphasis upon child Jane during the Lowood section of the novel. Neither is the film's laboured attempts to foreground its identity as an adaptation of Brontë's novel given particular prominence in its marketing posters. However, the original trailer for the film, shown to cinema audiences of the forties during the interval between B movies and the main film, foregrounds its relationship with classic literature in general and *Jane Eyre* in particular. And yet it is encoded as a product specifically for women: the domesticated, magazine-reading female of the trailer becomes our cipher – we scan the bookshelves with her as the voiceover lists for us other successful screen adaptations of classic texts, implying that this is going to be yet another successful translation from page to screen, of a type that will appeal predominantly to a female audience whose reading habits align the classic with the more reader-light narratives of magazines. Our access to the film text in this trailer comes via the moving pages of the novel. Its words are swiftly translated to on-screen images and its star casting is foregrounded as Welles and Fontaine perform in a number of the source text's key moments. We are offered narrative 'hooks' that reassure us that what we will be experiencing is tangibly linked to our knowledge of Brontë's story. Producer David O. Selznick's fidelity-driven approach to the adaptation of classics is well documented; the appointment of revered novelist Aldous Huxley as screenwriter on this project was meant to ensure a certain literary pedigree, though the wisdom of giving the task of writing for film to a writer whose reputation is built on a very different medium was considered questionable. Selznick's earlier adaptation of Daphne Du Maurier's Eyre related tale, *Rebecca* (1940), is similarly 'faithful' to the novel, though the subtle directorial interventions of Alfred Hitchcock seep into the film text despite Selznick's fidelity-driven demands. In line with common Hollywood practice when adapting classics to screen in the forties, the source text appears as words on a turning page, lending the film product kudos but also reinscribing the authority of the written word as a consequence. Stevenson's recurrent use of this strategy tends to undermine the film's capacity to translate the narrative, via visual and aural means, and the problem is exacerbated by the fact that the words we see (and hear in a voiceover) are an inferior rewrite of what is penned by Brontë. The casting of Joan Fontaine as the lead in this film is an example of glamourized forties casting – a means to attracting an audience to the purely romantic elements of the narrative – but her earlier appearance as the submissive, cringing second Mrs DeWinter in *Rebecca* (Hitchcock 1940) makes it very difficult for an audience to then empathize with her as the strong, independent heroine of Brontë's *Jane Eyre*; Fontaine's disembodied voiceover in *Jane Eyre* (Stevenson 1944) cannot be dissociated from her earlier performance as the meek, submissive narrator of *Rebecca* (Hitchcock 1940).

The film's swift treatment of the Gateshead period of Jane's journey curtails our capacity to understand her future actions; her wilful determination to confront injustice is not illustrated via her altercation with John Reed – the first of many males whose unfair treatment of her is challenged – and her psychological traumas when imprisoned in the Red Room as a consequence are excised. Her *actions* do not form part of the opening narrative and we are given no access to her troubled state of mind: instead we see a naughty child who has been locked in the pantry. And yet, Stevenson's film devotes considerable time to the Lowood experience; paying particular attention to the relationship between Jane and Helen Burns, the film explores the juxtaposition of childhood innocence and vulnerability and institutionalized cruelty. But whilst the canonical text presents us with strong female role models like the independent Miss Templeton and the God-loving Helen Burns as more restrained exemplars of resistance during this part of Jane's journey, Stevenson's film gives us instead, a male hero as the antithesis of the evil Brocklehurst. Dr Rivers (a convenient amalgamation of Miss Templeton and St John Rivers) becomes Jane's protector and her escape from Lowood to Thornfield Hall is brought about not by her own actions but by Rivers. Jane's independent spirit is diminished by such narrative interventions but they reflect the era's desire for strong, reassuring images of masculinity. Liora Brosh argues that films of the thirties and forties appropriate the nineteenth-century canon in ways that 'project comforting domestic ideals for audiences undergoing profound social, economic, and political dislocations as a result of the Depression and the Second World War', suggesting that Stevenson's adaptation is conditioned by its time of production (13). It is a film product that is engineered to offer ultimately reassuring images of romantic union and harmony, no matter how dark and 'gothic' the journey towards that point may be. Brosh sees Jane's construction here as one conditioned by her maternal desires: we have an 'excessive[ly] cute Adele' and a romantic lead whose sexuality is 'constructed through her desire for "motherhood"' (11). Such a reconfiguration of Jane Eyre certainly negates the sexual politics of the novel, but even in White's TV adaptation, with its exploration of the feminist elements of the text, the closing moments centre on images of domestic harmony and present Jane within the context of marital bliss. In Stevenson's adaptation, Bertha Mason has only one function: she serves as a plot mechanism to introduce a point of conflict and a final resolution. Bertha has no onscreen presence throughout the film; she remains a disembodied voice identified only by her off-screen screams and spoken of only in the third person. The sexual politics embedded in Brontë's novel via the juxtaposition of a virginal, independent Jane and a sexualized, incarcerated Bertha find no place in this forties studio film, and the heroic women of the source text are replaced by heroic males like Dr Rivers and Rochester. Conversely, Brosh argues that through use of camera angles that align us with the gaze of the out of shot Bertha, Jane becomes the 'object of Bertha's gaze' (61) in Stevenson's film; she suggests that such cinematography implies a 'reversibility' in their relative positions – a cinematic doubling within the narrative, that results in a more radical engagement with the novel's sexual politics, offering in subtle ways a radical 'destabilizing counter-perspective on the romantic melodrama shown in the rest of the film' (63). However, the closing moments of the film reinforce the image of Rochester as our romantic hero; in a drawn out piece of exposition delivered by Mrs Fairfax to Jane on her return to the charred ruins of Thornfield Hall, we hear of Bertha's death through a narrative that focuses instead on the heroic actions of Rochester as he tries to save his mad wife from the flames. Bertha still functions as the dark secret of the gothic and Stevenson's film successfully presents us with a gothic landscape through its visual style, but her lack of presence leaves us with what is in essence an uncomplicated gothic romance. We are not asked to ponder Jane's internal growth as an independent woman. The Marsh End and Ferndean episodes are removed: only the romantic moments in Jane's journey are retained in the latter stages of this adaptation. Jane Eyre, as abused orphan, rises from the ashes of her cruel upbringing and is rewarded with safe romantic closure; like many of the films of this era, it is an adaptation that offers hope and comfort at a time when the world is a dangerous and unstable place. It is an adaptation that is influenced by the preoccupations of its production era and the expectations of its medium within a forties Hollywood studio system.

Geraghty argues that 'classic' adaptations connect with their source 'not only by drawing on the author's name' but by inclusion of such referents as shots of the novel and its prose, especially in the opening sequences (15). In this respect, the 1944 *Jane Eyre* pays homage to its source. However, at the levels of narrative and thematics, the film text distances itself from its origins and becomes instead a populist gothic romance. Yet its emphasis upon the gothic in a visual sense – shot in black and white, with its chiaroscuro lighting design and its constant use of fogbound landscapes and austere architecture – also distances the film from the period detail of the costume drama we have come to associate with adaptations of such classic texts. Franco Zeffirelli's 1996 adaptation of *Jane Eyre* adopts a similarly gothic approach to its cinematic translation but unlike Stevenson, Zeffirelli also employs the visual tropes of the costume drama. Director Cary Fukunaga's recent film adaptation presents a realist rendition of the architecture of time and place, in a style more reminiscent of Joe Wright's *Pride and Prejudice* (2005) than costume dramas in vogue in the nineties, but it also plays the gothic card and it remains in many respects a piece that is preoccupied with period detail. Just as post-Davies adaptations of *Pride and Prejudice* (or indeed post 1946 David Lean adaptations of *Great Expectations*) owe a debt to this televisual forerunner, Fukunaga and the writer of the 2011 screenplay, Moira Buffini, acknowledge *their* debt to the 1944 *Jane Eyre*; in the marketing materials that surround the 2011 adaptation of Brontë's novel, Buffini and director Cary Fukunaga argue that Stevenson's film is the most successful cinematic adaptation of the novel thus far, and state the intention to emulate its very gothic treatment of the narrative. Buffini sees it as a 'gothic thriller', its romance centring on a 'Beauty and the Beast' premise (Focus Features: Buffini interview), despite the implications of casting child-like Mia Maikowski as Jane and charismatic Michael Fassbender as Rochester; Fukunaga sees it as both 'a period film and a romance with elements of horror' (Focus Features: a Passionate Adaptation). For certain viewers, the sexual feminist politics of the text remains an intertextual point of reference regardless of whether or not such matters are consciously dealt with in any given adaptation of *Jane Eyre*. Yet it is worth noting that the most recent BBC *Jane Eyre* (White 2006) is arguably the only moving image adaptation to date that seeks to explore such matters in any kind of sustained manner. Though produced within a similar post 2000, postfeminist context, Fukunaga's film does not engage with the novel's sexual politics in any overt manner: as with Stevenson's film, it treads instead the established adaptive romance path.

Buffini and Fukunaga may align their film with what they define as the prestige of the 1944 film (Focus Features: Buffini interview), but the narrative structure of this 2011 adaptation presents us with a very different way into the story of Jane Eyre. Buffini's screenplay picks up Jane's story at her point of dramatic departure from Thornfield Hall; we are introduced to an isolated, emotionally conflicted heroine and through a series of flashbacks we learn what has brought her to this crisis point. Buffini's rationale for such a radical shift in narrative momentum relates to the problems of adapting all of what she deems the essential elements of Jane's journey; unlike Huxley, Buffini is not prepared to sacrifice the Marsh End period of this bildungsroman plot, even though she acknowledges the difficulty of introducing another set of characters at such a late point in the story (Focus Features: Buffini interview). A cinematic adaptation is also constrained by time limits, and by shifting the point of entry, Buffini engineers a way of both including the Rivers family and foregrounding selective memories of what has brought the protagonist to Marsh End. We avoid a purely chronological unravelling of the plot, and as a consequence we can stand back and assess what has gone before from the relative calm of Marsh End, in a manner that emulates the novel's retrospective first person narration, without resorting to intrusive devices like voiceover. As a consequence, some of the novel's preoccupations are sidelined in favour of others: we have less focus on the Gateshead period of the novel, less screen-time devoted to the relationship between Jane and Helen Burns, and Miss Templeton is again excised from the story. The memories that are realized on screen do, however, give us access to defining moments: the solitary Jane's initial altercation with tyrannical John Reed is played out for us in a way that highlights the violence of the scene, and Jane's character growth as a consequence of her Lowood experiences remains central to the narrative's momentum.

Much time is, instead, devoted to the development of the relationship between Rochester and Jane Eyre: fireside conversations in which, according to Buffini, they 'just talk each other into love' (Focus Features: Buffini interview) play out alongside sunlit encounters in the gardens of Thornfield Hall, where Jane sketches and Rochester tends his plants. The focus is very much upon the growing relationship between Jane and Rochester; the sexual politics of Brontë's novel again become secondary to the film narrative's preoccupation with romance, and Bertha's screen presence is once more minimized. We are momentarily introduced to Bertha by Rochester after his plans to marry Jane Eyre are foiled; she is not the bestial creature of Brontë's novel, despite Fukunaga's stated interest in the horror elements of the text. Instead she appears to be well cared for and there is a certain tenderness in the way that Rochester handles her, even when she becomes violent. Rochester's heroic status is of paramount importance here and matters relating to sexual, postcolonial and feminist politics are seen as secondary to the film's identity as gothic romance. The closing moments of this adaptation echo those of Stevenson's 1944 *Jane Eyre*: in a very similar manner, Jane returns to the ruins of Thornfield Hall, where Mrs Fairfax gives an account of Rochester's courageous attempts to rescue his mad wife from the fire she has started, once again underlining the heroism of the film's invariably handsome lead. Stevenson's film is intertextualized, emphasizing each adaptation's desire to foreground the romance elements of the source text. However, though both are physically maimed as a consequence of the fire, Welles' Rochester retains his masculine energies as he enters the film space whilst Fassbender's Rochester is constructed as a much more passive figure during the closing moments. Where Welles strides into shot, still looking like the commanding, romantic lead who initiates the final embrace, a passive, decidedly unkempt Fassbender – fulfilling at last his role as Buffini's 'Beast' – sits waiting, and it is Jane who takes the initiative in what is a very understated yet poignant close. Brontë's 'Reader, I married him' becomes a succinct interchange between the protagonists, and the final words are given to Jane:

Rochester: I dream.
Jane Eyre: Awaken then. (Buffini 92)

It is interesting to note that, whilst all three adaptations discussed here are seen as 'classic' adaptations, their treatment of the narrative differs considerably. Even though Fukunaga acknowledges a cinematic debt to Stevenson's earlier adaptation, the resultant film text has a very different tone. The general colour palette of the 2011 film is muted and the colour red, so central to the symbolism of the 2006 BBC adaptation as a means to foregrounding the relationship between Jane Eyre and her alter ego Bertha Mason, plays no visual part in Fukunaga's film. He is, however, conscious of highlighting the visual differences between Gateshead and Thornfield Hall; the former is shot in stark white light and the camera lingers upon the period detail of its rooms, whereas its interiors of Thornfield Hall are invariably shot in candlelight, replete with flickering shadows, the rooms' possessions becoming of secondary importance to the mood of the shot. In his treatment of the interiors and exteriors of Thornfield Hall, he highlights visually the contrast between tones suggestive of mystery and potential horror, and those of romance, openness and harmony. The darkly lit interiors of Thornfield Hall rely upon candlelight rather than direct lighting to lend even the fireside conversations between Jane and Rochester a double edge: the symbolic warmth and safety of the hearth is juxtaposed with the dangers inferred by the shadows cast around them. In contrast to the constantly fog-bound exteriors of Stevenson's film, when we move to the exteriors of Fukunaga's Thornfield Hall, we are momentarily given a sense of harmony as Jane sketches, Adele plays and Rochester cultivates his plants. The climactic point at which Rochester declares his love for Jane beneath the great oak is initially shot in bright sunlight, to the backdrop of the diegetic sounds of nature rather than an emotive orchestral score, and it is not until the next morning that we see the split tree. Unlike most adapters, Fukunaga relinquishes the gothic drama of this moment and highlights instead the sense of their natural union, doomed though it is from the outset by things we have no knowledge of as yet.

Despite the unromantic grittiness of its opening moments and the gothic edge established in its treatment of its Thornfield Hall location in general, much is made of the period detail of location and costume throughout the rest of this film. It also recycles film locations used by earlier screen adapters of the novel: Haddon Hall and Wingfield Manor provide the period settings for Thornfield Hall and its ruins respectively in both Zeffirelli's 1996 *Jane Eyre* and the 2006 TV adaptation. Whether any of these 'classic' adaptations aims for the kind of 'nostalgic gaze' we associate with costume drama/heritage cinema is open for debate: all three employ costume and setting as part of the temporal positioning of a narrative belonging to a specific moment from the nineteenth century, but none of these film texts foregrounds the period elements at the expense of its own cinematic agenda. Stevenson's film, with its choice of black and white film stock and its gothic look, is first and foremost a gothic romance;

White's TV serialization has its own political agenda and chooses to step outside the boundaries of costume drama at various points in the narrative, notably in its first introduction of Jane as one aligned with an alien desert landscape; Fukunaga's gritty realization of the historical moment ensures a level of authenticity rather than the kind of visual splendour we have come to view as an intrinsic characteristic of heritage cinema, but it is again the story's romantic momentum that drives this film product rather than any overt preoccupation with period detail. Each of these screen adaptations becomes part of a narrative continuum, recycling and intertextualizing the romance at the core of *Jane Eyre* ad infinitum.

Jane Eyre: Re-visioning the text (*Wide Sargasso Sea* and *Rebecca*)

Canonical texts like *Jane Eyre* permeate our culture, engaged in what Geraghty sees as:

> a layering process [that] involves an accretion of deposits over time, a recognition of ghostly presences, and a shadowing or doubling of what is on the surface by what is glimpsed behind. (195)

Jean Rhys's *Wide Sargasso Sea* and Daphne Du Maurier's *Rebecca* form part of this kind of 'layering process': they are haunted by and in turn they haunt Brontë's gothic romance, refracting and re-visioning its thematic concerns through the creative prism of adaptation. Though defined here as a 're-visioning' of the *Jane Eyre* narrative, both *Rebecca* and *Wide Sargasso Sea* may be seen instead as adaptations that function as 'radical rethinks'. As with all taxonomies, the placement of a text into a particular classification is problematic: all models serve only as a platform for discussion of the texts under review and offer us interesting pathways into a discussion of the relationship between those texts. However, in this instance they are identified as 're-visionist' adaptations as a matter of authorial intent and political agenda. Jean Rhys makes her position clear from the outset, stating:

> The Creole in Charlotte Brontë's novel is a lay figure – repulsive which does not matter, and not once alive which does. She's necessary to the plot, but always she shrieks, howls, laughs horribly, attacks all and sundry – *off stage*. For me she must be right *on stage*. She must be plausible with a past, a *reason*

why Mr Rochester treats her so abominably and feels justified, the reason why he thinks she is mad and why of course she goes mad, even the *reason* why she tries to set everything on fire, and eventually succeeds. (Rhys qtd in Wyndham and Melly 157)

In seeking to shift the narrative focus from Brontë's Eyre to the novel's Bertha Mason and her relationship with Rochester, Rhys repositions the reader, affording Antoinette (as she is referred to in *Wide Sargasso Sea*) a visible, complex presence – a presence that colours our reading of *Jane Eyre* and gives greater significance to Bertha's function within the precursor text. Though we may see it as a prequel it is also, in the parlance of Adrienne Rich, an act of 're-vision' that allows us to 'enter an old text from a new critical direction', that encourages us to 'know the writing of the past and know it differently', breaking with tradition as a means to challenging the canonical text's authority (18). Sanders notes Rhys's desire to 'go "after" canonical works', to 'question their basis in patriarchal and imperial cultural contexts' (157), and it is this desire that sets her adaptive agenda. Rhys is eager to position her novel in relation to Brontë's *Jane Eyre*, and for readers who have prior knowledge of *Jane Eyre*, the outcomes of *Wide Sargasso Sea* are intrinsically linked to those of the canonical text: we remain, to a certain extent, dependent upon our knowledge of it. But in this instance, Rhys's prequel does more than offer backstory: it is an adaptation that changes our perception of the canonical text's characters and its politics, and it becomes an influential part of the feminist/postcolonial discourse that surrounds Brontë's *Jane Eyre*.

Daphne Du Maurier's *Rebecca*, first published in serial form in British and American newspapers and subsequently released as a novel in 1938, has a less definitive relationship with *Jane Eyre*: at no point does the writer identify her novel as an adaptation of Brontë's text. Avril Horner and Sue Zlosnik note that she 'never refers to what most readers see as an implicit intertextuality with *Jane Eyre*' (112), and yet the narrative parallels, the Gothic tone and the striking similarities and contrasts between characters that people both novels identify it as a text which plays with Brontë's tale. Like Rhys, Du Maurier brings to the fore the complex 'presence' of the problematic first wife; in *Wide Sargasso Sea*, Antoinette is very much 'onstage', and yet despite the fact that Rebecca is deceased at the onset of Du Maurier's novel, her identity as a powerful and covertly subversive force is written into the narrative's subtext, and the narrator is constantly examined in relation to Rebecca. Such textual concerns engage with readings of *Jane Eyre* in which Bertha is viewed as Jane's mirror image, her sexualized, dangerous doppelganger, reinforcing the notion that Rebecca is all that the second Mrs De Winter longs to be yet cannot, much to the relief of Maxim. *Rebecca* may be deemed what Sanders terms an 'appropriation' rather than an 'adaptation' since its relationship with *Jane Eyre* is 'less explicit, more embedded' (2–3), but as with Rhys's *Wide Sargasso Sea*, once read, it has the capacity to infiltrate our relationship with the canonical text, leading us to reassess our understanding of the thematic preoccupations that dominate Brontë's novel.

However, both *Rebecca* and *Wide Sargasso Sea* are texts with an independent identity: they are not to be viewed as works which have relevance only in so far as they engage with *Jane Eyre*. *Wide Sargasso Sea* is seen as a canonical text, having attained the status of a modern classic, and though Du Maurier's novel is ostensibly a piece of populist romance fiction, it has both a certain literary status and an enduring place within the best seller list. It has also generated a body of adaptations in its own right, from a raft of novels (Susan Hill's *Mrs De Winter* 1993; Maureen Freely's *The Other Rebecca*; Sally Beauman's *Rebecca's Tale* 2001; Justine Picardie's *Daphne* 2008) to plays, films and televised serializations, some of which were produced within three years of the novel's publication. Whilst Alfred Hitchcock directed the now famous screen adaptation of *Rebecca* (1940), Du Maurier reinscribed her narrative for the West End stage as a detective story (1940) and Orson Welles Mercury Theatre produced a radio play version of the tale. That such interest surrounded the narrative at its initial time of release attests to its contemporary popularity and to the enduring allure of themes explored in Brontë's *Jane Eyre*. Hollywood producer David O. Selznick – a producer keen to monopolize on the literary kudos of existing narratives – seized upon its popularity and Hitchcock's cinematic reincarnation of Du Maurier's *Rebecca* has ensured its prominent place within popular culture as a well-known gothic romance. It is also a narrative that finds its place within very different cultures and cinematic arenas; there have been several Bollywood adaptations (*Kohra* 1964; *Anamika* 2008) both of which present us with melodramatic romance situated not in the gentrified English mansion of Du Maurier's novel but in Eastern palaces haunted by the ghosts of dead first wives. And whilst televised serializations have generally taken the well-trodden path of costume drama (BBC 1979; ITV 1997), as a consequence of greater sexual openness and acceptance in a mid-nineties context, opportunities to explore the sexual subtleties of the story in more overt ways have been seized upon with, for example, ITV's nineties adaptation foregrounding the lesbian leanings of

Mrs Danvers. The latest adaptation currently in pre-production and to be directed by Dane Nikolaj Arcel, may offer a similarly explicit exploration of the more ambiguous sexuality presented in Du Maurier's novel, but there is no guarantee that Dreamworks and Working Title's contemporary production will be more radical and no definitive indication as to whether it will function as an adaption of Du Maurier's novel, or a remake of Hitchcock's film.

Rebecca presents us with an alternative kind of bildungsroman, again told from a first person perspective by a heroine who mirrors Brontë's narrator in some respects; yet this narrator also serves as the antithesis of Jane Eyre in other vitally important ways. Indeed, it could be argued that the deceased Rebecca has more in common with Brontë's heroine than the novel's narrator. Like *Jane Eyre*, *Rebecca* is a novel that may viewed as what Ellen Moers terms the Female Gothic – a 'coded expression of women's fears of entrapment within the domestic and within the female body' (90). At a surface level, it shares with Brontë's novel its gothic manorial setting as a site of 'ghostly' visitations, dark secrets and past transgressions; similarly, the plot of each, revolves around the romantic union between a diminutive young woman of low social status and a wealthy, enigmatic older man, recounted through the former's first person narration. As with *Jane Eyre*, the tale of Bluebeard haunts the narrative, with its timid yet curious heroine, lurking in the gothic shadows, and the final revelation that the hero is a man of dark secrets who poses a threat to women – especially to wives. However, in both its prose and cinematic forms, whilst *Rebecca* appears to be an *uncomplicated* gothic romance, dealing in conservative values, it is on closer reading – especially when read as a text that intertextualizes the Eyre narrative – a complex critique of patriarchal society and its positioning of women. The institution of marriage (and the home) becomes a vehicle for female repression in which women are threatened or excised. Ostensibly, it is Rebecca, like Bertha before her, who threatens the position of the narrator within this narrative, but at a subtextual level we sense that it is Maxim, with his desire to control and infantalize the second Mrs De Winter who poses the greatest threat to her well-being. His 'love' of the narrator is predicated on her capacity to remain virginal and child-like, and one wonders from the outset what happiness can be attained in a marriage that is founded on the desire to suppress female maturity. Rochester's supposedly dangerous, lascivious wife Bertha is incarcerated as she poses a threat to herself and to others, but most of all to his own sense of English respectability; similarly, Rebecca threatens Maxim's manhood and uses his desire to maintain the image of a perfect society marriage as a means to blackmailing him into accepting her adulterous behaviour. But whilst Brontë affords Rochester both the foresight to love the mature, independent Jane of the novel's denouement, and hero status in his final dealings with his first wife as he tries to rescue her from the flames engulfing Thornfield, Du Maurier's Maxim presents us with the ultimate threat to females in marriage when finally revealed as Rebecca's murderer.

Du Maurier, like Brontë, also plays with our perception of female identity through the inclusion of the 'other' woman. However, whilst Brontë places her narrator centre stage, naming the text *Jane Eyre*, Du Maurier asserts the importance of Rebecca from the outset by inscribing her presence through the novel's title. Rebecca is never a mere plot device. Given Brontë's preoccupation with names and her protagonist's anxious reaction to the potential surrendering of that name as a consequence of her impending marriage, it is interesting to note that Du Maurier devotes time and attention to this very issue in *Rebecca*: in subtle ways, it is the invisible Rebecca whose identity and name remain inscribed throughout. The narrator remains nameless; she is the unnamed orphan child who, in marriage, gladly accepts the appendage of her husband and yet is always seen as the *second* Mrs de Winter, referred to repeatedly as a 'child', a 'little girl', afraid of the domestic duties thrust upon her and lacking confidence in her power to pass (unlike Rebecca) as 'a woman...dressed in black satin with a string of pearls' (Du Maurier 46). Conversely, we are invited to conjure images of Rebecca throughout firstly by constant references to her by other characters in the narrative and secondly by the prominence of her name, monocled on objects still to be found at Manderley: her name appears on her stationery, on pillows, on letters and inscriptions to Max. The shrine-like preservation of Rebecca's living quarters by the obsessive Mrs Danvers sets up an antithesis to Brontë's image of Bertha, imprisoned in her tower and tended by ambivalent gatekeeper Grace Poole; Rebecca's 'tower' is testimony to her power even beyond the grave, whilst Bertha's is evidence of her powerless incarceration and symptomatic of her descent into an almost non-human, invisible form. And unlike the narrator, she is not trapped in domestic spaces; rather, she commands them, even when she is dead.

It is through repositioning of the narrator's gothic double, Rebecca, that Du Maurier's darker purpose is explored in this text. Writing in the guise of populist romance fiction, Du Maurier's subtextual messages challenge accepted definitions of the position of women in 1930s western society.

By creating the public façade of a happy marriage and by playing the part of successful society wife, Rebecca is able to pursue her own transgressive desires within the private sphere. She rides, sails, travels unaccompanied and privately flaunts her adulterous affairs to her husband; there are also subtle hints of her bi-sexuality and of Mrs Danvers' lesbian obsession with Rebecca. Horner and Zlosnik note that du Maurier's own preoccupation with what she termed her 'boy-in the box' syndrome led her to write into existence a 'masculine personae through which she could express a desire for women' (110). Rebecca represents not only the gothic double of the second Mrs de Winter but of her creator – a married woman with children, writing about heterosexual romance for a conservative mainstream audience yet harbouring aberrant sexual desires within the taboo context of the 1930s. It is, however, disturbing to note that by posing a threat to societal norms, Rebecca, like her predecessor Bertha Mason, is ultimately sacrificed for threatening the sanctity of marriage.

For a twenty-first-century audience, bi-sexuality and homosexuality are no longer deemed problematic; instead, what may strike the contemporary reader as aberrant is the relationship between the narrator and her much older love interest. It will be interesting to see how Dreamworks' *Rebecca* will address this aspect of the text. Germaine Greer contests that 'women's erotic fantasy is so shocking, so subversive that it can only be written in code' and that it's main narrative trajectory involves a pseudo 'seduction of the father by the daughter', casting Du Maurier's narrator as the 'seducing child' who triumphs only as a consequence of her child-like persona and thus making this narrative a tale of paedophilic involvement in terms of twenty-first-century sensibilities. In many respects, the same is true of Jane Eyre: she is the virginal, inexperienced, fairy child who represents the antithesis of the worldly, sexually aware society women (from Bertha, to Celene Varens to the social-climbing Blanche Ingram) he has thus far been involved with and it is this that attracts him to her, whilst for Jane he represents the lost father figure. However, Du Maurier's construction of her narrator constantly reinscribes her child-like status and Maxim's desire for her to dress up as Alice in Wonderland for the Manderley Ball speaks volumes. His assertion that 'a husband is not so very different from a father' is similarly indicative of the nature of their relationship. This narrator is to be controlled and mastered in a way that Jane Eyre could never be; Jane Eyre has more in common with the outspoken Rebecca than with the subservient, passive second Mrs De Winter who must 'eat up [her] peaches' without asking 'any more questions' under threat of being 'put in a corner' (238). There are occasional lines which suggest her frustration at being seen in this manner, and she recounts a number of failed attempts to redefine herself as womanly, but she remains the pure, innocent child until the closing moments when her innocence is willingly sacrificed as a means to gaining control of her marriage and affirmation of Maxim's love for her. That the childlike Mrs De Winter transforms at this point into an adult does not bode well for the relationship given that Maxim's desire for her is built upon her capacity to remain innocent and unwomanly – a girl who will 'never wear black satin' (46). Her response is similarly problematic:

> I don't want you to bear this alone. I want to share it with you. I've grown up, Maxim, in twenty-four hours. I'll never be a child again … I'll be your friend and your companion, a sort of boy. I don't ever want more than that. (313)

The promised romantic closure falters; the language adopted by the narrator at this point does not speak of heterosexual romance but of accomplices, bound together by a secret pact rather than by mutual sexual attraction, and by referring to herself as a 'sort of boy', we are again reminded of the sexual ambiguities operating at a subtextual level throughout this novel. Whilst Brontë's nineteenth-century text subverts expectations of the gothic protagonist through her questioning of the roles of women in Victorian society, Du Maurier's twentieth-century narrator epitomizes the genre's persecuted heroine; but the seemingly down-trodden narrator, dwarfed by both the invisible presence of the first Mrs De Winter and the very real presence of Rebecca's loyal housekeeper, Mrs Danvers, and Maxim, her domineering husband who revels in her child-like stature, ultimately emerges at the end of this warped bildungsroman as a woman in control, secure in the knowledge that she is loved yet willingly culpable in the guilty secret that surrounds the murder of Rebecca.

In this novel of secrets and disguise lurks, according to adapter Frank McGuiness, a far less gullible narrator. McGuinness argues that Du Maurier's meek narrator is more 'tiger' than 'mouse' and sees her as 'a master of disguise'. Rather than being a put upon girl who chooses, in the name of love, to acquiesce in the cover up of a murder, she is 'an intelligent woman who completely wrong-foots the reader by brilliantly disguising her victory as a defeat and herself as a victim when she is actually a victor'. His contention that 'the more you want to shake her, the cleverer she's being' has some validity and, in his 2005 stage adaptation of the novel, McGuinness creates a far more feisty narrator with whom his contemporary audience readily identify, giving her lines of dialogue that challenge the dominance of characters like Mrs Danvers (McGuinness qtd in Sooke). In Du Maurier's novel she may remain annoyingly compliant and afraid but her final response to the knowledge of Rebecca's murder suggests that her attempts to 'masquerad[e] as blameless victi[m] of a corrupt and oppressive patriarchal society' (Smith and Wallace 2) are just that: her compliance results in her triumph over that system, leaving Maxim dependent upon her willing participation in a cover-up. The narrator's story, couched in a style of writing more readily associated with pulp fiction of the type a character like the second Mrs De Winter may read, is perhaps yet another disguise; the very constructed 'voice' of the narrator should immediately signal to us a certain unreliability, or at least a suspicion that, like the protagonist of Henry James' The Turn of the Screw', our narrator is self-dramatizing.

Du Maurier takes the traditional bildungsroman structure and subverts our expectations. Instead of witnessing the narrator's growth towards a moment of uplifting maturity, we follow on a trajectory, from 'innocent child' to 'corrupt woman', and though Rebecca is excised through the parallel plot point of destruction by fire – of all traces of her existence and of Manderley, the site of gothic haunting – there is no comfortable closure of the kind characteristic of the Female Gothic: despite the excision of Rebecca and the realization that Maxim hated his first wife, his secret becomes a shared burden, the lovers must live in exile, and the reader is left to question the heroic value of a protagonist who seizes the opportunity to aid her husband in the cover up of a murder. Du Maurier's initial ending envisaged a much closer correlation to that of *Jane Eyre*, with Maxim disabled as a result of a car accident, and the second Mrs De Winter gaining strength from her position as his lifelong carer, but the decision to remove this echo of the Eyre story encourages us to retain our doubts as to the stability of this relationship: whilst Brontë's narrator reveals 'Reader, I married him' in the closing section of the novel, Du Maurier chooses to make her reader privy to the marital outcome at the onset, and what follows is less about the emerging romance than about the problems endured within it. Whilst *Jane Eyre* is a narrative that alludes to aspects of the 'Bluebeard' tale, with its referencing of a husband with dark secrets and an unravelling of the mysteries surrounding former wives, Rebecca follows a narrative trajectory that revolves as much around the unravelling of Maxim's Bluebeardesque secret as it does around notions of romance, despite its classification *as* romance fiction.

Du Maurier's forties detective thriller stage adaptation of *Rebecca* was consciously 'unfaithful'; as an adapter aware of the need to shape narratives according to their time of production and their medium, she sacrificed the novel's gothic edge in favour of a dialogue-driven murder-mystery spin that excised its subtextual subtleties but proved popular when first staged in the West End during the Second World War. Manderley, the novel's symbol of a degenerate English aristocracy, became instead symbolic of 'unity, stability and defeat of threatening forces' for an English audience in the throes of the Second World War (D'Monte 2), and the play ends with the De Winters still in residence rather than in exile, Manderley still intact and Mrs Danvers suitably banished. And yet at Du Maurier's insistence and as part of his own continuing pursuit of literary kudos, when adapting the novel to forties Hollywood cinema, producer David O. Selznick aimed to create a 'faithful' cinematic version of *Rebecca*. Given the financial implications of large scale cinematic production – *Rebecca* cost $1,288,000 – Selznick also aimed his film at forties cinema's predominantly female audience, creating a 'woman's film with a direct appeal to romantic fantasies' (Modleski 44). Though already a success in the British film industry, Alfred Hitchcock was a relative newcomer to the Hollywood scene when appointed director of this film, and despite his posthumous status as an auteur, his control of the project was limited. Questions of authorship within the very collaborative film industry continue to generate debate: who has the creative ownership of the final film product? Some may argue here that it is Selznick the producer with his interventionist strategies; many see *Rebecca* as a Hitchcock film, despite the director's claim that it is not a Hitchcock picture; but what of those involved in the adaptation of Du Maurier's prose to screenplay format? The first screenplay, rejected by Selznick, was written by Philip MacDonald and Joan Harrison whilst the revised version was penned by Harrison in collaboration with Hitchcock and Michael Hogan, but Selznick hired yet another writer, Robert E. Sherwood, to draft the final script. Unlike his producer Hitchcock was averse to adapting classic novels – he preferred to work with little known texts over which he had creative control. For a director who covets 'authorship', the lack of control exercised over this film caused problems, and yet it is the one Hitchcock film that has garnered any kind of Oscar, securing the academy award for Best Picture of 1940. Seen as a film that brought into vogue the forties cycle of the Gothic Woman's film, characterized by its preoccupation with marriage as an institution haunted by murder, it was both critically acclaimed and a huge box-office success. It generated a body of films in the forties now classified as Women's Gothic;

from *Suspicion* (1941), *Jane Eyre* (1944) and *Gaslight* (1944) to *Dragonwyck* (1946) and *Secret Beyond a Door* (1948), these films revolve around the damsel in distress within a romance plot that echoes the narrative trajectory of 'Bluebeard', adding yet again to what Geraghty terms a 'layering process [that] involves an accretion of deposits', of 'ghostly presences' that 'shad[ow]' earlier narratives (109).

And yet despite Selznick's 'fidelity' edict and Du Maurier's insistence that this Hitchcock adaptation of her work (unlike his 1939 film adaptation of *Jamaica Inn*) must remain faithful to her novel, Hitchcock's *Rebecca* is ultimately a Hitchcock film with the auteurist flourishes of his later work in evidence throughout, if only in subtle ways. Turning to his advantage Selznick's somewhat limited reading of the novel's narrator as 'a little girl' whose 'nervousness' and 'self-consciousness' make her a protagonist for whom every reader has 'cringed with embarrassment' and yet 'adored' (Selznick qtd in Modleski 43), Hitchcock amplifies the diminutive, child-like status of the narrator and builds upon the novel's identity as gothic horror. With her prim, school girl attire and her submissive body language, Joan Fontaine's narrator becomes the 'cringing' child bride, her victim status and her innate fear of all things womanly and adult permeating her performance. Her role as gothic heroine, menaced within the confines of the domestic space, is exaggerated throughout, and in Hitchcock's film it is not a Bluebeardesque husband who provides us with the gothic fear factor but a hauntingly present Rebecca and the obsessive Mrs Danvers. Maxim's role as romantic lead is emphasized and even his final reveal is tempered by plot amendments that are a consequence of the restrictive and highly moralistic Hays 1930 Production Code, one of its guiding principles being:

> No picture shall be produced that will lower the moral standards of those who see it. Hence the sympathy of the audience should never be thrown to the side of crime, wrongdoing, evil or sin. (Brooke, BFI Screenonline)

Rebecca's murder becomes an act of manslaughter, and her pregnancy becomes late stage cancer, allowing Maxim to emerge as one who, within the parameters of the code, can be rewarded with romantic union, whilst Rebecca remains the sinner, punished for her misdemeanours. Further plot amendments serve to establish Maxim as a more vulnerable hero; his first meeting with the narrator places him precariously on the edge of a cliff, seemingly contemplating suicide, his reasons for being so distraught becoming part of the tale's narrative momentum. He is also the romantic lead who rescues the gothic damsel in distress as the film places the second Mrs De Winter in the burning Manderley *alongside* the evil Mrs Danvers and the ghostly remains of her nemesis, Rebecca, during the film's final scene.

As well as intervening through plot excisions and additions, the adapter of a first person narration must circumnavigate the difficulties of translating this internalized prose into film's visual vocabulary. The realism of cinema dictates a third person narration via the filter of the camera's lens, and though voiceover may mirror the internalized mode of expression afforded by the novel's first person narration, it is a device used sparingly by filmmakers. Fontaine's voiceover takes us into the story initially but we soon move into flashback. As a consequence of taking away her all-pervasive narrative 'voice', Hitchcock reinscribes the narrator's position as powerless interloper in her own tale. At every opportunity her diminutive status is heightened: even the height of the doors and their handles appear to dwarf her, creating an Alice in Wonderland image that echoes Maxim's desire to see her dressed as Alice at the Manderley ball. Hitchcock also amplifies the gothic properties of the narrative by shooting in black and white with low level lighting, permeating the visuals of the film text with shadows and dark corners and utilizing camera angles and frames that heighten the claustrophobic atmosphere, especially when the focus of the shot is the narrator or the narrator and Mrs Danvers. Just as Joan Fontaine's performance plays to the submissive nature of the heroine in a manner that defines her as victim, Judith Anderson brings to the role of Mrs Danvers an other-worldly quality as she glides into and out of shot, appearing as if from nowhere and always in disquieting close-up. Hitchcock's treatment of the moment in which Mrs Danvers taunts the narrator with the Rebecca's silken underwear provides a subtle yet powerful exploration of the novel's sexual dalliance with homosexual desire at a time when such matters could not be addressed openly, and the addition of a scene in which the tormented narrator is encouraged by Mrs Danvers to commit suicide adds a further layer of menace to the tale, affording Hitchcock the opportunity to realize the horror dynamics he intended. Like Maxim, the narrator is pushed to the edge of self-destruction by the forces of evil (Rebecca and Mrs Danvers) at work in Manderley, making their romantic closure a conclusion that we anticipate and applaud in a way that is not possible when one reads the subtext of Du Maurier's novel. The narrator matures instantaneously during Maxim's confession scene: the alice band and twin set look is replaced by more womanly loose curls and dark coat, and the cringing body language and tortuous facial expressions are excised.

However, though visibly changed we are unable to see throughout the film text any sign of the intelligent woman who according to McGuinness lurks within the subtext of Du Maurier's novel and emerges triumphant at its close (McGuinness quoted in Sooke).

Whether we view the romance at the centre of this narrative as an appropriation of the female Oedipus complex (Raymond Durgnat qtd in Modelski 44) or, as Tanya Modleski suggests, the Electra complex, the patriarchal control exercised by Maxim in this relationship, and the narrator's incapacity to define herself within the domestic spaces of Manderley until the 'mother' figure Rebecca is destroyed, are visibly reinscribed in Hitchcock's film (45). Hitchcock's insertion of the 'projector' scene and his treatment of the Boat House confession scene have generated much scholarly debate. Hitchcock chooses not to present us with any onscreen image of Rebecca, even though film's third person narration mode presents him with the capacity to do so. She remains a figure whose onscreen realization is achieved through the recollections of others and through objects, from her preserved wing at Manderley to her possessions both there and in the house in general, many bearing her monocle and shot in close up. The closing moments, for example, place her centre stage as the camera tracks in to the pillow on her bed, her burning initials held in the camera's gaze. The final image reinscribes the presence of Rebecca, highlighting her significance within this telling of the tale, and throughout the film she haunts the edges of the frame, 'lurk[ing] in the blind space of the film' (Modleski 53). Though the story is temporarily hijacked as we move towards its final moments, becoming a crime thriller dominated by males in pursuit of the truth and order, it is the invisible Rebecca who commands the cinematic space at the close rather than the men involved in this restoration of patriarchal order or the romantic couples who form the final focus in both *Jane Eyre* and Du Maurier's *Rebecca*.

A comparison of the two scenes identified reveals the very different ways in which the narrator and Rebecca are constructed within this film text. Both have generated heated critical debate amongst feminist scholars. Prior to the addition of the projection scene in which Maxim presents his second wife with the kinds of images of her sanctioned by him – feeding geese and giggling in a childlike manner – the narrator has tried to reinvent her image: we move from the pages of a style magazine to the image of the narrator, emulating the magazine model and looking very much like the kind of woman abhorred by her husband, 'dressed in black satin with a string of pearls'. Her anticipated approval is met by his humiliating indulgence of her but it masks his desire to control her persona and we swiftly move to the projected images *he* has constructed for her gaze. Mary Ann Doane argues that though she 'enters hoping to beco[me] a spectacle for Maxim' she is 'relegated to the position of spectator-spectator of the images Maxim prefers' (202), and when at this point we see the very first signs of her questioning his authority, Maxim 'castrates' her gaze, placing himself in front of the projected images and obliterating all trace of her (203). Through this addition to the tale, Hitchcock is able to create, via cinematic shorthand, the sense of masculine menace that permeates Du Maurier's gothic romance. The narrator becomes what Mulvey terms 'the image of woman as (passive) raw material for the (active) male gaze' (6–18) but what is most interesting here is that she seeks this as a means to becoming more womanly; it is Maxim's rejection of this invitation to gaze upon her as a woman that is most disturbing, reinscribing at a subtextual level at least, the paedophilic qualities of this romance.

Conversely, the womanly Rebecca remains outside the parameters of the male gaze. She is at all times unseen and thus escapes any sense of being set up as 'sexual object', the 'leif-motif of erotic spectacle' (Modleski 62). Modleski notes that 'in *Rebecca*, the beautiful, desirable woman is not only never made a part of the film's field of vision, she is actually posited within the diegesis as all-seeing', placing her in a position of power. Such power is realized in the scene in which Maxim confesses to her manslaughter; Rebecca may not be present, but by placing us with Maxim as he recounts the movements of Rebecca on that day, we experience via the camera's tracking, her presence as she controls his and our gaze. Doane argues that, since it is still Maxim who narrates the moment, ventriloquizing Rebecca's voice and giving us his version of events, it is Maxim who retains ultimate control, 'inscrib[ing]' her 'absence' by 'constructing a story about [her] which no longer requires even her physical presence' and thus hi-jacking female power (210): even as the invisible femme fatale figure takes centre stage, that stage is managed by a male. However, though we initially enter this story via the retrospective narration of the second Mrs De Winter, there is no return to her voiceover in the film's closing moments; rather, we close in on the image of Rebecca's burning bed as her monocled pillow is devoured by flames. It is Rebecca's demise that takes centre stage at this point. Maxim may have been recast as the hero who saves his damsel in distress from the flames that destroy both Manderley and Rebecca, but the gothic romance plot is superseded by the powerful presence that is the dead wife and we are left to ponder whether she can ever be excised. Hitchcock successfully amplifies the horror of the text over and above its romantic leanings, foreshadowing the emergence of a cycle of forties Hollywood films dealing in the Female Gothic.

Though intent upon giving a voice to the marginalized Bertha of Brontë's *Jane Eyre*, Rhys's *Wide Sargasso Sea* has a more ambivalent close. Despite the fact that Rhys has succeeded in bringing Antoinette 'on stage', affording her a credible past and a rationale as to why she descends into madness, by the end of her novel Antoinette is renamed Bertha and is incarcerated in the tower at Thornfield. She refers to herself as 'the ghost … the woman with streaming hair … surrounded by a gilt frame' (Rhys 154), suggesting that she is not only held within the confines of the frame but that the mirror image refracted within it is one that redefines her as someone she barely recognizes. Caroline Rody sees Antoinette's narrative as one that ultimately leads a 'revolt against the master text' of *Jane Eyre* (Rody qtd in Kimmey 129), but Deborah Kimmey argues that the 'gilt frame' functions here as a veiled authorial reference to the canonical text that similarly frames and contains Rhys's narrative (127), implying that just as Antoinette is defined ultimately by Rochester, the novel remains a text that is defined by its relationship with Brontë's 'master narrative'. Kimmey views such alignment as detrimental, and yet Rhys has, from the outset, purposely foregrounded the interdependence of her story and her desire not only to present her own tale but to *redefine* our perception of the 'grand master text' that precedes it. As an adapter with a particular agenda, Rhys adopts a subversive proactive engagement with the canonical precursor text, giving voice to a different kind of subjugation to that explored in *Jane Eyre* by handing the first person narration to Brontë's 'mad woman in the attic', relocating the narrative to the referenced colonial outpost, and rewriting its politics as a consequence of both by drawing upon postcolonial and second wave feminist critiques of the 'master text'. And despite Antoinette's changed appearance and her incarceration, there is again an inference that, as with Rebecca, this 'other' woman is in charge of her final destiny: having awoken from a prophetic dream of fire spreading through Thornfield, she states 'at last I know why I was brought here and what I have to do (Rhys 155–156)'. It is construed as a final, empowering act of rebellion by some, the inference being that she will burn down Thornfield Hall and all that it stands for in terms of patriarchal and colonial power; but for others it is seen as an act of self-destructive despair that, engineered by her jailor-husband, reinscribes the disturbing dominance of Empire and of patriarchy. Whichever reading of the text prevails, Antoinette's statement functions as a loaded echo of the author's re-visionist adaptive strategy: Rhys has brought the bestial Bertha of the canonical text 'on stage' and in so doing changes our perception of the so-called 'master narrative'.

Adapters reconfigure Brontë's Bertha Mason in accordance with their own agenda: whether secreted into the narrative subtext of an adaptation or foregrounded as first person narrator of her own story, she emerges as a construct of ideological significance. Even when excised in the name of the romance plot in mainstream Hollywood films, her absence provokes debate. Rhys takes us to a point in the narrative which precedes that of *Jane Eyre*: this is Antoinette Mason's bildungsroman, retrospectively recounted and ending on an ambiguous note that denies us the form's neat closure – a closure that traditionally reasserts the social status quo and places the narrator back into the fold, her character arc completed. The fragmented nature of Rhys's narrative works contrary to the norms of the realist structural mode of the bildungsroman plot; Antoinette's narrative dominates but her unnamed husband is also given a narrative voice that provides us, as the writer intended, with an understanding of (though not a justification for) his treatment of his wife. But it is Antoinette who is given narrational authority, rather than Jane Eyre who is this time the character excised from the plot. Rochester is also given a narrative space to relate his own tale; however, Antoinette invades his story, reinforcing her authorial power as her earlier lines, presented in italics, hijack his:

> I saw the hate go out of her eyes. I forced it out. And with the hate her beauty. She was only a ghost. A ghost in grey daylight. Nothing left but hopelessness. *Say die and I will die. Say die and watch me die.* (140)

However, when Antoinette's capacity to control the narrative disintegrates in Part three she descends into madness, suggesting that the power to narrate one's own story is crucial to existence. By addressing such issues, Rhys not only deals with matters of feminist importance but of postcolonial significance: Jane Eyre is able to maintain control of her narrative but the culturally 'other' Antoinette cannot, and it is Rochester, symbol of Empire, who orchestrates her silence.

Whilst Rebecca remains an invisible and thus indefinable force within the text, Antoinette is systematically reconstructed and diminished by her husband as the story unfolds; Jane Eyre becomes emblematic of female resistance, defying all male attempts to redefine her, but Antoinette lacks the power to resist her husband's systematic assault upon her identity. Rhys engages in debates surrounding the importance of narrative ownership and like Brontë she is concerned with the significance of names. Antoinette's husband, initially echoing the seemingly weak and ineffectual narrator of *Rebecca*, remains *unnamed* and as such we view him as one who is less defined within the narrative, but as the story unfolds we see him turn his position of narrative powerlessness into a position of dominance. Like Jane Eyre, Antoinette is aware that 'names matter' and that her husband's refusal to call her by her name results in a loss of self; she sees 'Antoinette drifting out of the window with her scents ... her pretty clothes and her looking-glass', leaving her to question her own identity (147). It is Rochester's reductive renaming of Antoinette that brings about his psychological victory. Allusions to the master-slave relationship between Jane Eyre and Rochester are also written into *Wide Sargasso Sea* but in this instance the slavery reference is heightened by the colonial setting and the diminished social standing of the white planter class of the 1830s. Antoinette's husband assumes the role of the slave-master, renaming his purchase. The white plantation class is viewed in Brontë's contemporary England as immoral due to its connection to slavery, but by building upon the significance of names and the colonial practice of renaming slave 'commodities', Rhys is able to add another dimension to the debate – one that critiques the Empire and highlights its hypocritical, moralistic stance by creating empathy for Antoinette, the story's representative of the deserted planter class.

Unlike Jane Eyre, the protagonist's 'otherness' is not a simple consequence of her class or gender. Rather, it is her cultural 'otherness' that Rhys chooses to highlight – an 'otherness' that is at odds with the unnamed husband's sense of self and nationhood. She has 'long, dark, alien eyes' and is a 'Creole of pure English descent', yet she is not 'English or European' (56). Her beauty and what he sees as her emotional excess add to his sense of her as 'alien', but it is his own alienation within the colonial environment that exacerbates the problem. It is a place that is similarly associated with excess – where 'everything is too much ... too much blue, too much purple, too much green' (59) too 'wild, untouched, with an alien, disturbing secret loveliness' (73), but with a 'loveliness' that is 'unreal' and 'dreamlike' (67). This pseudo Rochester shares Bertha Mason's position of relative powerlessness and geographical displacement but he also shares Jane Eyre's position of relative social inferiority. Rhys highlights his resentment of a system that treats younger sons of wealthy men as commodities to be brokered in marriage; he states that, contrary to the widely held belief that it is women who are treated as acquisitions to be bought via marriage, it is Antoinette who has 'bought [him]' for 'thirty thousand pounds' leaving him to feel that he has 'sold his soul' in order to escape the dependency of being the younger son (59). He is, as are Blanche Ingram and Du Maurier's Rebecca, a packaged commodity. As a woman of the 1930s Rebecca must present a public façade in order to realize her private desires, but as a nineteenth-century male, Antoinette's husband is able to exercise control in a more direct way since, once married, she and her wealth are his: he becomes what Chin-Ping Chen terms 'the imperialist curator of a colonial body' (379), disquietingly intent upon controlling what he does not understand. The brooding enigmatic Rochester of the canonical text is revealed as a complex individual with a backstory that constructs him first as 'victim' and then as arbiter of male, colonial power. No matter how much we empathize with his 'position' we are inevitably drawn to the realization that his treatment of Antoinette is self-serving, fuelled as it is by his identity as a white European male.

Antoinette's emotional 'excess' extends to her sexual openness, redefined here by her husband as aberrant behaviour and yet another example of her lack of European restraint. She fails to fit his image of English womanhood: she is more 'whore' than 'angel' and as such, 'lacking a proper English wife he cannot imagine himself as a proper English husband' (Kendrick 241). His rejection of her is, according to Vivian Halloran, more about maintaining the 'purity of [his] given or acquired Englishness' (87). She is defined by her lack of 'Englishness' – a lack that is, conversely, associated with sexual appetite and excess of the kind identified in the canonical text as so dangerous for women that it results in insanity and incarceration. What Rhys foregrounds here is the way that natural sexual appetite, when associated with women other than whores, is redefined as deviant behaviour within the strictures of nineteenth-century Europe.

There are few screen adaptations of *Wide Sargasso Sea*: an Australian production in 1993 was both a financial and a critical failure but the 2006 BBC adaptation achieved greater acclaim. Aired in the relative obscurity of BBC Four, it served as a companion piece to its big budget BBC One counterpart, *Jane Eyre* (2006), which was shown on the broadcaster's main channel during the peak Sunday evening viewing slot. Such scheduling suggests that a traditional costume drama type adaptation of Brontë's seminal text continues to attract a wide audience whilst a postcolonial re-visionist reading of that narrative, even when delivered in a similar costume drama format, will attract a niche audience. The appeal of televised costume drama serializations of realist nineteenth-century texts seems inexhaustible. However, Rhys's text is indebted to a very different kind of cinematic realization of *Jane Eyre*. Rhys intertextualizes the image of the female zombie found in Val Lewton's *I Walked with a Zombie* (1943), 'lin[king] the tale of a sexualised, hybridized zombie woman with a narrative of imperial domination' (Aizenberg 464) by not only relocating the narrative to a colonial outpost but by loading the text with references to the living dead. There are distinct parallels between Antoinette Mason and the film's zombified Jessica Holland, and each story unfolds in the exotic 'otherness' of the West Indies, rather than a gothic country mansion. *Wide Sargasso Sea* is littered with references to Antoinette's ultimately comatose state. Her husband's description of her casts her as a zombified 'doll', her smile 'nailed to her [white] face', her eyes 'dazed'; he refers to her as 'one of them', who 'walk and talk and scream or try to kill, then disappear', as others 'wa[it] to take their places' in what is 'a long long line' (Rhys 140–142). Each text references Obeah, underscoring the connection between these seemingly very different narratives. Antoinette's husband reads, from *The Glittering Coronet of Isles*, the definition of a 'zombi' as 'a dead person who seems to be alive or a living person who is dead' and equates this figure with his wife; yet he fails to recognize his own part in her reconfiguration, from dangerous exotic 'other' to inert, controllable zombie. In *both* narratives, it is the sexually aware wives who, deemed morally and sexually aberrant, are punished for their transgressions whilst husbands attain a position of patriarchal dominance and relative happiness. Wives are first incarcerated and then excised, so that husbands can be liberated.

Jane Eyre: A radical rethink (*I Walked with a Zombie* and *The Governess*)

But how *do* we move from a realist, female-centred bildungsroman that employs romance as part of its narrative trajectory to a low budget forties horror movie? The shift may certainly be deemed 'radical' given the very different generic platform cinematically realized in Val Lewton's *I Walked with a Zombie*, but for a writer like Rhys, its capacity to evoke *Jane Eyre* on several levels is undeniable, and the thematic connections between this film, Brontë's novel and Du Maurier's *Rebecca* are written into Lewton's film text in more than a subliminal fashion. In Wagner's terminology the film is an 'analogy' rather than an adaptation based on 'borrowing', and it does present us with what is here termed a 'radical rethink' of the narrative template of the canonical text. In Sanders' terminology it is deemed an appropriation since it 'affects a more decisive journey away from the informing source into a wholly new cultural product and domain': as an 'appropriated' text its relationship with a text like *Jane Eyre* is not 'clearly signalled or acknowledged' but is present in a 'far less straight-forward context' (26). Similarly, Sandra Goldbacher's *The Governess* (1998) has a tenuous relationship with Brontë's novel, signalled by the ways in which it explores issues of female identity and class rather than by any overt identification as a film text that 'adapts' *Jane Eyre*. It plays with the governess trope and offers a neo-Victorian re-vision of the position of women during this period. As such it adapts history as much as it adapts any particular story, but Goldbacher's 'appropriation' of concerns central to Brontë's canonical text remain an identifiable part of this film's subtext for viewers familiar with this nineteenth-century novel.

For Lewton, the connections between *Jane Eyre*, *Rebecca* and his film are written into the narrative of *I Walked with a Zombie* at a very fundamental level, though for studio executives at RKO they a far less visible. It remains ostensibly a B horror movie, produced at speed for a swift financial turnover, but its growing cult status and its importance as a seminal horror text has afforded it a much wider audience platform than that envisaged by the studio, and its relationship with the aforementioned classic texts adds another layer of fascination. Lewton joined RKO in the early forties having already worked on successful screen adaptations of classic texts with Selznick (*A Tale of Two Cities* 1935; *Prisoner of Zenda* 1937; *Gone with the Wind* 1939; and *Rebecca* 1940). His move to RKO heralded greater production control but brought with it very specific constraints: RKO productions were all low budget affairs with a maximum of $150,000 available for each film, a seventy-five minute running time (governed by its B movie status), and a preordained sensationalistic title designed to foreground the product's horror appeal in order to attract the forties teen horror audience. Building on the popularity of the zombie film, first generated by *White Zombie* (1932) back in the early 1930s, the studio handed down to Lewton the rather limiting title, *I Walked with a Zombie*, and expected him to produce for them a derivative zombie tale based on an article from a contemporary magazine, *American Weekly*. Inez Wallace's article, titled 'I Walked with a Zombie' is a piece of similarly sensationalistic journalism that reports a tale of 'zombies' encountered by the author in Haiti, and Lewton was instructed to employ the stock zombie narrative template of threatening plantation owner turns wife into zombie when her plans to leave him come to light. The first script, penned by Curt Siodmark employed Universal Studio's successful stock horror format, but with the help of screenwriter Ardel Wray, Lewton transformed the formulaic first draft into a much more complex story. His intention was to 'make it high class horror' (Lewton qtd in Dyson 103) and in order to do this, he turned his attention to two classic tales more readily associated with the female gothic and romance than with the kind of formulaic horror films produced by Universal or RKO. However, if as Robin Wood argues, the horror film locates its horror at 'the heart of the family' characterized by its 'sexual repressiveness in the cause of preserving the family unit' (Wood qtd in Bansak 156), then both *Jane Eyre* and *Rebecca* may be read, in part, as 'horror' narratives.

But whilst Hitchcock's *Rebecca* and many screen adaptations of *Jane Eyre* primarily play upon the gothic horror of the tale by employing a noiresque cinematic style, Lewton works instead from the narrative starting point of the zombie horror template and cleverly embeds the more complex and disturbing thematic preoccupations of *Jane Eyre* and *Rebecca* into what is ostensibly a low budget mainstream crowd pleaser. Despite his role as producer of B movie horror films, Lewton, like Hitchcock, is afforded authorial 'ownership' of the films he works on: whilst it is the norm within the film industry to credit directors (deemed auteurs rather than metteurs) as authors of the final film text, the films produced by Lewton during his time with RKO are regarded as works of his creation – a 'rare thing in Hollywood and a valuable indicator of how able an individual Lewton was' (Dyson 150). Scripting amendments resulted in the production of a cult classic that employs the zombie format but adds complex thematic layers by drawing upon concerns of central significance to both *Jane Eyre* and *Rebecca*. Questions of identity and the position of women within the confines of the patriarchal institutions of marriage and family are part of its subtext. Lewton adds another layer of complexity to his construction of Jessica: she is the unfaithful wife who embarks on an adulterous affair with her brother-in-law and so is doubly guilty of crimes against the family. Functioning as the film's pseudo Bertha Mason, she is incarcerated not only in a similar 'tower' but also in her zombified body. Bertha's insanity and 'bestial' form is replaced by a zombification that is even more debilitating since Jessica retains her former beauty and the resultant gaze. She remains the focus of the cinematic gaze, trapped in her zombified state, unable to react even as either the maniacal Bertha of Brontë's text or the proactive Rebecca of Du Maurier's text. She becomes the voodoo doll effigy manipulated as part of voodoo rituals at certain points in the narrative, and these disquieting images foreshadow moments in Rhys's *Wide Sargasso Sea*, when Antoinette's husband speaks of her as a doll and she equates *his* actions with Obeah (Rhys 121). Like Bertha and Rebecca, Jessica is symbolic of what happens to dangerous women who transgress but, divest of any spirit, any capacity to act, she presents the most disturbing exemplar of all. She remains a physical presence throughout the film yet has less 'presence' than Du Maurier's 'bad wife' or Hitchcock's invisible *femme fatale*. However, whilst some cinematic Berthas are reduced to the level of plot device, Jessica is central to this film's identity as a zombie movie: she must stay centre stage, even if her function on that stage is that of inert body. Though kept in a gothic 'tower' her existence is not a secret, and her transgressive behaviour is common knowledge.

I Walked with a Zombie is marketed as pure horror but the romance thread is built into this tale from the outset; even the ambiguities of its opening sequence signal romance as a couple strolling along the seashore come into shot, and the gentle voiceover of Nurse Betsy unfolds to a backdrop of wistful orchestral strings. It is not until the couple walk into closer focus that we see the giant-like proportions of the zombie Carrefour alongside Nurse Betsy. There are no stock horror devices here, other than the figure of Carrefour with whom the female figure walks at ease. The usual narrative focus of the zombie genre does not incorporate romance: it tells of repressive marital relationships in which the husband metes out rough justice to the adulterous wife by turning her into a zombie. However, in this story, we eventually learn that it is not the husband who 'incarcerates' his wife but the matriarch of the family: it is Mrs Rand who believes she is responsible for the zombification of the daughter-in-law who betrayed the family, leaving Paul Holland to assume the role of enigmatic and ultimately blameless hero of the film's romance plot – a hero who continues to care for his wife, despite her adulterous behaviour and her zombified state. He is a less developed character than either Rochester or Maxim, yet is alienated by his environment in a way that again foreshadows Rhys's complex male protagonist in *Wide Sargasso Sea*. The opening voiceover suggests that Betsy will be our narrative filter, though this is not sustained throughout, and Lewton again plays with expectation in the closing moments of the film when the voiceover is handed to one of the islanders for delivery of a summative and morally loaded commentary. Her narrative voice is also invaded when her thoughts are 'read' by Holland. During their journey to St Sebastian he challenges her perception of the island: where Betsy sees Caribbean beauty, Paul sees decay as they sail into St Sebastian. Rhys's male protagonist in *Wide Sargasso Sea* echoes Paul's sentiment, and like Nurse Betsy, he is unable to retain control of first person narration as Antoinette's voice seeps into his lines at strategic moments. The relationship between Lewton's film and Rhys's novel showcases the way in which adapters continue to intertextualize not only the canonical text but those texts that radically reshape it, whether at the level of narrative, characterization, temporal and geographical location, or ideology. Lewton employs a further intertextual reference to the governess trope that hints at its horror format; the opening flashback, as Betsy is interviewed for a mysterious post in the Caribbean, echoes the interview scene from Henry James' 'The Turn of the Screw'.

However, whilst both of these narratives are shrouded in mystery, Nurse Betsy is presented as a much more forthright and level-headed individual than James's unstable governess. Betsy is the modern woman of the forties, able to realize many of the freedoms Brontë's Jane Eyre desires yet cannot attain within the context of nineteenth-century England. Though a nurse rather than a governess or a companion, she is cast in the role of supportive carer, yet she is able to exercise greater control of her life than either Jane Eyre or Du Maurier's narrator, and she appears to be far more worldly-wise. The bildungsroman format is not employed in this film as it is not a 'coming of age' story. Betsy's role is to recount Jessica's story but she also functions as the story's romantic female lead and the parallels between Betsy and Jane Eyre are telling: both are constructed as adventurous, courageous, morally good characters, and both are ultimately rewarded romantic closure.

Though operating as a tale of repression and horror, the zombie film may be read as a text that deals with the insecurities of its contemporaneous United States, with its warped justification for its own expansionist, imperialist designs on places like Haiti (occupied by the United States at the time). By defining the voodoo practices of such cultures as 'barbaric' the United States could validate its own interventionist strategies as part of a 'civilizing mission' (Aizenberg 461–466). Like the Empire builders of nineteenth-century Europe, forties America could present expansionist ambition as moralistic mission. But both Lewton's film and Rhys's novel give us a very different picture of island life; Christophine, who is associated with Obeah, is the voice of reason and relative compassion in *Wide Sargasso Sea*, and (within the context of the times) Lewton presents us with a non-racist portrayal of islanders for whom voodoo worship is as valid as Christian worship: there is no inference that voodoo ceremonies are aligned with evil. Instead they are presented as part of the fabric of island life, the ceremonies themselves contrasting with the everyday realities of such a belief system as demonstrated by Alma who tells Nurse Betsy that islanders cry at the birth of a child and celebrate death as a release. He constructs a film text that is structured around a series of binary oppositions – superstition/science, good/evil, black/white, christian/voodoo, death/birth, growth/decay, and the lines between them are constantly blurred. The binary oppositions explored at a thematic level are also employed visually. Gothic country mansions shrouded in fog are replaced by an opulent plantation house set in the lush, alien landscape of the Caribbean, and Lewton amplifies the gothic horror not only through his use of low key lighting and shadows, creating what we now call a noir edge to the film but by presenting us with on-screen images that offer a stark contrast with the dialogue of speakers found in these scenes. When, for example, Betsy speaks of the beauty of her room, the onscreen image contradicts her commentary: she is dwarfed within the frame, and shadows fall across her, cutting through her image and infusing the scene with menace. There are numerous internal shots of empty rooms that signal isolation, and the gates leading to the plantation house resemble those of Manderley, echoing the ghostly presence of Rebecca. Lewton is also known for his signature horror technique – the 'Lewton walk' – which is employed successfully in this film as Betsy leads Jessica through the fields of sugar cane; consisting of extended, lateral tracking shots devoid of non-diegetic sound, the moment is infused with a tension that builds as they approach the voodoo ceremony. The film's close provides a pattern of punishment and reward similar to that found in *Jane Eyre* and *Rebecca*: those who transgress are excised and those deemed morally good are united in love as Wesley and Jessica are sacrificed to make way for the film's romance subplot. In this narrative Jessica's fellow transgressor, Wesley, becomes the ultimate 'keeper of [her] bestial body'. However, in keeping with Lewton's blurring of opposites, this too may be read as romantic closure since they are united in death and Wesley's behaviour may be seen as a self-sacrificing romantic gesture.

Lewton's *I Walked with a Zombie* was marketed as a low budget horror film, part of the emerging zombie sub genre: its relationship with *Jane Eyre* and *Rebecca* is encoded rather than foregrounded. Though the film is now considered a seminal cult horror text that appears on Film Studies courses at undergraduate level, at the time of its release it was unlikely to have appealed to an audience with prior knowledge of either of the literary novels we now associate with it. Linda Hutcheon concludes that, in order to be defined as 'adaptation', a text must offer 'an extended, deliberate, announced revisitation of a particular work of art' (170); within the strictures of this definition Lewton's film fails to qualify: it may play with the canonical text(s) in an 'an extended, deliberate', manner due to Lewton's interventions, but it is not an 'announced revisitation of a particular work of art'. Does this mean then, that this is not an adaptation? Do the canonical texts alluded to function instead as intertexts embedded within this very different cultural product? More importantly, does that matter? Onega and Gutleben argue convincingly that what we should focus on is the 'textual dialogue' at work in the production of narrative, 'analys[ing] pragmatically and semantically two (or several) texts using one as a reading prism for the other' (9) in order to avoid innate hierarchical and evaluative distinctions of the kind inherent in any comparison between a canonical text like *Jane Eyre* and either a film like *I Walked with a Zombie*, with its radical reconfiguration of a classic nineteenth-century gothic romance into something decidedly 'other' or a neo-Victorian film like *The Governess* with its similarly different spin on cultural positioning. Neither of these film texts announces its relationship with any precursor text. Furthermore, writer-director Sandra Goldbacher does not signal her 'extended, deliberate' engagement with *any* specific literary forerunner: her idea is developed from her fictional diary of a Victorian woman. Yet for the consumer of this type of art house costume drama a number of canonical narratives permeate the text, 'shadowing' and 'doubling' facets of Goldbacher's story, and whether intentional or not, these other narratives become part of what Geraghty terms a 'layering process [that] involves an accretion of deposits over time' (195). *The Governess* presents 'a shadowing or doubling of what is on the surface' in Brontë's *Jane Eyre* both by (consciously or subconsciously) reinscribing its romance plot and by playing with a number of its central ideas. The film's romance plot, revolving around a young, sexually inexperienced 'governess' and her, older, enigmatic employer, echoes not only the central relationship in *Jane Eyre* and Du Maurier's *Rebecca* but that of George Elliot's Dorothea and the emotionally inept Casaubon in *Middlemarch*. The film also trades upon its title to a certain extent; though there is no direct reference to Brontë's tale – either by naming the film for its heroine or its anti-heroine as is the case in *Jane Eyre* and *Rebecca* respectively – *any* reference to 'governess' evokes a host of images and narrative threads for its art house audience.

However, it adapts the Victorian past as much as it adapts the realist novels of that era, injecting a twentieth-century sensibility into the 'voice' of its heroine and presenting us with a different version of Victorian womanhood, constructing what Cora Kaplan terms 'a *virtual* relationship between past and present' (9). *The Governess* builds on a nineties trend for cinematic adaptation of the nineteenth century – *Little Women* (1994), *Sense and Sensibility* (1995), *The Portrait of a Lady* (1996), *Mary Reilly* (1996), *Washington Square* (1997) – yet unlike the majority of such films, it does not adapt a specific novel. Rather, it references Jane Campion's *The Piano* in many ways, as both present a version of Victoriana that is 'a kind of fictional reparation of a past supposedly denied its libidinal birthright' (Caplan 134); the female lead in each asserts her right to be sexually curious, standing in stark contrast to expected modes of behaviour for the Victorian woman. They are neither angels nor whores but women with a sexual appetite, and in this both Goldbacher and Campion take us to an imaginative place that goes beyond known, historically recorded fact or fiction related to the Victorian period. Neo-Victorian literature of this kind 'adapts' a specific historical era, playing with the past and refocusing history's lens in order to bring marginalized voices centre stage. It seeks to rectify, revise, refract, rewrite and reclaim those voices silenced by historical discourse and to build upon the societal critiques of the quietly subversive heroines of the Victorian novel.

Their purpose, according to Kate Mitchell, is not to 'mak[e] sense of the Victorian past' but to 'off[er] it as a cultural memory, to be re-membered, and imaginatively re-created' rather than 'revised or understood' (7). John Fowles' *The French Lieutenant's Woman* and Rhys's *Wide Sargasso Sea* are amongst the earliest examples of what is now termed 'neo-Victorian' literature and each shares with *The Governess* a desire to bring to the narrative foreground women seen as marginal, whether as a result of their gender, class, race or culture. Goldbacher's Rosina shares with Jane Eyre a desire to be treated as an intellectual equal, despite contemporaneous social and gender inequality. Reviewer Alan A. Stone aptly dubs Rosina a '"back from the future" governess…dropped as if by a time machine into the world of Jane Eyre'. She enters a narrative that charts her coming of age in a sexual and experiential sense as she journeys towards the postmodern realization that to be a thriving, successful woman, she must walk away from anticipated romantic closure, having learnt that her emotionally crippled and sexually repressed lover is willing to betray her, spiritually and intellectually. Within the backdrop of Empire and the moral confines of Victorian society, sexual curiosity sets women like Bertha, Antoinette and Rosina apart from the heroines of the nineteenth-century realist novel and brings them into conflict with the sexually repressed males of each text. The tower that imprisons Bertha Mason, Antoinette Cosway and Jessica Holland is entered willingly by Rosina in her pursuit of knowledge – intellectual and sexual – but unlike the 'mad' ghosts of former narratives who are punished for their sexual transgressions, she is liberated by the experience and escapes having acquired it. She is also aligned with Rhys's Antoinette on another level: both are culturally 'Other'. As a Sephardic Jew living in the seedier confines of London, Rosina, like Antoinette, experiences a very different kind of upbringing and outlook on life. Goldbacher places Rosina within the warmth and vibrancy of her Jewish culture in the bustling heart of London before moving her story to the cold remote backdrop of the Isle of Skye with the prerequisite 'country mansion' and 'tower' shrouded in mystery. The vitality of her Jewish culture offers a striking contrast to the emotional inertia of the Cavendish family, and in her disguise as Protestant governess, Rosina becomes the 'plain Jane' of Brontë's tale, though she retains her true identity and appearance during her private moments, unlocking from her chest the sensual fabrics and colours associated with 'home'. Whilst Antoinette's cultural 'otherness' and Rebecca's sexually transgressive 'otherness' pose a threat within the context of their relationships with their husbands, Rosina's 'otherness' is acknowledged but for the audience it is not presented as alien or a threat.

This shared 'otherness' offers intriguing parallels between the various adaptations we are exploring, but the most intriguing 'textual dialogue' at the core of this film involves a shared thematic preoccupation with the gaze across a number of these texts. With part of its narrative momentum focusing on the emergence of photography, the film positions itself as a narrative that is intrinsically linked to matters relating to the photographic and the cinematic gaze. Whilst Lewton presents us with a traditionally male gaze in his horror film, the camera lingering on the eerie yet still beautiful form of Jessica, Goldbacher subverts the traditionally male gaze, placing a naked Cavendish, posed by Rosina, at the centre of the lensed shot, thus giving her control of what we see and how we see it – a control that again echoes other adaptations of *Jane Eyre* for it bears comparison to the way in which Hitchcock's Maxim manipulates images of his second wife in the now infamous projection scene from *Rebecca*. Here, though, the power rests in female hands. Cavendish's reaction to 'control' of his image speaks volumes: it heralds the end of their affair. By introducing this thread, Goldbacher connects her film not only to adaptations of *Jane Eyre* but to *The Piano* in which Campion is similarly preoccupied with female sexuality and repositioning of the gaze. Neither of these films are presenting us with the traditionally nostalgic gaze of the period drama: there are no lingering shots of country mansions and regency dining rooms in either. Instead these postfeminist films seek to question matters relating to the nature of the gaze; they challenge Mulvey's notion that the gaze is inherently male, placing naked men – sometimes vulnerable, naked men – within the frame. Taking her lead from Campion, Goldbacher also engages us in debates concerning the very nature of film's voyeuristic identity: shots of eyes in apertures, holding for our gaze the inert and constructed body allude to controversies surrounding Michael Powell's *Peeping Tom* (1960) which caused outrage in the film industry on its release due its inference that cinema as a medium is perversely voyeuristic. By aligning Rosina's story with the emergence of photography (and by inference cinema) the significance of the medium itself is foregrounded throughout and is connected to Rosina's final liberation: she is a successful photographer, able financially and emotionally to reject Cavendish. Though a romance of sorts, built on its allusions to other romance narratives, any sense of romantic closure is avoided, leaving Rosina triumphantly independent. She has achieved, within the context of a nineteenth-century tale, the kind of freedoms Brontë's nineteenth-century heroine could only dream of. *The Governess*, like Campion's *The Piano*, offers the kind of radical reconfiguration of Victorian literature heralded by Stam as capable of ' "de-repressing" ' these nineteenth-century realist narratives in 'sexual and political terms', providing 'a feminist sexual liberationist dynamic' that 'releases the latent feminist spirit of the novels, of the characters, or even the author, in a kind of anachronistic therapy or adaptational recuperation' (42).

Analysing text: Exercises related to *Jane Eyre*/adaptations of *Jane Eyre*

Close critical reading: *Jane Eyre*

Step one

Read the following extract from *Jane Eyre*, 140–141 (Penguin edition, 1980).

Anybody may blame me who likes, when I add further, that, now and then, when I took a walk by myself in the grounds; when I went down to the gates and looked through them along the road; or when, while Adele played with her nurse, and Mrs. Fairfax made jellies in the storeroom, I climbed the three staircases, raised the trap-door of the attic, and having reached the leads, looked out afar over sequestered field and hill, and along dim sky-line – that then I longed for a power of vision which might overpass that limit; which might reach the busy world, towns, regions full of life I had heard of but never seen – that then I desired more of practical experience than I possessed; more of intercourse with my kind, of acquaintance with variety of character, than was here within my reach. I valued what was good in Mrs. Fairfax, and what was good in Adele; but I believed in the existence of other and more vivid kinds of goodness, and what I believed in I wished to behold.

Who blames me? Many, no doubt; and I shall be called discontented. I could not help it: the restlessness was in my nature; it agitated me to pain sometimes. Then my sole relief was to walk along the corridor of the third storey, backwards and forwards, safe in the silence and solitude of the spot, and allow my mind's eye to dwell on whatever bright visions rose before it – and, certainly, they were many and glowing; to let my heart be heaved by the exultant movement, which, while it swelled it in trouble, expanded it with life; and, best of all, to open my inward ear to a tale that was never ended – a tale my imagination created, and narrated continuously; quickened with all of incident, life, fire, feeling, that I desired and had not in my actual existence.

It is in vain to say human beings ought to be satisfied with tranquillity: they must have action; and they will make it if they cannot find it. Millions are condemned to a stiller doom than mine, and millions are in silent revolt against their lot. Nobody knows how many rebellions besides political rebellions ferment in the masses of life which people earth. Women are supposed to be very calm generally: but women feel just as men feel; they need exercise for their faculties, and a field for their efforts, as much as their brothers do; they suffer from too rigid a restraint, too absolute a stagnation, precisely as men would suffer; and it is narrow-minded in their more privileged fellow-creatures to say that they ought to confine themselves to making puddings and knitting stockings, to playing on the piano and embroidering bags. It is thoughtless to condemn them, or laugh at them, if they seek to do more or learn more than custom has pronounced necessary for their sex.

Step two

Now return to the first paragraph and ask yourself the following questions:

- What tone of voice does Jane Eyre adopt in this opening paragraph?
- How does her choice of vocabulary reflect her state of mind?
- How does the sentence structure employed here reflect her state of mind?

Jane Eyre continues to strengthen her line of argument.

- How does she do this?
- What is the impact of her use of a strategically placed rhetorical question?
- What do words like 'relentless, silence, solitude, visions, heaved, exultant, swelled, expanded, life, imagination, created, quickened, life, fire, feeling, desired, existence' add to the tone of the piece at this point in her speech?
- How does Eyre shift the tone of her address here from the passionate 'voice' of the opening paragraphs to the 'voice' of logic and reason?
- How – and to what end – does she widen out the debate to encompass her fellow man at this point in the argument?
- What gender issues are raised at the close of this extract?
- Would such a speech be considered radical when this text first appeared in print? Why/why not?

Controlling the gaze

Step one

Watch these two scenes from Rebecca:

- Narrator & Projection Scene http://youtu.be/SyK3lhP9CZA?list=PLEE 71622A1E463B83
- Scene of Maxim's Confession http://youtu.be/3AqHRcXr8wk

Consider the following in relation to each scene:

- Mise en scène
- Camera movement/positioning
- Positioning within frame
- Lighting

- Sound
- Performance

How are we positioned as viewers of these scenes? What does each tell us about the relationships unfolding on screen? (i.e. between Narrator/Maxim AND Rebecca)

Step two

In 'Visual Pleasure & Narrative Cinema' (*Screen* 1975), Laura Mulvey introduces the term 'scopophilia' – a term which refers to the pleasures experienced in using another person as an object of sexual stimulation through the act of looking. Mulvey argues that women in classic Hollywood cinema are constructed as passive objects of male desire, the voyeuristic male gaze serving to construct woman as either 'whore' or 'madonna'. Many critics (and Mulvey later) argue against this belief that only males glean pleasure from female 'to-be-looked-at-ness', but Mulvey's theories provoked meaningful critical debate about the cinematic construction of women within the context of seventies feminism.

Step three

Now explore two feminist critiques of the scenes we are focusing on and:

- summarize in your own words the key points raised by each writer;
- decide whether you agree with all/some of the points raised by these writers, giving justification/s for your response.

Narrator & Projection Scene

(Mary Ann Doane, '*Caught* and *Rebecca*: The Inscription of Femininity as absence', in *Feminism and Film Theory*, ed. Constance Penley. New York: Routledge, 1988. 202–204)

The home movie sequence depicts a process of projection constituted as an assault on the diegetic female spectator. This scene as well is preceded by the delineation of female desire in relation to the fixed image of the fashion magazine. A preface to the projection scene, the shot of the fashion magazine whose pages are slowly turned is here unlocalized. *Rebecca* elides the establishing shot which would identify the woman as viewer and, instead, dissolves immediately to her transformation into the image, an image she had previously promised Maxim she would never appropriate for herself – that of a woman 'dressed in black satin with a string of pearls' … the heroine enters the cinema in the hope of becoming a spectacle for Maxim but is relegated to the position of spectator – spectator of the images Maxim prefers to retain of her, those taken on their honeymoon … . Maxim is in control in this scene – of lighting and projection … . The images of Fontaine feeding geese constitute a denial of the image she has constructed for herself by means of the black evening dress, while Maxim's binoculars give him a mastery over the gaze even within the confines of the filmic image … . Maxim abruptly walks between Fontaine and the screen, blocking the image with his body and effectively castrating her look. Substituting himself for the screen, he activates an aggressive look back at the spectator, turning Fontaine's gaze against itself. The absolute terror incited by this violent re-organization of the cinematic relay of the look is evident in her eyes, the only part of her face lit by the reflected beam of the projector. Furthermore, the image revealed as he finally moves out of the projection beam to turn on the light is that of himself, once again holding the binoculars (202–204).

Scene of Maxim's Confession
(Tania Modleski, *The Women who Knew too much*. London: Routledge, 1988. 52–55)

It's impossible for any man to gain control over [Rebecca] in the usual classical narrative fashion [because] the sexual woman is never seen. We have no shot-reverse-shot formations in which men look at women … In *Rebecca*, the beautiful, desirable woman is not only never made a part of the film's field of vision, she is actually posited within the diegesis as all-seeing … She is said by Mrs Danvers to come back to watch the newly weds together … . Rebecca herself lurks in the blind space of the film … . she never becomes 'domesticated' (53).

Adaptation, the Genre?

Thomas Leitch proposes an alternative means of exploring adaptations. Rather than considering them in relation to their so-called source texts, Leitch argues that adaptations can be defined as belonging to a specific genre, with distinctive identity markers ('Adaptation, the Genre' 106).

Leitch notes four markers or 'cues' that '*encourage* filmgoers to experience adaptations as adaptations', even if they know nothing of their sources:

1 period setting/emphasis on costume and period detail;
2 a foregrounding of its status as an adaptation, sometimes listing authors of source texts in the titles in an attempt to 'identify [itself] *as* adaptation';
3 a 'fetishizing of history' connected to an 'obsession with authors, books, words'; and
4 use of 'utterly distinctive' intertitles as a means of 'reminding the audience' of its status as an adaptation ('Adaptation, the Genre' 106–120).

Step one

Ask yourself the following:

• Do we recognize adaptation as a genre in the way that we recognize such industry-driven genre labels as horror, western, rom-com or road movie and so on?
• If not, can we still use the term in any legitimate sense within the very commercially driven medium of film?
• Is it feasible to argue for a body of common markers shared by products of such diverse origin/product type? What of adaptations of contemporary/populist texts? What of remakes/prequels/sequels?
• How does this genre proposed by Leitch differ from already established genres like the costume drama or heritage cinema?

Step two

Watch the following marketing trailers for each of the 'classic' examples of *Jane Eyre* explored in this section:

http://youtu.be/fupUKF9SEy4
http://youtu.be/xV4qpvF-e80
http://youtu.be/8IFsdfk3mlk

Now ask yourself:

- How does their presentation differ? What forms the focus of each trailer?
- To what extent can we categorize them as film products that belong to what Leitch terms the genre of 'adaptation'?
- What other genre labels could we apply to each of these films?

References

Aizenberg, Edna. '*I Walked with a Zombie*: The Pleasures and Perils of Postcolonial Hybridity'. *World Literature Today* 73.3 (1999): 461–466. Print.

Andrews, Emily. 'Reader, I ravished Him …'. *Mailonline. Daily Mail Australia*, 17 Jul. 2012. Web. 5 Feb. 2013.

Angelini, Sergio. 'TV Literary Adaptation: From Page to Screen'. *BFI Screenonline*. Web. 20 Feb. 2013.

Bansak, Edmund G. *Fearing the Dark: The Val Lewton Career*. Jefferson, NC and London: McFarland and Company, 1995. Print.

Botting, Fred. *Gothic*. London and New York: Routledge, 1996. Print.

Brontë, Charlotte. *Jane Eyre*. Harmondsmith: Penguin, 1980 [1847]. Print.

Brooke, Michael. 'The Hays Code'. *BFI Screenonline*. Web. 8 Feb. 2013.

Brosh, Liora. *Screening Novel Women: From British Domestic Fiction to Film*. Houndmills: Palgrave MacMillan, 2008. Print.

Buffini, Moira. *Jane Eyre: Screenplay* (2nd draft, 6 Mar. 2008). The Internet Movie Script Database (IMSDb). Web. 5 May 2012.

Cardwell, Sarah. *Adaptation Revisited: Television and the Classic Novel*. Manchester: Manchester University Press, 2002. Print.

Chen, Chih-Ping. '"Am I a Monster?": Jane Eyre Among the Shadows of Freaks'. *Studies in the Novel* 34.4 (2002): 367–384. Print.

D'Monte, Rebecca. 'Changing Form: Stage, Film and TV Adaptations of Daphne du Maurier's *Rebecca*'. *Adaptation in Contemporary Culture: Textual Infidelities*. Ed. R. Carroll. London: Continuum, 2009. 163–173. Print.

Doane, Mary Ann. '*Caught* and *Rebecca*: The Inscription of Femininity as Absence'. *Feminism and Film Theory*. Ed. Constance Penley. New York: Routledge, 1988. 202–204. Print.

Donaldson, Elizabeth J. 'The Corpus of the Madwoman: Toward a Feminist Disability Studies Theory of Embodiment in Mental Illness'. *NWSA Journal* 14.3 (2002): 100–119. Print.

Du Maurier, Daphne. *Rebecca*. London: Victor Gollancz Ltd., 1988 [1938].

Dyer, Richard. 'Heritage Cinema in Europe'. *Encyclopedia of European Cinema*. Ed. Ginette Vincendeau New York: Facts on File Inc., 1995. 204–205. Print.

Dyson, Jeremy. *Bright Darkness: The Lost Art of the Supernatural Horror Film*. London: Cassell, 1997. Print.

Focus Features. 'Jane Eyre: A Passionate Adaptation of a Classic Novel'. Web. 5 Jan 2011.

Focus Features. 'Unlocking Charlotte Brontë's *Jane Eyre*: An Interview with Screenwriter Moira Buffini'. Web. 15 March 2012.

Geraghty, Christine. *Now Major Motion Picture: Film Adaptations of Literature and Drama*. Lanham, MD: Rowman and Littlefield, 2007. Print.

Gilbert, Sandra M., and Susan Gubar. *The Mad Woman in the Attic: The Woman Writer and the Nineteenth-Century Literary Imagination*. 2nd ed. New Haven, CT: Yale University Press, 2000 [1978]. Print.

Greer, Germaine. 'Mad About the Girl'. *The Guardian* 28 Jun. 2006: Culture. Print.

Halloran, Vivian Nun. 'Race, Creole, and National Identities in Rhys's *Wide Sargasso Sea* and Phillips's *Cambridge*'. *Small Axe* 21 (2006): 87–104. Print.

Higson, Andrew. 'Representing the National Past: Nostalgia & Pastiche in the Heritage Film'. *British Cinema and Thatcherism*. Ed. Lester Friedman. London: UCL Press, 1993. 109–129. Print.

Horner, Avril, and Sue Zlosnik. *Daphne du Maurier: Writing, Identity and the Gothic Imagination*. Basingstoke: Macmillan, 1998. Print.

Kaplan, Cora. *Victoriana: Histories, Fictions, Criticism*. Edinburgh: Edinburgh University Press, 2007. Print.

Kendrick, Robert. 'Edward Rochester and the Margins of Masculinity in *Jane Eyre* and *Wide Sargasso Sea*'. *Papers on Language and Literature* 30.3 (1994): 235–256. Print.

Kimmey, Deborah A. 'Women, Fire, and Dangerous Things: Metatextuality and the Politics of Reading in Jean Rhys's *Wide Sargasso Sea*'. *Women's Studies* 34.2 (2005): 113–131. Print.

Leitch, Thomas. 'Adaptation, the Genre'. *Adaptation* 1.2 (2008): 106–120. Print.

Mitchell, Kate. *History and Cultural Memory in Neo-Victorian Fiction: Victorian Afterimages*. London: Palgrave Macmillan, 2010. Print.

Modleski, Tania. *The Women Who Knew Too Much: Hitchcock and Feminist Theory*. New York: Methuen, 1988. Print.

Moers, Ellen. *Literary Women*. London: Women's Press, 1978. Print.

Monk, Claire. *Heritage Film Audiences*. Edinburgh: Edinburgh University Press, 2012. Print.

Mulvey, Laura. 'Visual Pleasure & Narrative Cinema'. *Screen* 16.3 (1975): 6–18. Print.

Onega, Susana and Christian Gutleben, eds. *Refracting the Canon in Contemporary British Literature and Film*. Amsterdam and New York: Rodopi, 2004. Print.

Patmore, Coventry. 'The Angel in the House'. *Victorian Web*. 2 Jul. 2009.

Plasa, Carl. *Critical Issues: Charlotte Brontë*. Houndmills: Palgrave Macmillan, 2004. Print.

Rhys, Jean. *Wide Sargasso Sea*. Harmondsmith: Penguin, 1985 [1966]. Print.

Rich, Adrienne. 'When We Dead Awaken: Writing as Re-Vision'. *College English* 34.1 (1972): 18–30. Print.

Rigney, Barbara. *Madness and Sexual Politics in the Feminist Novel: Studies in Brontë, Woolf, Lessing, and Atwood*. Wisconsin: University of Wisconsin Press, 1980. Print.

Sanders, Julie. *Adaptation and Appropriation*. Abingdon: Routledge, 2006. Print.

Showalter, Elaine. *A Literature of Their Own: British Women Novelists from Brontë to Lessing*. London: Virago Press, 2003. Print.

Smith, Andrew, and Diana Wallace. 'The Female Gothic: Then and Now'. *Gothic Studies* 6.1 (2004): 1–7. Print.

Sooke, Alistair. 'Still Haunted by the Ghost of Rebecca'. *The Telegraph* 24 Jan. 2005. Print.

Stam, Robert. 'Beyond Fidelity: The Dialogics of Adaptation'. *Film Adaptation*. Ed. James Naremore. New Brunswick, NJ: Rutgers UP, 2000. 54–78. Print.

Stone, Alan A. 'On Film: Governing Passion'. *The Boston Review: A Political and Literary Forum*. Dec. 1998.

Wyndham, Francis, and Diana Melly, eds. *Jean Rhys Letters, 1931–1966*. London: Andre Deutsch Ltd., 1984.

Filmography

I Walked with a Zombie. Dir. Jacques Torneur. Prod. Val Lewton. 1943. DVD.

Jane Eyre. Dir. 1934. Christy Cabanne. DVD.

Jane Eyre. Dir. Robert Stevenson. 1944. DVD.

Jane Eyre. Dir. Campbell Logan. 1956. BBC.

Jane Eyre. Dir. Rex Tucker. 1963. BBC.

Jane Eyre. Dir. Delbert Mann. 1970. DVD.

Jane Eyre. Dir. Joan Craft. 1973. DVD.

Jane Eyre. Dir. Julian Amyes. 1983. DVD.

Jane Eyre. Dir. Franco Zeffirelli. 1996. DVD.

Jane Eyre. Dir. Robert Young. 1997. DVD.

Jane Eyre. Dir. Susanna White. 2006. DVD.

Jane Eyre. Dir. Cary Fukunaga. 2011. DVD.

Rebecca. Dir. Alfred Hitchcock. Prod. David O. Selznick. 1940. DVD.

The Governess. Dir. Sandra Goldbacher. 1998. DVD.

The Piano. Dir. Jane Campion. 1993. DVD.

3

Adapting *Great Expectations*: A Creative Practice-Based Approach

Charles Dickens' *Great Expectations* has attracted the attention of adapters since its initial serialization. Like many of his narratives, it was swiftly adapted by his contemporaries, and the recent rash of adaptations of *Great Expectations*, produced as part of the Dickens' bicentennial celebrations in 2012, demonstrates both its enduring popularity and the continuing relevance of its universal themes. First appearing in thirty-six weekly instalments in Dickens' periodical *All Year Round*, from December 1860 to August 1861, *Great Expectations* was his thirteenth novel, the third of his major works to employ a first person narrator and, according to biographer Peter Ackroyd, his most autobiographical novel to date. This opening discussion of the canonical text is informed in part by the postcolonial discourse that surrounds the novel, and by debates about its ongoing commodification, but it also foregrounds more 'writerly' ways of engaging with adaptations of *Great Expectations*, both here and in a series of practical exercises placed at the end of the chapter.

By the time he wrote *Great Expectations*, Dickens had become a known and distinguished author with a capacity for self-promotion of the kind we more readily associate with today's celebrity culture; he had a dedicated fan-base, eagerly awaiting his stories and keen to engage in debate as to how these stories should unfold. Creating what was commonly termed 'The Boz Cascade' or 'The Dickens Deluge' (Fawcett 44), a volume of theatrical adaptive spin-offs regularly circulated Dickens' serializations, even before their completion, attesting to both his popularity and his 'celebrity status'. Dickens, claims Jay Clayton, was 'never averse to commercializing his enterprises' and always 'understood the publicity value' of products that fed off of his stories (4): his *Great Expectations* (or more specifically the implications circulating its title) is referenced in a whole host of twenty-first-century media products and forms by advertisers, sketch writers, fashion chains, dating web sites, and so on (147). It has become a culturally loaded term in contemporary times and the publicity-conscious Dickens would no doubt have applauded such inventive appropriation. Cora Kaplan attributes the current popularity of 'neo-Victorian' texts – texts which adapt both the past and the literary world of the nineteenth-century realist novel – to the 'currency of Dickens and his work' (81): novels like Michel Faber's *The Crimson Petal and the White*, Sarah Waters' *Fingersmith* or Jane Harris's *The Observations* with their complex plots and gritty realism remain indebted to this *Dickensian* currency.

Linda Hutcheon compares our postmodern interest in adaptation to that of the Victorians who had a 'habit of adapting just about everything' (2006 xi). Unauthorised 'borrowing' was widespread: copyright laws covered only stage-related works back in the 1830s and 1840s, and novelists were afforded little protection. Though instantaneous borrowing of his works added to the 'cult' of Dickens the populist writer, he sought to curtail such practices initially by giving his own very popular public readings of the texts and by providing proofs to selected 'pirate' theatre companies. In an effort to retain some control, Dickens released *Great Expectations* as a stage play in 1861; whether authored by or commissioned by Dickens, *Great Expectations: A Drama in Three Stages* was covered under copyright law in a way that the novel was not. However, rogue productions still appeared both here and in the United States where no less than four had been staged before the novel's final instalment was released. These Victorian adaptations were, according to Natalie Neill, 'manifestations' of an 'emergent mass culture'; already popular narratives, Dickens' stories became commercially viable commodities, regularly appropriated in 'the highly commercialized world of early Victorian entertainment' (72–73). Stage productions of Dickens' works are still popular, though the stage success of *Great Expectations* has been limited in comparison to staged adaptations of texts like *Nicholas Nickleby*, *Oliver Twist*, *David Copperfield*, *Pickwick Papers* and *A Christmas Carol*. Many of his novels have been adapted as musical theatre; building on the melodramatic sentimentality at the heart of Dickens' writing, these musical adaptations have helped to shape popular perception of his work. However, *Great Expectations* is notably his least sentimental novel; its lack of emotional exhibitionism (of the kind so characteristic of Dickens' prose in general) explains in part its more limited success as a stage production in contemporary times. The most recent theatrical adaptation of *Great Expectations* by Jo Clifford was staged in the West End at the Vaudeville Theatre in 2013 but its run was cut short, and the RSC's 2005 *Great Expectations*, adapted by Declan Donnellan and Nick Ormerod, did not receive universal praise, unlike the RSC's highly acclaimed 1980 production of *Nicholas Nickleby*.

The appropriation of existing narratives as a mainstay of film production from the early days of the medium to current times is an extension of Victorian theatrical practice rather than a trend established by Hollywood financiers. Cinematic adaptation of Dickens' novels dominated the early days of silent cinema: over 100 silent films were produced, and many had been seen in Magic Lantern Show formats prior to this (Eaton). In the twenties, with the arrival of sound, an adaptive trend of 'epidemic' proportions ensued (Dennett 54), whilst the thirties heralded the arrival of the Hollywood treatment with commercially successful productions by David O. Selznick (*David Copperfield* and *A Tale of Two Cities* 1935). A similar interest in Dickens' narratives emerged post World War Two, with the release of *Great Expectations* (1946), *Nicholas Nickleby* (1947), *Oliver Twist* (1948), *Scrooge* (1951) and *Pickwick Papers* (1952). *Great Expectations* continues to attract adapters working in the film and television industries. It has been adapted for the cinema on seven occasions thus far, three of which pre-date the now famous Cineguild adaptation directed by David Lean: two silent adaptations (1917 and 1921) were produced in the early days of cinema, and Universal Studio's under-whelming adaptation, deemed by Brian McFarlane a 'filming-by-numbers exercise' with 'a conventional, toothless Hollywood resolution' (*Text to Screen* 83) appeared in 1934. But it is Lean's Cineguild adaptation that is regarded as the seminal cinematic realization of Dickens' *Great Expectations*, and all films – past, present and future – are measured against it; indeed, Michael Johnson claims it has a stronger presence in the 'critical unconscious' than the original novel (63).

In this instance our relationship with the story may well be predicated on having first experienced it in its adapted form, as a piece of cinema rather than as a piece of canonical literature. The oft-cited parent/child relationship between the so-called 'source' text and its adaptation lacks credibility in such instances since it is the canonical text which is 'haunted' by its adapted text, 'its presence shadowing the one we are experiencing directly' (Hutcheon 26). Similarly, moving image adaptations that follow on from Lean are inevitably explored through the lens of Lean's adaptation; from animated versions (1947, 1983) and televised serializations which were particularly popular in the eighties (1959, 1967, 1974, 1981, 1983, 1986, 1999, 2011) to feature films, some of which offer a close reading of Dickens' novel (1971, 1975, 2012) while others, like Tim Burstall's *Great Expectations: The Untold Story* (1986) or Alfonso Cuaron's 1998 *Great Expectations*, move the narrative a long way from Dickens' tale in a temporal, cultural or geographical sense. With the exception of Cuaron's film, screen adaptations of *Great Expectations*, for both film and television, operate within the novel's contemporaneous timeframe and as such may be classified as costume dramas, lensing the past in all of its period detail. However, though there may be lingering shots of ballrooms and carriages, the settings for Dickens' tale contradict our expectations of the genre: lush countryside and immaculate country mansions are replaced by bleak moors, a dilapidated Satis House and the grimy streets of London, and it is the novel's gothic associations that visually dominate the screen. Adapter Michael Eaton sees Dickens as 'central to the very notion of "English Heritage"', but the depiction of that heritage adds a different dimension to both our perception of the Victorian period and to heritage cinema.

Joss Marsh notes that Dickens' novels have 'spawned more film adaptations than those of any other author' (204). His relationship with cinema as a medium of expression is central to an understanding of how and why his work is so frequently adapted to screen. Marsh, like Eisenstein before him, argues that 'there is a more striking affinity between Dickensian modes of narration and film's developed techniques of story-telling (including editing, camerawork, and design) than exists between film and any other author' (205). Dickens' work has long been regarded as highly cinematic and has attained 'an almost mythic status since Eisenstein all but enshrined [him] as the forefather of cinematic narrative' (Novel to Film 105). In his seminal essay, 'Dickens, Griffith, and The Film Today', Eisenstein credits Dickens with not only the title of 'forefather of cinematic narrative' but with the pre-empting of film techniques like parallel editing, shot types and dissolves that create a film language of similar optical quality to that of Dickens' prose (144–146). The writer of the most recent screenplay adaptation of *Great Expectations* (2012), David Nicholls, speaks of the relationship between Dickens and cinema as one in which cinema, as a medium, is the obvious choice for translation of his stories because it 'draws on the same effects that Dickens note[s] and describe[s]' in his prose, offering the adapter the capacity to 're[ad] the books and s[ee] the sequences' simultaneously. He cites the tense, action-packed pursuit of Magwitch in the novel's final stage as one that possesses the montage qualities identified by filmmakers like Eisenstein and Griffith:

> At the same moment, without giving any audible direction to his crew, he ran the galley aboard of us ... In the same moment, I saw the steersman of the galley lay his hand on his prisoner's shoulder, and saw both boats were swinging round with the force of the tide, and saw that all hands on board the steamer were running forward quite frantically. Still in the same moment, I saw the prisoner start up, lean across his captor, and pull the cloak from the neck of the shrinking sitter in the galley. Still in the same moment, I saw that the face disclosed was the face of the other convict of long ago. Still in the same moment, I saw the face tilt backward with a white terror on it that I shall never forget, and heard a great cry on board the steamer and a loud splash in the water, and felt the boat sink from under me. (Dickens 330–331)

The cinematic quality of the prose is undeniable: it lends itself to visual realization on screen and to the action-packed sequence that it becomes in Nicholls' resultant film adaptation. Dickens does, as Nicholls claims, present us with 'a kind of prose storyboard' with its own 'in-built energy and pace': we do indeed 'read and see them in the same moment'. Citing instead the opening moments of Lean's *Great Expectations* to illustrate her point, Kamilla Elliott observes that if we invest in this 'myth of the cinematic novel', circulating Dickens' novels in particular, the inevitable inference is that *film* is 'the glorious fulfilment of what is only a seed of promise in the novel' (115). While the novel's prose, no matter how vivid, remains static on the page, Lean's translation of the novel's opening sequence is energized through use of the visual and aural signifiers available to him in the medium of cinema, and even though Lean reverently presents Dickens' prose by focusing on shots of the words as they appear on the page, and by giving prominence to the words via Pip's opening voiceover, it is the 'flip-book animation' quality of the turning pages and the fade into the immediacy of the graveyard moment that captures our interest as viewers, giving the film text both 'cultural and representational dominance' as a consequence (115). Dickens is present in a 'parental' role but a less dominant role nonetheless. The relationship between the canonical text and its adaptive 'offspring' is clearly a complex one; though the language employed to discuss that relationship still revolves around matters of genealogy and 'parentage', there is an acknowledgement here that when stories are adapted to a different medium, they evolve and grow rather than replicate and stagnate.

Fairy tale tropes are embedded within a story like *Great Expectations*. Dickens' story tells of the abused and motherless child saved by the interventions of a fairy 'godmother': it is both 'a Victorian rendering of the Dick Whittington legend' and a 'male version of Cinderella', with Miss Havisham as 'witch', Magwitch as 'ogre' and Estella as the 'siren' (Samuel 48). It bears striking resemblance to Dickens' own 'boy makes good' past, and his attempts at 'self-analysis and self-knowledge' are woven into the text's thematic preoccupations (Ackroyd 997). Despite its fairy tale allusions, no matter how potentially positive the revised ending of *Great Expectations* may be, it is the darker, self-reflective side of this tale to which adapters, past and present, are often drawn. Nevertheless, there are a number of spin-offs that play with the text's humorous intent: Jasper Fforde's *The Well of Lost Plots*, the third novel in his *Thursday Next* series, introduces a feisty Miss Havisham, and due to the success of novels spurned by *Pride and Prejudice and Zombies* (2009), Sherri Browning Erwin's *Grave Expectations: The Classic Tale of Love, Ambition and Howling at the Moon* followed in 2011, reconfiguring Pip and Estella as werewolves, and Miss Havisham as a vengeful vampire. Satirists Trey Parker and Matt Stone also presented a truncated spoof of *Great Expectations* as a one-off episode of their cult teen television series, *South Park*. There have been a number of adaptations that explore the themes and characters found in the story, many shifting the narrative focus from Pip to Estella (Sue Roe's *Estella: Her Expectations* 1982; Alanna Knight's *Estella* 1998 and *Miss Havisham's Revenge* 2012) to Magwitch (Peter Carey's *Jack Maggs* 1997; Tony Lester's *Magwitch* trilogy 2010–2012), or Miss Havisham (Dominic Argento's opera, *Miss Havisham's Fire* in 1979, Carol Ann Duffy's 'Havisham', from her *Meantime* collection, 1998), and there are numerous cinematic reincarnations of Miss Havisham, from *Sunset Boulevard*'s Norma Dinsmoor (1950) to Bette Davis' Baby Jane Hudson in *Whatever Happened to Baby Jane* (1962).

Scholarly interest in all things Dickensian peaked during his bi-centennial celebration; academic conferences like 'The Other Dickens: Victorian and Neo-Victorian Contexts' (University of Portsmouth's Centre for Studies in Literature) in July 2012 and 'Adapting Dickens' (De Montfort University's Centre for Adaptations) in February 2013 marked the occasion, as did special issues of journals. Dickens' 200th birthday celebrations saw the publication of Ronald Frame's *Havisham*, a fictitious prequel to the canonical text, first adapted for radio broadcast on BBC's Radio 3 in 1998, and two screen adaptations. Mike Newell's film adaptation of *Great Expectations* (2012) swiftly followed on from a three part BBC TV adaptation broadcast as part of its 2011 Christmas programming. That so much attention was focused on Dickens' *Great Expectations* in his bi-centennial year attests to its enduring capacity to engage and entertain audiences, whether Victorian or contemporary.

Whilst Brontë's *Jane Eyre* is preoccupied with issues related to the position of women in her contemporary England, and thus continues to attract the attention of feminist scholarship, Dickens' *Great Expectations* is predominantly preoccupied not with feminist but with humanist issues. Focused here on the concept of 'the gentleman', rather than the 'Angel in the House', it inevitably concerns matters related to class and to the corrupting power of wealth and status. According to Dickens' contemporary, Cardinal Newman, a gentleman is 'one who never inflicts pain' (Landow); it is not a stature defined by class but by behaviour, and this is the lesson that Pip must learn during the course of the narrative. His coming-of-age story revolves around his clearly structured journey towards becoming a 'gentleman' in more than a class-based definition of the term. Pip's initial motivation is to acquire wealth and position as a means to securing Estella's 'love', but his journey is ultimately one of self-discovery. Dickens presents us with inherently good characters who by class-based definition are not deemed 'gentlemen': both Joe Gargery and Herbert Pocket do not have the prerequisite wealth to be seen as gentlemen in the eyes of Victorian society, and yet they epitomize 'gentlemanly' behaviour. The backstory of criminals Magwitch and Compeyson further illustrates the discrepancies between status and behaviour of the 'gentleman' in society; through this narrative aside Dickens highlights the injustice of a system that treats criminals differently according to their class status, presenting the coarse working-class Magwitch as the more benevolent and ultimately more 'gentlemanly' of the two.

Pip's failure to recognize this sets him up as a very unsympathetic protagonist but because the tale is narrated by the mature, reflective Pip, the narrator's concerns about his own behaviour are foregrounded from the outset, and by the novel's close he has acquired self-knowledge and emerges as a more humane individual. Even though a romance plot of sorts lies at the heart of this narrative, Pip's love interest remains secondary to his journey towards becoming a 'gentleman'. Romance may provide motive here, but it does not provide closure for Pip as the novel's protagonist. Pip states, 'it is the most miserable thing to be ashamed of home' (Dickens 86); he shares his feelings of guilt and frustration with the reader throughout, noting how he would 'decide conclusively that [his] disaffection to dear old Joe and the forge was gone, and that [he] was growing up in a fair way to be partners with Joe and to keep company with Biddy – when all in a moment some confounding remembrance of the Havisham days would fall upon [him] like a destructive missile and scatter [his] wits again' (105). Through use of a first person narration, Dickens is able to communicate Pip's self-doubt, and his constant assessment of his own behaviour endears him to the reader, allowing us to forgive him for his lack of judgement and his questionable behaviour at the various stages of his journey towards adulthood. The gentle wit and humour of his delivery ensures audience empathy, despite the questionable nature of his actions.

Dickens' female characters in general tend to be either cloyingly pure 'Angels in the House' of the Esther Summerson variety who are rewarded for their stoicism or evil caricatures punished by their excision. In *Great Expectations*, Dickens' women are more complex: there is no central 'Angel' figure: the eccentric Miss Havisham and the emotionally redundant Estella emerge as far more complicated females than those found in his earlier novels. Most of the female characters in this tale – Mrs Joe Gargery, Molly, Miss Havisham, Estella – subvert traditional expectations of the contemporaneous 'Angel in the House', and yet each of them remains bound within a 'domestic' space. Only Biddy and Clara Pocket emerge as conventional Victorian women whose eventual matrimonial status is just reward for a life time of stoicism. Mrs Joe is trapped in a domestic role that infuriates her: she is not only the wife of a lowly blacksmith but the unwilling mother of her orphaned nephew, and like Miss Havisham (and Brontë's Bertha Mason), she is a woman who is ultimately removed from the narrative for failing to conform.

Although Miss Havisham plays a pivotal role within the story, she is not a visible presence throughout; she may dominate the opening section but she has a less prominent part to play in Pip's realization of his expectations during his London days, and it is his relationships with other males within the text – Joe Gargery, Herbert Pocket, Jaggers, Wemmick, Bentley Drummle and ultimately Magwitch – that are most central to the narrative trajectory. Yet, she is a character who constantly haunts his story, and her currency within that story remains a central preoccupation of adapters working with this text. Dickens' Miss Havisham makes a mockery of marriage: she is the virginal corpse bride whose mission is to destroy the hearts of male suitors, but here it is Miss Havisham who is destroyed and women who go against the norms of Victorian society invariably meet violent ends in this novel. She is seen as 'the most sinister, spectacular bride in Victorian fiction' (Regis and Wynne 37), one of a number of 'evil and unnatural dominatrices – Miss Havisham, Mrs Joe and Magwitch's wild mistress – who are eventually beaten into submission or written away as irrelevant' (Mukherjee 114). On-screen Havishams have become part of the folklore of the novel. Concerns relating to her casting, costuming and performance tend to dominate the discourse of academics and film reviewers alike. The most recent screen adaptations, starring Gillian Anderson (2011, BBC) and Helena Bonham Carter (2012) as Miss Havisham, provoked heated debate as to which performance best reflects Dickens' infamous 'Witch' (Dickens 69), but whatever the merits and demerits of each actor's performance, Miss Havisham remains Pip's ever present and grotesque 'fairy godmother'. Gillian Anderson, describes her as 'an iconic character who pervades our world in various forms', and our preoccupation with issues relating to the casting and costuming of cinematic screen Havishams becomes central to our judgement of a production's success or failure. There is, according to Georges Letissier, a 'mnemonic persistence attached to her image' that 'has repeatedly reasserted her centrality in film adaptations' (33), and her appearance continues to subvert expectations of traditional heritage cinema, offering a 'complex visual rejection of all that traditional costume drama stands for' (Regis and Wynne 38).

Both Miss Havisham and Mrs Joe serve as the stepmother of fairy tale, each with her own brand of cruelty. Mrs Joe's physical violence against Pip is equalled only by Miss Havisham's emotional mistreatment and manipulation of Estella. Raised to be emotionally distant by a disturbed adoptive parent, Estella's unconventional behaviour and rejection of romantic notions of love make her an unlikely heroine and an even more unlikely bride, yet marriage remains the only life choice for her; her marriage to the violent Bentley Drummle serves as a further example of the ways in which women who fail to conform are punished in this text, but Dickens does afford Estella a level of control in the matter. The decision to marry Drummle is made by Estella; she is affronted when Pip pleads with her not to 'let Miss Havisham lead [her] into this fatal step' and assures him that it is her 'own act' (Dickens 271). In the original ending Estella survives the violence of her first marriage to Bentley Drummle and is married off to a country doctor: she is never going to be the 'angel' of Victorian society but she is at last safely and conservatively integrated into the community, and Pip does observe that she 'had been given a heart to understand what [his] heart used to be' (359), even if not the capacity to feel the same emotion. At the urging of Bulwer-Lytton, however, Dickens revised his ending to ensure audience satisfaction, creating a close that did not necessarily serve as a natural and inevitable conclusion to Pip's tale, but that did deliver the possibility of romantic union for Pip and Estella. Ever seeking to please his readership, Dickens willingly conceded and produced an even more conservative conclusion: Pip states, as he takes her by the hand, that he 'saw the shadow of no parting from her', inferring that they will be together forever from this point onwards. In service to the desired romantic closure, the emotionally redundant Estella has, it seems, overcome a life time of conditioning and is now capable of returning Pip's love.

Adapters are constantly drawn to the disturbing figures of Miss Havisham and Estella; they are rarely removed from the adapted narrative, unlike Biddy and Clara Pocket. The gothic setting provided by a neglected Satis House, its decaying rooms in which time has stood still and the presence of the macabre bride offer the screen adapter in particular a wealth of visually loaded detail through which to narrate Pip's tale, whether recreating its gothic propensity through the lens of film noir as in Lean's 1946 film or by playing with images of rebirth and decay as in Alfonso Cuaron's *Great Expectations*, where Satis House becomes a dilapidated Florida mansion, aptly named Paridse Perduto (Paradise Lost). Similarly, Dickens' dialogue is invariably treated with a reverence usually reserved only for Shakespeare's verse. The dialogue in Part one, between Pip, Miss Havisham and Estella is, for example, traditionally reproduced in its entirety. When Estella remarks that Pip is 'a common labouring boy' who 'calls the knaves Jacks' or when Miss Havisham tells her she 'can break his heart' (51–52), we are already primed to anticipate these lines as knowing consumers of the tale. Adapters also remove Joe's 'What larks' line at their own peril: the phrase, though comedic, captures his humanity, and it makes an appearance even in the darkest of rewrites.

Whilst Charlotte Brontë resorts to the anonymity of an authorial pseudonym, Dickens is at pains to highlight his authorship, and adapters of *Great Expectations* continue to address issues related to the importance of authorship and of writing oneself into a narrative. Biographer Peter Ackroyd claims *Great Expectations* is 'a novel in which [Dickens] is engaged in exorcising the influence of the past by rewriting it' (930): disturbing childhood memories of working in a blacking factory and of his family being imprisoned in Marshalsea Prison as a result of his father's debts haunt this text. Adapters Peter Carey (*Jack Maggs*) and Lloyd Jones (*Mr Pip*) experiment with *Great Expectations* by returning to these notions of authorship and of rewriting the past as a process of reclamation and affirmation. As postcolonial writers they interrogate the significance of authorship, foregrounding the importance of storytelling and its capacity to heal. Like Jean Rhys's Antoinette, Carey's Jack Maggs authors his own past, battling his demons by *writing* his experiences into existence, reclaiming ownership of both personal and colonial history and building on Dickens' dark vision of nineteenth-century England. Like Rhys, Carey repositions his reader, forever influencing our perception of and relationship with the precursor text. The postcolonial colonization of the Ur text in Jones's *Mr Pip* further emphasizes the ways in which adapters challenge the authority of the canonical 'source' and their respective authors. Postcolonial fascination with reclaiming of the experiences of those silenced by their position within the colonial outpost can also be found in earlier film adaptations of the text: in 1986 the Australian Broadcasting Corporation financed, *Great Expectations: The Untold Story*, a production detailing the experiences of Magwitch post transportation. It is a tale that foreshadows Carey's interest in this much maligned and underdeveloped character from Dickens' novel. In postcolonial rewrites, Magwitch, like Rhys's Antoinette, no longer functions as plot mechanism but as the central narrative voice, yet whereas Antoinette is eventually submerged in former narrative outcomes, both Tim Burtsall (director of the ABC production) and Carey create upbeat endings in which their protagonists rise above their criminal past and are rewarded rather than removed from the story.

Postmodern authors like Carey, Jones and Kathy Acker find what Sanders terms 'a useful metafictional method for reflecting on their own creative authorial impulses' (129) by means of spinning a different version of Dickens' *Great Expectations*. Postmodernist and feminist, Kathy Acker appropriates Dickens' *Great Expectations* in her own semi-autobiographical novel of the same name (1982); her works are a pastiche of appropriations from canonical literature and though her novel identifies itself through its title and its opening lines as a text that has a relationship with Dickens' narrative, she proceeds to challenge established literary forms by reinventing the tale as something completely different. She openly rejects notions of authorial originality, and like Carey's fictional Maggs, uses her writing as a vehicle for self-affirmation that in turn asks us to question the validity and veracity of earlier stories we think we already know. Her story's relationship with *Great Expectations* is tentative and speculative, yet it serves to disrupt accepted notions of narrative ownership and originality and in so doing poses interesting questions about the relationship between canonical literature and texts that rework that literature within a very different cultural backdrop. *Great Expectations* is a novel that presents us with a conservative ideology that does not engage with the feminist preoccupations of an adapter like Acker; however, Acker challenges its conservatism by hijacking its title and invading the narrative space with her own, very different authorial agenda.

Dana Shiller notes that the Victorian writer has an 'unfettered enthusiasm for plotting' and claims the popularity of today's neo-Victorian novel is in part due to the form's similar preoccupation with the unravelling of complex plotlines (84). *Great Expectations* is seen as a novel of 'the golden age of plot' (Brooks 114), full of convoluted yet credible coincidences and purposely misconstrued or misguided beliefs that add to the mysteries surrounding his stories. Miss Havisham, for example, chooses not to contradict Pip's belief that she is his secret benefactor, whilst Pip purposely refuses to accept that Estella is incapable of 'love', and Jaggers' presence gives credence to some of the story's more fantastical plot points surrounding matters like Estella's parentage and adoption. In the hands of a less competent storyteller, the coincidences could become contrived, but Dickens seamlessly weaves the plot intricacies into the fabric of his narrative, and they form part of its natural outcomes. The serialized nature of Dickens' tale prescribes the need to incorporate certain structural elements into Pip's journey: each instalment must advance the action, resolve issues raised in the previous instalment and pose new difficulties, leading us to a cliff-hanger moment that anticipates the narrative thrust of the next episode. The structure of *Great Expectations* lends itself to cinematic narrative patterning as the story divides into three distinct acts – childhood and the acquiring of 'expectations'; realizing those expectations; and the disruption of said expectations.

It is, according to Nichols, a text that embodies all elements noted as essential within the 'jargon' of screenwriting manuals, with its 'three acts, an inciting incident, a series of obstacles, a crisis at the end of the second act'. Each section (or act) builds towards a moment of dramatic climax and leads to the ultimate point of closure. It adopts a story design of the type identified by narrative theorist Tzvetan Todorov as a simple cause and effect narrative structure that lends itself to the medium of film. We begin with what Todorov terms a brief period of 'equilibrium' that establishes the status quo within the story world, followed by a disruption to that equilibrium; the remainder of the narrative deals in the consequences of that disruption and works towards restoration of order or 'equilibrium'. Mainstream cinema's classical story design mirrors that of the classic realist text which dominates writing of the nineteenth century. Both adopt the kind of cause and effect narrative patterning defined by Todorov, but the plotting complexities of the nineteenth-century realist novel add multiple layers to the story as it unfolds, without losing its ultimate goal of narrative closure and restoration of order. Scriptwriting guru Robert McKee defines the classical design (or 'archplot') as:

> a story built around an active protagonist who struggles against primarily external forces of antagonism to pursue his or her desire, through continuous time, within a consistent and causally connected fictional reality, to a closed ending of absolute, irreversible change. (45)

It is a model narrative consisting of the prerequisite 'series of events, causally linked', and involving a 'continuing set of characters which influence and are influenced by the caused events' (Novel to Film 12). In his seminal text, *Novel to Film: an Introduction to the Theory of Adaptation*, McFarlane offers a theoretical methodology for exploration of the processes at work in the translation of literature to screen. Taking the observations of narratologist Roland Barthes as his starting point, McFarlane notes that all stories consist of 'the linking together of cardinal functions' which 'provid[e] the irreducible bare bones of the narrative', or its narrative 'hinge points' (13–14). Adapters work predominantly with these hinge points in order to produce a story that is, to a greater or lesser degree, recognizable as a reconfiguration of a particular tale. Hence adapters who are primarily concerned with fidelity to a source text will incorporate most of what are seen as its major narrative 'hinge' points in order to signal the connections between the adaptation and its 'source' text, whilst those seeking a less definitive relationship with the precursor text will incorporate its narrative elements to a lesser degree. McFarlane notes that *Great Expectations* is 'complex in its structure' with its 'multiplicity of narrative strands, and consequently of major cardinal functions' (112). He identifies no less than 54 'narrative hinge points' (or 'major cardinal functions'), each 'linked consequentially as well as sequentially to other events and actions in the narrative' (115). However, whilst an adapter like David Lean chooses to follow this narrative patterning closely, others like Alfonso Cuaron select fewer points of direct narrative connection, signalling its very different relationship with Dickens' tale. McFarlane identifies only nineteen of the novels' fifty-four hinge points in Cuaron's film, though this is open to interpretation and as with Acker's adaptation, the film does signal its relationship with the novel in a very direct manner through its retention of the title, *Great Expectations*. Other adapters, like Carey, Frame or Duffy choose to relate the tale from a different point of view and often from a different temporal or geographical place. The permutations are endless, and this is what makes adaptation as a process so intriguing.

Narratologists differentiate between narrative and narration. Seymour Chatman defines narrative as 'story' that relates to 'the content of the narrative expression' while narration or 'discourse' relates to 'the form of that expression' (23–24). Russian formalists define it instead as the *fabula* (narrative/story) and the *suzet* (narration/discourse), but whatever terminology we employ, it is through *narration* – the *how* as opposed to the *what* of storytelling – that the adapter can make significant changes to the ways in which we receive the story, especially when operating in a different medium like film with its additional visual and aural signification system. Even when working within a similar signification system, adapters' employ the signifiers in different ways to produce very different creative outcomes: the playwright's creative tools are not the same as those of the screenplay writer, though both create a written document for a performance which ultimately relies upon visual, aural, verbal and performative means of communication; similarly, the poet employs a different mode of expression to that of the novelist with a different set of expectations for its readership, just as the short story writer creates within different parameters, despite the fact that the novel and the short story as forms share many features. Chatman argues that it is the 'transportability' of the narrative that offers the 'strongest reason for arguing that narratives are indeed structures independent of any medium' (20), thus ensuring their amenability to constant reinvention and adaptation. However, it is the ingenious *ways* in which adapters translate that portable narrative structure within their chosen medium that determines the adaptation's capacity to become a stand-alone text: it is less a matter of what is told and more a matter of how it is told.

Great Expectations adheres to cinema's classical design in terms of its structure, though it is less easily defined in terms of cinematic genre: it does not fit neatly into mainstream generic templates unlike a novel like *Jane Eyre* which, when translated to screen, is so often presented as romance. It may be considered a text book melodrama since it deals with family situations (no matter how convoluted and problematic these family situations appear to be), and the story does focus on the private emotions of its protagonist who must suffer as he journeys towards self-knowledge and reintegration into the community; but *Great Expectations* is also part mystery, part romance, part satirical social commentary, part gothic horror and thriller. There is always a sense of the wider world at work in Dickens' narratives and of his protagonists' engagement with that world. Pip becomes our Everyman, through whom we experience the social injustices at the heart of Victorian England. Moreover, his journey remains of interest to adapters and their audiences because of its universality rather than its placement within a particular historical moment: the social injustices continue, the desire to aspire to greater things – whether in matters of romance, social mobility or conscience – remains central to our humanity, and it is for these reasons that a story like *Great Expectations* has continued to attract the interest of writers since its initial serialization.

Great Expectations: The 'classic' treatment (screen adaptations of *Great Expectations*: 1946, 2011 and 2012)

Great Expectations has historically received the classic treatment on screen; though some screen adapters use the novel's structure, characters and themes in a purposefully unfaithful and irreverent manner, so-called 'fidelity' to Dickens' canonical text has, on the whole, been a primary goal of both feature film and television adapters. However, though all of these 'faithful' adaptations employ the anticipated period setting, each one adheres to its own socio-cultural agenda as a consequence of its time of production. The most acclaimed film adaptation of *Great Expectations* remains Cineguild's 1946 movie, directed by David Lean and released in post-Second World War Britain during a time of post-war nation building. It is a product of its time and though it is a film that does not shirk the moral complexities of Dickens' story, with its exploration of the darker side of Victorian England, ultimately it presents us with a coming of age story that speaks of hope and regeneration. Lean's film sets the benchmark against which other film adaptations of the novel are measured. Placed fifth in the BFI's top 100 British films of the twentieth century, it has become a cinematic canonical text in its own right and has been constantly appropriated in film and television adaptations since its release in the forties. The forties was the 'golden age' of British cinema during which time directors like Lean had far greater creative and financial freedom than directors working in a post-forties context, in which filmmakers had to compete with the growing presence of television.

From 1945 to 1949, Lean directed five films for Cineguild all of which are adaptations of literary classics, including *Great Expectations* and *Oliver Twist* (1948), both of which reflect the social upheavals of post-war Britain as it tries to regenerate. However, like a number of films produced in the forties by the Gainsborough Studios, they adopt a Gothic edge; they present a 'kind of English counterpart to Hollywood film noir' and in so doing, argues Raphael Samuel, the comedic, sentimentalized Dickens of the Victorian era is superseded by the 'dark Dickens' – a Dickens created by twentieth-century 'highbrow critics attempting to reclaim the novels from a sentimentalized popular taste' in order to 'assimilate them into the canon of modernism' (44–51). Like Shakespeare, Dickens has undoubtedly been co-opted as a writer of high art, and the populist nature of his work is sacrificed to a certain extent as a result of its placement within the literary canon. Despite attempts to present a moment of cathartic rebirth via *Great Expectations'* very optimistic closing scene, the general tone of the film remains downbeat. This preoccupation with the darker side of *Great Expectations* is still apparent as we move on to adaptations in the twenty-first century, though the most recent offerings dwell upon the novel's romance plot as opposed to its exploration of social injustice, moral dilemmas or its comedic potential and thus may be seen as returning the novel to its melodramatic and populist 'roots', even if through the rather different vehicle of romance cinema.

Lean's film pays homage to the novel from the outset: Dickens' words dominate visually and aurally, foregrounded through Pip's voiceover as he reads to us from the pages of the novel. Like other forties film adapters of classic tales, Lean adopts a reverential treatment of the canonical text. Elliott notes the visual sophistication with which Lean treats the process of adaptation from page to screen in these opening moments; Dickens' text remains a presence yet the static nature of the written word is superseded by the 'dynamic animation processes of film', and the visually dominant energies of the scenes that follow 'showca[se] film's visual and aural vivacity' (113). The powerful impact of the opening moments of Lean's *Great Expectations* is so great that it has become part of the adaptive landscape of screen adaptations – a template of sorts for subsequent films and televised serializations, from Cuaron's 1998 film to the most recent film adaptation released in 2012 or in TV products as diverse as BBC adaptations in similar periods (1999 and 2011) and episodes of *South Park*. It becomes a film text that is 'appropriated' in its own right. The eerie, gothic tone of the first formative encounter between Pip and Magwitch as realized by Lean seeps into later visualizations of the scene, with its open marshlands, neglected graveyard, its creaking, wind tossed tree and stark gibbet. However, despite Samuels' claim that there is a dilution of humour in cinematic adaptations of Dickens' work in the forties, Lean's depiction of the graveyard encounter does incorporate the same kind of humorous edge found in Dickens' writing. It is an understated humour – and one that is inevitably overpowered by the darker tone of the scene – but Pip's polite requests to be put back on his feet when held upside down and shaken, have a certain comedic edge to them. The camera positions itself with child Pip's perspective, even though the voiceover narration that initially cues us into the scene is that of an adult giving a retrospective point of view. Unlike later screen adapters, Lean does incorporate the humorous notes of Dickens' prose both here and in the moments leading up to Pip's second encounter with Magwitch, when his imagination is made manifest via menacing talking cows that accost him en route.

Working within the time constraints of forties cinema, Lean condenses this coming of age story into 118 minutes without sacrificing what Barthes terms its narrative hinge points. The majority of screen time is devoted to the early sections of the novel and Pip's formative years (approximately forty-five minutes), with his arrival in London and his reunion with Magwitch taking up the remainder of the running time. This preoccupation with the formative years and childhood innocence is shared by a number of forties film adapters working with canonical texts: Stevenson's 1944 *Jane Eyre*, for example, dedicates a disproportionate amount of time to Jane's Lowood experiences. The orphan narratives of Dickens and Brontë strike a chord with postwar cinema audiences of the forties; both Lean's *Great Expectations* and Stevenson's *Jane Eyre* monopolize on images of the enduring orphaned child as a symbol of hope and regeneration for nations recovering from the trauma of a Second World War. Pip's journey from childhood innocence to adult awareness remains the focus of Lean's streamlined narrative. However, certain plot points are inevitably excised as part of this streamlining and there is the prerequisite cinematic focus on one central romance. Here, the relationship between Pip and Biddy has no grounding in childhood romance: there is no rival for Pip's love and, in keeping with cinematic expectations, Lean realizes a far less complicated romantic closure than is implied in Dickens' novel. Neither is the relationship between Herbert Pocket and Pip so central. Lean's Pip seems a much more likeable protagonist in less need of correction. He is the Everyman character of film narrative with whom we choose to journey: he is ready to see the error of his ways and is much more willing to embrace Magwitch than Dickens' Pip at first appears to be.

However, it is a film in which, according to Regina Barreca, the 'most interesting relationship is not among men but between women, Estella and Miss Havisham' (39). Mrs Joe is removed from the plot at a much earlier point in the narrative and her death by natural causes softens the traditionally harsh treatment of females in this story. Similarly, Molly's role is not explored fully. Instead, Lean focuses more directly on Estella and Havisham, whose physical and spiritual impact is amplified in this film. Miss Havisham dominates visually and just as Lean's opening scenes have become part of the story's cinematic lore, Martitia Hunt's Miss Havisham has become the prototype for subsequent screen Havishams. Recently cast Havishams, Gillian Anderson and Helena Bonham Carter, have spoken of their initial concerns about playing this role as they both felt that they were too young to be cast as the story's notorious crone. Yet Miss Havisham has historically been played by women of a similar age. Hunt was only in her mid-forties when cast as Lean's Miss Havisham, and Charlotte Rampling in her early fifties when she appeared in the role in the 1999 BBC adaptation. Indeed, Dickens' eccentric recluse is only twenty-seven when jilted, and thus in her mid-forties when she first meets Pip. So where does our sense of the aged Miss Havisham come from? Rather than being the sole product of Dickens' imaginative prose, she is an imagistic combination of Dickens' language *and* Lean's cinematic reincarnation of her. The work of costume designer Sophie Devine is also instrumental in our perception of Miss Havisham; Regis and Wynne note that the emphasis on Havisham's gothic excesses here negates the usually nostalgic propensities of the costume drama and its 'sanitized' look (45). Dickens prose descriptors are infiltrated by the visual energies of cinema: when we think of Miss Havisham, we picture her as Hunt's timeless, deceptively aged gothic 'witch', and we consider her successors in relation not only to the image inscribed by Dickens but to the 'otherness' generated by Lean's film text. Subsequent screen adaptations continue to add layer upon layer to our perception of this character, whether she is realized through the visuals of cinema or television, stage performance or imagistic prose and verse.

As with Miss Havisham, in the public imagination Estella is seen as central to the tale. She is the love interest that spurs Pip on in his quest to become a gentleman. In the marketing posters for Lean's film, the romantic image of Pip and Estella staring into each other's eyes dominates, despite the various surrounding images (of Compeyson and Magwitch mid brawl, or of an intimate Estella and Miss Havisham, a fearful Pip and Magwitch or a wide-eyed child Pip) which depict other relationships within the story.

The tagline emphasizes the novel's affiliation with its source text. It is 'from the vivid pages of Charles Dickens' masterpiece', and the adjective 'great' appears repeatedly: it markets itself as a 'faithful' adaptation of the tale. But in its quest to pitch itself as an appealing romance, the incongruous image of a submissive Estella, dressed in a modern, off the shoulder evening gown, overpowered by a handsome male lead takes centre stage. The anachronistic costuming on the poster suggests that the film is not seen by its promoters as costume drama, and though its marketing emphasis is upon romance, it does sell itself as a mix of genres from 'romance', to 'thriller', and 'adventure' film, full of 'suspense'. It is much more than a romance. Jean Simmonds' performance plays to the precocious nature of Miss Havisham's adopted child. Lean places great emphasis upon the formative years of the relationship between Miss Havisham, Estella and Pip. The warped nature of the relationship between Miss Havisham and her charge is highlighted as a means to amplifying the endearing innocence of Pip and offers a stark contrast to the openness and camaraderie of Pip and Joe in this film adaptation. Lean's Miss Havisham nurtures in Estella an incapacity to engage emotionally with others and occupies a privileged 'male' position, orchestrating the ebb and flow of the relationship between Pip and Estella, though Estella retains her feisty individuality. She delivers the lines inscribed from Dickens' novel with a disdain yet to be equalled by her on-screen successors, and her mistreatment of the young Pip serves to further ingratiate him as the audience's troubled Everyman. However, the proud, wilful, captivating Estella of the earlier scenes is usurped by an adult Estella who becomes a parody of her benefactor; she returns to a Satis House that has survived the fire which kills Miss Havisham, and she awaits a similar fate. Miss Havisham, like Bertha Mason, is the final barrier to romantic closure and she too is excised by fire: images of burning witches who represent the unconventional image of female 'otherness' inevitably prevail in these texts.

Up until this point, it seems that Estella is also portrayed as 'other', but this is subverted by the much debated closing scene, in which Pip is cast as the returning hero who rescues his 'princess' from the decaying tower. It is a close that is viewed by many academics as a betrayal of the narrative's inevitable outcome. Pip is proactive here, Estella being left in the role of the inert damsel-in-distress of the romance genre, despite her earlier depiction as one who does not have the capacity to return Pip's affections and who ultimately is in control: for reasons of narrative consistency, the inferred romantic union written into Lean's closing shot of Pip and Estella, fleeing hand in hand from the dark ruins of Satis House and into the daylight, may be seen as flawed. Yet like Dickens, Lean is responding to the politics of his time and the expectations of his audience. Pip is the orphan child who rises from the ashes and makes good, and in so doing he becomes a symbol of hope and rebirth for a socialist Britain emerging from the horrors of the Second World War. Michael Klein and Gillian Parker conclude, as do a number of critics, that the moral to Lean's film is that 'women are weak and need a man to tell them what to do' (152), but it is perhaps unfair to judge Lean's film within the prism of second wave feminist values when it is a product of an era that predates such preoccupations. Furthermore, it is a film that in a forties context foregrounds other concerns, and as an adaptation it responds to those concerns. Thus far, Lean has amplified the dark, gothic qualities of the narrative, using low key lighting to exaggerate the shadows, positioning his characters in relation to the vastness of their surroundings as in the opening scene, or Pip's first visit to Satis House or by highlighting the cluttered, claustrophobic nature of the mise en scène, particularly in moments shared with Miss Havisham. In contrast, the closing shot highlights a way out of the film's overarching noir-like framework, leaving us on a note of postwar optimism as Pip and Estella move away from the 'ashes' of Satis House and into a brighter future.

Televised serializations of the nineteenth-century realist novel have historically presented comforting costume drama mini-series, aired in the favoured Sunday evening viewing slot and targeting a female audience. However, a much more complex relationship between the televisual text and its audience is emerging; Cardwell argues that rather than presenting us with distant images of a past situated solely within its own historical context, many contemporary period drama serializations both 'affi[rm] and renegotia[te] our relationship with the past' through 'constant affirmation of the present' (162). Adaptations of Dickens *Great Expectations* continue to thrive as a consequence of the novel's capacity to engage us in dialogue between past and present, as is evidenced by Lean's optimistic re-visions at the end of the 1945 film adaptation in response to the values and the political context of the era of its production. Televisual adaptations engage in a similar process of negotiation, often generating the same kind of critical dismay that attaches to the close of Lean's film. The most recent televised adaptation of *Great Expectations* produced for the BBC (2011) was met with critical animosity on the whole, some lamenting its lack of humour (Singh), while others questioned what are deemed its 'soap opera' qualities (Lott). However, what is sorely lacking from these critiques is any sense of the ways in which this production 'negotiates' the past through the lens of the 'present'. Instead of interrogating the revisions and amendments made during the adaptive process as part of its journey to the screen of a twenty-first-century audience, critical discourse has focused on the liberties taken with the novel, returning yet again to tired debates concerning 'fidelity'. It is, claims contemporary novelist Howard Jacobson, 'a witless three part traducement of *Great Expectations*, designed to make good the claim that had Dickens been alive today he would have written for Eastenders'. Whether screenwriter Sarah Phelps' amendments 'feminiz[e], Jane Austeni[se] and se[x] up' the canonical text (Lott) to its detriment remains debatable, but such amendments forge intriguing avenues for discussion about what is taking place here as the text moves from page to screen, and from the reading experience of the individual to the viewing experiences of the six million people who tuned in to watch the mini-series during its 2011 Christmas transmission.

Despite the traditional heritage look established by the opening credits, the dark, gothic quality of Dickens' prose dominates here as in the majority of screen adaptations of *Great Expectations*. Satis House is perpetually shrouded in fog, and the marshes remain emblematic of Pip's initial fear and foreboding. The forge is constructed as a place of similarly murky and troubled possibilities rather than a refuge of any kind, and the menacingly humorous moments set in Pip's home are removed. The opening wide angle shots, accompanied by an eerie musical score and the diegetic sound of something moving through water, emphasize the vastness of the wet marshlands that surround the forge and establish the adaptation's overarching visual schema which is built upon notions of rebirth, renewal and entrapment. When the camera moves on to the graveyard scene, the sound of a creaking tree dominates, echoing the audio properties of Lean's adaptation, but the opening moments also intertextualize elements of Alfonso Cuaron's 1998 *Great Expectations*. Like Robert De Niro in the latter adaptation, Ray Winstone emerges from the watery depths of the vast landscape, but whilst De Niro's entrance is given the classic horror treatment, the entrance of Winstone's Magwitch sets him up as a more vulnerable, empathetic character from the outset. Visual allusions to baptism and birthing infer, at least at a subliminal level, that his encounter with Pip will bring about some kind of change. Phelps' script highlights the humanity of both Pip and Magwitch and engages with the class issues at the centre of the narrative; in this adaptation, as well as providing Magwitch with the requested file, Pip brings food without being asked to do so, and it is this simple act of kindness that stays with the recaptured convict. Scenes involving Pip and Magwitch are shot in close detail: we witness the inhumane treatment of Magwitch, and Pip's worried reaction, as he is welded back into his leg irons, and the camera holds on a close up shot of Magwitch as he asks Pip his name, underscoring the significance of the moment for him. The possibilities of a future bond between them is clearly signalled from the outset.

As the opening credits roll the screen is littered with images of chrysalids and butterflies, implying that there will be a natural evolution for characters within the narrative – certainly for Pip, from working-class orphan to wealthy gentleman. However, the whimsy of this heavy-handed visual shorthand is tempered by the equally dominant (and similarly loaded) image of inanimate objects encased in glass domes: collected, neglected and left to fade. Stuffed glass-domed animals, insects and birds clutter the mise en scène during Miss Havisham's first meeting with Pip, and Estella and Miss Havisham are visually aligned with the atrophied trophies inside Satis House. The camera lingers repeatedly on framed shots of Estella as she peers out of the window with her hand pressed against the glass; Miss Havisham mirrors Estella's pose later in the narrative. The new beginnings inferred by the images of chrysallids and butterflies – for the orphan Estella, the bride-to-be Miss Havisham and for Pip – are constantly undermined by images of entrapment. Its laboured visual signification may lack subtlety, but the symbolism provides a visual means to highlighting the cyclical nature of the journey undertaken by Pip. It also serves to introduce feminist issues related to the objectification of women, 'affirming and renegotiating' our relationship with Dickens' narrative through the prism of the present.

By casting Gillian Anderson in the role of Miss Havisham, the production instantly signals its intent to reposition her as an object of beauty rather than as the witch-like ogre of fairy tale; she may, as a consequence, play the part as 'more cougar than crone' (Wollaston), yet Anderson presents a Havisham who is not only unstable and other-worldly but complex. On her first entrance she glides into the frame, barefoot, and her lines are delivered in a slow, high-pitched whisper as she takes Pip into the room littered with glass-cased specimens collected by her brother. The specimens become the focus of added dialogue: Miss Havisham informs a bewildered Pip that men seek to contain and preserve beauty as a spectacle, only to neglect it once they have it. She questions the validity of such control and ownership. The script contextualizes her grand plan to reverse the cruelty by turning Estella, whom she refers to as her very own object of beauty – '[her] jewel, [her] prize' – into a destroyer of men. She has a powerful, haunting screen presence in this adaptation; edits between Satis House and the forge are threaded together by her voiceover, as she states: 'Your eyes have been opened and now you cannot close them.' Later, we hear her voice beyond the edges of the frame as adult Pip returns to Satis House to visit Estella, suggesting that she has control of the narrative at such moments. However, she becomes increasingly anxious and unhinged; unable to breathe, scratching her hands until they bleed, she deteriorates physically in front of the camera presenting a stark reversal of earlier images of butterflies emerging from their cocoons. By this stage, both Pip and Estella are beyond her control. Her death is construed as a wilful act of suicide – perhaps a final act of self-assertion or of madness as she chooses to burn Estella's returned letters and makes no attempt to escape from the flames.

Yet again, Dickens' females take centre stage during the transition from page to screen, and as in all screen adaptations other than Tony Marchant's *Great Expectations* (1998), we build towards a romantic climax, despite the series' earlier preoccupations with matters of female agency. Whilst darker elements of the narrative such as Orlick's violent attack of Mrs Joe are retained, conflicting love interests are removed: Biddy does not emerge as a potential rival for Pip's love, and Joe remains alone. Any dilution of the central romance is avoided; rather it is enhanced at every opportunity, and the insertion of a scene in which Pip and Estella disrobe and frolic in the river as a prelude to their 'stage kiss' does leave the production open to claims of 'sexing up' the text unnecessarily (Lott). Yet through this insertion, Phelps provides a rare moment of unencumbered happiness, a glimpse of what might have been had both Pip and Estella been free from the constraints of their upbringing. The addition of scenes which 'sex up' the canonical text also has precedence: the once controversial and now much anticipated 'Darcy wet shirt' moment smuggled into Andrew Davies' televised adaptation of Jane Austen's *Pride and Prejudice* has become a ploy emulated by a number of contemporary writers working with canonical texts as a means to reflecting the cultural norms of the production era rather than its Victorian antecedent. As in Lean's film, Satis House survives the fire and on Pip's return Estella appears again at the window, echoing the earlier images of entrapment. However, in this adaptation Pip is not her heroic rescuer: instead Estella walks out of the ruins of Satis House of her own accord. The anticipated romantic close is realized but Phelps' ending reflects the postfeminist values of its contemporaneous moment.

Pip's friendship with Bentley Drummle (and their visit to a whore house in particular) is another questionable addition to the narrative, but it serves as a means to foregrounding Pip's cultural displacement; his dubious friendship with Drummle is contrasted with the warmth and openness of the friendship between Wemmick and Herbert Pocket. Wemmick exclaims 'I don't know who you are!' in one of his altercations with Pip, and it is Wemmick and Herbert Pocket who must persuade Pip to help protect his benefactor, Magwitch. Pip returns to the start of his journey, when an act of kindness on his part sets him on the path towards learning what it means to be a true gentleman; the time devoted to the establishment of the relationship between Pip and Magwitch at the start of the series, through a slight repositioning of the way in which Pip *chooses* to come to the escaped convict's aid, makes his transition from uncaring 'gent' to humane and dutiful 'son' much more credible. The hinge points of the narrative are retained but a minor amendment like this adds to the story design, and in execution of that story in a visual medium the camera is all important as it directs our gaze, showing us, through a series of close up reaction shots, the impact of the opening moments upon both Pip and Magwitch.

The release of Mike Newell's *Great Expectations* soon after the airing of the BBC mini-series can perhaps be viewed as a marketing error, even in the context of bicentennial celebrations of the birth of Dickens. Both adaptations work within the genre conventions of the costume drama and so to sell the same type of screen product twice within similar markets is always going to be difficult. The film was not a huge success in terms of critical response or box office takings. Where the 2011 TV adaptation is criticized for its lack of fidelity to Dickens' novel, this film adaptation is roundly criticized for being too dependent upon it, returning us yet again to reviewers' preoccupation with the so-called source text. The inference is that no matter how the screen adapter processes the canonical text, the end product will always be measured as a failure: it is either too reverential or too radical. The main criticism of Newell's film from many British reviewers is that in its attempt to remain faithful to the novel, it fails to establish its own identity; it is scathingly labelled a 'York Notes adaptation' that provides a 'whistle-stop tour' of the text (Shoard), an 'open-top bus tour trundling dutifully past all of the familiar sights' (Collin). Its reception in the United States was similarly underwhelming; again it is charged with being too reverent, Dickens 'sacred text' serving as 'a crutch', when it could and should 'benefit from being imaginatively interpreted for the screen' (Chang). Both of the recent screen adaptations fail to engage with the humorous undertones found in Dickens' prose, and both are measured unfavourably against Lean's canonical film adaptation, but Mark Kermode defends Newell's adaptation, speaking fervently of the need to move beyond this fixation with Lean's film and arguing that it is neither necessary nor productive to have one canonical version of the story; according to Kermode, Newell's adaptation plays successfully and unashamedly to the audience's emotions and identifies itself as a 'romantic melodrama in the gothic sense'.

Newell's film is haunted by earlier reincarnations of the novel on screen but in its defence, it does attempt to take us beyond the prescribed confines of the adaptations which precede it. Despite claims that it is a lack-lustre painting-by numbers copy of the canonical text, traduced to 128 minutes and employing expected narrative hinge points and anticipated dialogue, it incorporates seamlessly a number of interesting intertextual allusions to earlier adaptations of *Great Expectations* on screen and uses a series of flashbacks as a means to visually conveying moments of exposition found in the novel. The backdrop to the first encounter between Pip and Magwitch references Lean's 1946 film, and as in Lean's film, Dickens' comical cows make an appearance though without the comic effect. There are also echoes of the BBC's BAFTA award-winning television film adaptation directed by Julian Jarrold (1999); both films employ wide angle panning shots of the landscape, frequently cutting to images of screaming gulls before moving in to a shot of Pip running directly into the camera's lens. Whilst Lean employs voiceover as a cinematic device that situates us with Pip as the narrative's Everyman, Newell and Jarrold rely upon a more visual and less invasive means of identifying Pip as the main 'voice' of the text: his direct gaze into the camera lens places him at the centre of the story that is about to unfold. Like all of its post-forties predecessors – including Alfonso Cuaron's modern take on the story – it shares a dark gothic edge, and Pip's first arrival at Satis House presents the prerequisite shots of the towering gates that lead into the overgrown gardens of a decaying Satis House. Yet Newell's visualization of the grimy, makeshift streets of Victorian London, with Jaggers' law firm's hand-painted sign and its streets thronging with people, mud and refuse ensures that the film remains far from the realms of prettified costume drama throughout, whereas the 2011 adaptation shifts inexplicably from the dark tones of its first act to a second act that presents a touched up image of London, devoid of the anticipated squalor and dirt and shifting inexplicably to a heritage look avoided thus far.

Sometimes the production resorts to unnecessarily loaded visual shorthand: on his arrival in London Pip, in his strikingly white finery, presents a stark contrast to his grimy surroundings, highlighting his social displacement and naivety in a far from subtle manner. This aligns with Newell's declared intent to focus on the humanity of Pip's character and his sense of cultural isolation, yet his Pip does not want to be Pip of the forge from the outset: his desire to move beyond the confines of his working-class origins robs him of the childlike innocence of Lean's and Dickens' orphan boy, and the later rivalry between Pip and Bentley Drummle again focuses on Pip's overriding preoccupation with matters of class. In its defence, Dickens' adult Pip is a similarly objectionable individual during the middle section of the narrative, but to ask a film audience to identify with a dislikeable Everyman is far more problematic. We have to care about him in order to follow him on his journey. The dubious actions and attitudes of Dickens' Pip become the focus of his own critical commentary through the use of first person narration delivered from a retrospective adult point of view; for the screen adapter, there is no easy or constantly workable substitution for such narrative recount without resorting to intrusive voiceover. Film, by its very nature, relies upon visual and aural modes of storytelling. Interestingly, the compulsion to employ voiceover for Pip is resisted, yet it is used as a device to introduce the backstory of both Miss Havisham and Magwitch in this production. By introducing flashbacks that detail her past and her early relationship with an infant Estella, Newell provides us with Miss Havisham's motivation. Through use of voiceover and the onscreen realization of past events, Newell conjures additional backstory without resorting to heavy-handed exposition. When a much younger Miss Havisham in the flashback brings Estella under her wedding veil, the initial inference is that she intends to protect her, but her voiceover contradicts the womb-like safety of the on-screen image: we are told that she is 'seduced by Estella's beauty' and feels compelled to use that beauty as a weapon in her own revenge quest. Magwitch is also afforded extra screen time and backstory through the same kind of flashback visualization and in each case, the audience is given greater insight into the characters of Miss Havisham and Pip's convict benefactor, and as intended their humanity is brought into sharper focus, but there is a danger here of these enigmatic characters losing their mystery, and a hint that the casting of Bonham Carter and Ralph Fiennes has dictated the inclusion of more screen time for them whether or not to do so furthers the narrative momentum or detracts from its pace and natural progression.

As with Kirk's 2011 production, the gifting of voiceover to Miss Havisham can place the narrative too directly into her control. Pip's story is in part eclipsed by characters who, though central to the text and to its intricacies of plot, are not its intended focus. Yet this ever-present preoccupation with screen Havishams has been part of cinema's response to the character since

Martitia Hunt's performance in the forties. By casting Helena Bonham Carter as the reclusive benefactress, Newell highlights the gothic properties of the narrative. Bonham Carter is associated with the gothic through her performance in films as diverse as *Mary Shelley's Frankenstein* (1994), Tim Burton's animated *Corpse Bride* (2005) and *Sweeney Todd: the demon Barber of Fleet Street* (2007). She brings to the role a quirky, other worldly edge. The worryingly caricatured opening shot of Miss Havisham as waxwork figure brought to life suggests that Bonham Carter will be revisiting her performance as the Corpse Bride, but despite the initial shot, her Havisham is played as a credible, damaged individual rather than as the psychologically disintegrating yet similarly convincing Havisham portrayed by Gillian Anderson in the 2011 mini-series. The fairy tale tropes of the novel are encoded in this film text, many of them at the insistence of Bonham Carter: she carries a wand-like monocle, has stars in her long, tangled hair, angel wings sewn to her wedding dress, and wears only one shoe, the latter as prescribed in Dickens novel. Warped allusions to fairy tales like Rapunzel and Cinderella, and to her role as Pip's fairy godmother abound, but there are conscious attempts to ensure her humanity.

However, rather than realizing the declared intent to produce an adaptation that foregrounds Pip's humanity, Newell's film identifies itself as a romance: this *Great Expectations* is one of the few screen adaptations of Dickens' novels that could make an appearance in one of the many youTube fansite tributes to costume drama romance. Other screen adaptations of the novel have given greater prominence to the romance elements of the story but here the narrative arc builds to the romantic climax in a manner that is far more central. The initial relationship between Pip and Estella is constructed as one of mutual interest from the outset; Pip's fight with Herbert Pocket becomes a matter of protecting Estella's honour, and the traditionally emotionless Estella cries when Miss Havisham tells him that he will no longer visit Satis House. When they meet again as adults, Nicholls' script introduces additional dialogue in which Estella questions Pip's misguided belief that he is the 'knight from a children's story' who will 'marr[y] the princess', and in a later encounter, when Estella in turn defends Pip's honour during an altercation with Drummle, she signals her love for him but insists that she must do what Miss Havisham demands of her. The adult Estella is a more likeable character than is the norm in either the novel or screen adaptations; Holliday Grainger's Estella is less ice-queen, more flirtatious tease, and her conversations with Pip cast her in the role of princess to his heroic prince, even as she denies the validity of those roles. Her disdain for men, cultivated by Miss Havisham, does not extend to him: she tells him that she will 'deceive all men but [Pip]'. When he learns of her betrothal to Drummle, Pip declares his undying love for her in a fashion more readily associated with Hollywood romances and the scene ends in the prescribed stage kiss.

By playing to the conventions of the romance genre, this adaptation may dilute the novel's complex preoccupation with the whole debate related to social engineering versus heredity, but it does, as Kermode argues, establish its own identity as a romantic melodrama for a twenty-first-century audience. All romantic threads are neatly brought together: Joe and Biddy are set up as poor but in love, and Estella and Pip are reunited. There is no mention of the violence of her former marriage to Drummle, and Pip voices his love for her in true romance fashion. However, Estella, in line with postfeminist expectations of a twenty-first-century audience, is given some control of narrative outcome: it is Estella who sends for Pip, Estella who reaches for Pip's hand; the final shot, holding on a close up of their joined hands, infers that they are now inseparable. Like Dickens and most other screen adapters of this text, Newell and Nicholls play the romance card. The only exception to this romantic narrative outcome is presented in Tony Marchant's 1999 television screenplay. Marchant's Estella is by far the most consistently drawn of all screen Estellas; her character arc leads us to the kind of inevitable close initially envisaged by Dickens – one in which emotionally redundant Estella and humbled, penniless Pip cannot realize a romantic close to the narrative. Estella does not languish in the saved ruins of Satis House, passively awaiting the story's knight in shining armour. Pip returns to a Satis House that is slowly being restored by Estella, and the closing shot of them, returning to the innocence of their childhood card game, suggests that these damaged individuals can share friendship rather than love. Marchant's close returns us neatly to the relative innocence of their initial meeting, underscoring the cyclical nature of Pip's journey and suggesting that there is no idyllic escape from the shadows of the past. Here, there is no fairy tale end, no hint of society rising from the ashes as in the final moments of Lean's film. Unlike her screen counterparts and the Estella Dickens finally decided to deliver, Marchant's Estella emerges as the strong but inherently damaged woman that the narrative arc of the canonical text leads us to anticipate.

Classic screen adaptations of *Great Expectations* situate the narrative within Dickens' contemporary timeframe; as such they are in part costume dramas and they often foreground romance for the modern cinema-going and TV viewing audience. However, they do stand out from the usual heritage fare, particularly in terms of their dark tone and their gothic, noir-like visual style. 'Classic adaptations' of canonical texts *retain* their own identity. Even though inevitably judged against Lean's adaptation – an adaptation that has now found its own place within the growing canon of classic adaptations on screen – each of the classic adaptations considered in this section is seen as a new response to the text, whereas screen adaptations of populist texts and their cinematic or televisual reincarnations are invariably referred to as 'remakes'. Whether this is due to the canonical status of the source text it adapts or to the quality of the adaptation itself is debatable, but 'classic adaptations' are afforded a reverence and a screen identity that is often denied to film and television products that revisit a populist narrative. Elitist matters related to a product's status as either a work of 'high art' or of mainstream popular culture tend to define its critical reception and the language employed to critique it *as* an adaptation. Even when the classic adaptation on screen leans towards its populist potential, its capacity to identify with the status of a canonical work of 'high art' prevails.

Great Expectations: Re-visioning the text (Cuaron's *Great Expectations* and *Jack Maggs*)

Stories now deemed part of the canon of English Literature seep into the collective consciousness: knowledge of certain Shakespeare plays, Austen novels, works of the Brontës, Dickens or Henry James for example are known in some guise, whether that knowledge is detailed and gleaned via close reading of the written work or vague and absorbed through some other adaptive filter such as film, a cultural referent on an advertising billboard, a song lyric. Like myths and fairy tales, these stories become part of the cultural landscape. Adaptations that play with facets of these tales in order to create a new product with a re-visioned ideology, narrative point of view or cultural/temporal/geographical backdrop employ difference as a starting point. Reverence to any prior text is of secondary importance to the adapter and the appropriation of certain elements of that text is conditional upon its capacity to serve the newly created story.

By employing the title of Dickens' famous narrative, Alfonso Cuaron's *Great Expectations* signals its allegiance from the outset; by referencing the prior narrative in such a visible, forthright manner, the film product draws inevitable comparison with that novel, with the classic adaptations that precede it and with those that follow. In terms of its story design, this film stays close to the narrative template and character arcs of Dickens' *Great Expectations*. It employs the anticipated lead characters: Pip/Finn, Estella, Miss Havisham/Miss Dinsmoor, Magwitch/Lustig, Joe Gargery. And yet Cuaron's film is not reliant upon its relationship with Dickens' text or the classic cinematic adaptations that precede it: it has its own cultural, temporal, geographical and cinematic context. Its thematic preoccupations echo those of the canonical text but are defined primarily by its identity as a story set in late twentieth-century United States: matters loosely related to class and journeying beyond the confines of that class remain central, as does the intensity of the protagonist's love of an unobtainable woman, but Cuaron as director and Mitch Glazier as screenwriter are not concerned with matters of fidelity, despite the fact that by employing the title *Great Expectations*, expectations of that nature are written into its critical reception. Reception, perhaps as a consequence, was negative on the whole and the box-office take was similarly disappointing.

As with a number of film adaptations of this tale, Glazier's script foregrounds romance as its central concern, and as a consequence of its casting and its marketed identity as a tale of romantic 'desire', it becomes a product destined for mainstream consumption, despite Cuaron's Art House credentials and his distinctive cinematic style. Cuaron's interest in retaining a discussion of class through a closer referencing of the plight of fisherman affected by the decline of the Gulf's fishing industry is eclipsed by marketing and production considerations (Katz 97). Such considerations continued to influence narrative momentum during shooting; Gwyneth Paltrow, as emerging star commodity, was given increased screen time, and her less appealing character traits were softened in response to audience reaction to pilot screenings (99). Financially driven interventions are part of industry expectation but in this instance the impact is detrimental to the product's identity and as a consequence of these interventions, its intended audience remains unclear. In its marketing materials, it is projected first and foremost as a love story with the tagline 'Let desire be your destiny' and visuals that foreground Paltrow as star body, and despite the costume drama inferences of its title within a cinematic context, its temporal placement means that it is not a piece of heritage cinema. Matters related to class are inevitably less central since the story is relocated to a supposedly classless contemporary American society. Here, the narrative emphasis is upon the current preoccupation with celebrity culture, and just as Paltrow's Estella becomes a less acerbic woman, Pip/Finn becomes a more proactive cinematic Everyman whose rise to fame is, at least in part, the result of his own artistic endeavours.

In terms of story design, the film does stay very close to Dickens' narrative template. However, by constructing a proactive protagonist whose view of the world is filtered through his own visualization of it, this adaptation signals its identity as a mode of expression that is first and foremost concerned with storytelling via visual means. For Cuaron as film-maker and for Emmanuel Lubeski as cinematographer, the cinematic mode of narration becomes all important, and unlike other film adaptations of *Great Expectations*, much of its telling is achieved without recourse to dialogue. Just as the novel's first person narration gives us access to Pip's self-reflective voice, the images drawn by Finn give us a clear insight into his state of mind. Where Lean presents a close-up shot of the turning pages of the novel, Cuaron focuses on the turning pages of Finn's sketch book, implying that what is of significance here is the world view as visually represented by this boy: it serves as the cinematic equivalent of the novel's first person narration, and it is a 'voice' that remains similarly constant throughout. The device of cinematic voiceover is not required, and yet Finn *is* afforded a voiceover. Added during production and written by David Mamet, it could have been the kind of intrusive add-on that labours the positioning of audience with protagonist but in this instance, the words we hear serve to do more than this. Finn states that he is 'not going to tell the story the way it happened' but as he 'remember[s] it', signalling the adaptive intent to create this narrative afresh, from a different and very particular perspective, through selective 'memory'. It encapsulates what adapters do each time they approach the adaptation of an existing story: they select, they shape, they edit and 'tell it' in a manner that suits their purpose rather than 'tell the story the way it happened' in a former text. As in numerous neo-Victorian fictions, the act of remembering becomes all-important. For Cuaron, the film is more an 'elaboration' than what he terms 'pure adaptation' (*Urban Cinephile*).

In homage to the American literary canon, Cuaron's protagonist is named Finn rather than Pip, referencing Mark Twain's iconic child protagonist from *Huckleberry Finn* rather than Dickens' representative orphaned child: each is emblematic of the very different cultures from which their narratives emerge, and this contemporary cinematic orphan is, like his American counterpart, at ease in his surroundings. Cuaron subverts what has become a traditionally dark opening to the narrative and places Finn in an open expanse of wetlands that is for him, like Huckleberry Finn, a place of familiarity and ease, where memory is associated as much with the aural and visual signifiers of his surroundings as with any particular story. The film's opening credits present pencil drawings which, via the edits to Finn and his sketch book, signal from the outset that this is his memory and that his memory works in a kinaesthetic manner akin to the medium of film rather than prose. In this regard, it is an intellectualized work of adaptation that interrogates the very nature of the relationship between prose and cinematic space. Though seen by some critics as a 'pop overhaul' of Dickens' novel that indulges in 'visual exoticism' to the detriment of narrative clarity (Maslin), it is a film that employs its visuals as its central mode of delivery; Cuaron notes the 'perhaps over-stylized' edge to the cinematography with its saturated colour palette (Hitfix) but the narrative clarity is achieved as much through what we see as through story events and dialogue. Stark marshlands become open water, and the grim church and its graveyard are replaced by natural imagery in the film's establishing shots: unlike Pip, Finn is at peace in his world and he engages with it through his drawings. It is as he gazes into the water, sketching all that he sees, that his world is irrevocably changed; his world view is literally shattered as convict Lustig rises from the water. He is, in Finn's eyes, the villain of horror movies, and for the knowing audience the scene alludes to Martin Scorseses' disturbing thriller *Cape Fear* through both the casting of Robert De Niro and his appearance in the staple convict outfit in each. Cuaron engages his audience in the act of making meaning through the visuals on screen: drawings of birds and fish recur throughout the narrative, reminding the viewer at a subliminal level that all of this is as Finn 'remembers' it, taking us back to his initial gaze into the waters and the skies of his homeland, and to that life-changing moment when Lustig invades his line of vision. The loaded visuals become part of the film's style but they also provide a constant reminder that the story is filtered through Finn: it presents a cinematic equivalency to first person narration. Satis House becomes Paradise Perdito, and the dark gothic images associated with this location, whether generated by Dickens or Lean or both, are replaced by the fecundity of nature untamed in Cuaron's film. Finn's arrival at the house again alludes to Lean's film as the ornate fretwork of the iron gates loom into shot, its gardens similarly overgrown and unkempt, almost exotic in their wildness and thus indicative of Finn's bewildered state of mind. Cuaron cuts to shots of insect life teeming beneath the decay, shots of pathways engraved with the tell-tale images of the fish and birds of Finn's imagining. It takes on a dream-like status that echoes the gothic other worldliness of former *Great Expectations* narratives, but it does so through lush, overpowering, colour-saturated visuals associated with the mind-set of emerging artist, Finn. The film's green-tinged colour palette remains synonymous with Finn as artistic creator, signalling through association that what we see is filtered through his eyes: from the green backdrop of the opening moments, its credits shimmering and oscillating on the surface, to the green-themed costuming of both Estella and Ms Dinsmoor.

Finn's gaze is all-important: it mediates our viewing throughout. Estella becomes the object of his painterly gaze – his muse and his reason for seeking to move beyond his present circumstances. The camera lingers on her body, dissected, enlarged, held within frames constructed and directed by Finn and as such her function is in part reduced to that of sexualized object, positioned by and for the male gaze. Pamela Katz notes that Estella's role as art dealer in Glazier's screenplay is removed during the production process leaving her with a purely sexual function within the film text and thus reducing her 'modernity' (98). Instead, she is constructed as a high society woman with a decorative function only, creating a screen Estella who is even less powerful than her forties counterpart. The increased screen time devoted to Paltrow as star body suggests that she is a marketable commodity that must be exploited to full advantage. Yet her distanced, emotionally vacuous on-screen persona is successfully conveyed by this objectification, and from a postfeminist perspective, her power lies in her capacity to use her body as she sees fit. Any sexual advances – even as children – come from or are withheld by Estella: she encourages Finn to paint her, and she chooses to stand naked, framed by the arched window in his apartment. It is Estella who directs Finn's and the audience's gaze at such moments, prompting Michael K. Johnson to argue that rather than presenting Estella purely as object of the male gaze, the film 'facilitates a feminist reading by encouraging its spectators to interrogate the male-centred story the movie (and Finn) purports to tell on the surface' (63). To a certain extent her willingness to be looked at does encourage the audience to consider its position in relation to the eroticized body held in this frame – and by inference its position in relation to other painterly and cinematic frames presented as 'art'. Whether this Estella can carry the weight of such claims remains debatable but she is representative of late twentieth and early twenty-first-century postfeminist attitudes to sexuality and the sedentary pursuit of wealth. Perhaps the least convincing facet of her characterization within the film is her final acquiescence to romance; however, this is a narrative flaw that is also present in Dickens' novel and the majority of screen adaptations of it.

The film's treatment of its other female characters is less condemnatory. Finn's sister is a non-descript late twentieth-century woman who, unlike her Dickensian counterpart, can and does choose to leave an unfulfilling marital situation. The darkly humorous edge to her characterization is removed but so too is her violent demise. Similarly the disturbingly retributive elements of Miss Havisham substitute, Nora Dinsmoor, are excised. She is an equally eccentric recluse, but her eccentricities are couched in different ways. The inert Miss Havisham, surrounded by the decaying remnants of her wedding day, is replaced by an animated, dancing, cigarette wielding Miss Dinsmoor who both performs for and directs her audience of two. Though her plight is similar and her neglect of her surroundings results in the same decay and stoppage of time, there remains a certain vitality to her characterization. Garish clown-like make-up and constant costume changes visually present a woman who is locked in the past, in bygone eras, but she is less witch-like. Anne Bancroft plays her as kookie rather than threatening, and the stress upon revenge of the male sex via Estella is far less pronounced: in this narrative, Estella – now niece rather than adopted orphan – seems to be in control of her own destiny from the outset, echoing the film's marketing tag line, 'Let desire be your destiny', as a central premise for both Finn *and* Estella. In this film, Dinsmoor serves in part as a foil to the beauty of Estella: she represents the aged female body and thus another kind of fear, one that is more tangible within a contemporary context in an age that is preoccupied with image and commodity culture. Regis and Wyne note that 'Dickens' original conception of the bride as failure' is often employed by film-makers to signal 'the failure of femininity and the uncanniness of the aging woman's body in an era when health and beauty are presented to cinema audiences as the desirable norm'. They cite Billy Wilder's Norma Desmond from *Sunset Boulevard* (1950) as a film text that appropriates both Dickens' and Lean's Miss Havisham as a means to critiquing the treatment of ageing stars, no longer seen as fit for purpose, and argue that Cuaron's Dinsmoor is an amalgamation of all three (38–39). Cuaron intertextualizes Wilder's film through both his particular construction of Havisham and through a less than subtle name change, Wilder's Norma Desmond becoming Cuaron's Nora Dinsmoor. Dinsmoor's capacity to leave Paradise Perdito, however, and her closing apology to Finn undermine her mystique, and the production again acquiesces to an unspoken desire to make its characters more appealing, less distant. Ultimately, Dickens crone appears old, frail, harmless and above all, superfluous in this adaptation.

Other female characters like Biddy and Molly are also deemed superfluous: to include another potential love interest for Finn would detract from his obsessive pursuit of Estella, and the ironic twist that reveals Estella's criminal parentage is excised from a plot that no longer focuses on class. The film does, however, pose interesting questions about femininity within a contemporary cinematic context. It is Finn's erotic obsession with his muse, Estella, that drives this narrative rather than Finn's journey from boyhood naivety to adult self-knowledge, and as such the role of its benefactors (anticipated and known) takes second place. Finn as artist requires none of the camaraderie provided by the novel's Herbert Pocket or Wemmick, and the interventions of both Dinsmoor and Lustig, though furthering his capacity to realize his artistic goals and to acquire Estella, seem to facilitate the desired end rather than become the sole vehicle for its realization. The shape of the narrative here is defined by 'desire' and 'destiny': Finn's all-consuming desire for Estella and his destiny as artist. As cinematic Everyman, Finn is expected to shape his own destiny in a way that the inexperienced Pip of Dickens' novel cannot. His rise is a consequence of his own ability, coupled with opportunity; rather than being reliant upon the interventions of an unknown benefactor as sole initiator of his changed expectations, Finn is presented as a credible, proactive twentieth-century Pip. Cuaron's romantic ending may be disappointingly predictable, but it neatly draws its narrative threads to its anticipated close and is no different to other such endings which similarly undercut the plausibility of the central female character.

Supposedly happy endings abound in both Dickens' novel and adaptations associated with it. However, though Peter Carey's *Jack Maggs* ends on a similarly upbeat note, the narrative journey that precedes it is far removed from that of *Great Expectations* as we know it. The 1998 film adaptation is the end product of a collaborative exercise, its outcomes shaped by a number of factors beyond the control of any one creative contributor; its thematic and narrative shape evolves during the filmmaking process in response to matters both pragmatic and financial, and the vested interests of any one 'adapter' – whether director, screenwriter, cinematographer or star performer – become secondary to the demands of the collaborative venture as a whole. Cuaron's desire to relocate Dickens' preoccupation with class to the struggling fishing community of contemporary Gulf Coast America is, for example, jettisoned; it becomes simply the backdrop to Finn's early years, and the film's exploration of class focuses instead on the protagonist's rise via celebrity culture. But Carey, operating as sole adapter of Dickens *Great*

Expectations, has a very clear and unfettered intent. His is an 'act of looking back, of seeing with fresh eyes' (Rich 18) that is prompted by his position as a postcolonial writer. Just as Jane Smiley in her novel *A Thousand Acres* feels the need to revisit Shakespeare's *King Lear* in order to give a voice to the much maligned elder sisters of that text, Carey is responding to the compulsion to rewrite the narrative of his ancestors, represented in *Great Expectations* by the marginalized, criminally defined and forcibly transported Magwitch. Carey acknowledges that, like most readers, he has 'read' Magwitch as the dark 'other' of Dickens imagining, but voices his frustration at finding himself in such a position. In his adaptation, Carey vows instead to 'act as [Magwitch's] advocate, to give to Magwitch some of the tender sympathy' that Dickens affords his orphaned protagonist (Powell's Books).

Writers of the British Empire form part of Australian literary heritage, with many of its early fictions coming from England, but Anthony J. Hassell notes the late twentieth-century desire of authors writing within a postcolonial context to '[re]claim and [re]write those English stories which constituted their first meta-narrative', as a means to '[re]mythologis[ing] Australia in its own terms' (134). Carey produces a story which is more than an adaptation in the direct sense: it is a writing back to the fictionalized history of his 'ancestors', a posthumous challenge from one author to another. It becomes his '*Wide Sargasso Sea*: an act of postcolonial retaliation against a parent culture' (Woodcock 120). Dickens' Magwitch is brought centre stage in Carey's narrative in order to present an alternative 'history' that the canonical text suppresses, but in his struggle to record his own story Carey's Maggs also becomes emblematic of the postcolonial writer's struggle to forge a literary identity beyond that of the colonial 'father'. It is a novel which is as much about the act of writing, the power of words, the role of the writer as it is about the hidden narratives of marginalized characters from Dickens' *Great Expectations*. Like other neo-Victorian fictions, Carey's *Jack Maggs* gives voice to those who remain silent in the Victorian realist novels that precede them, but here, Carey's re-visionary intent is fuelled by his desire to also interrogate the importance of writing and the ownership of [hi]stories.

Carey's tale does not follow the narrative trajectory of Dickens' novel but there is a purposeful imitation of both Dickens' writing style and of the Victorian realist novel's use of complex plotlines. It is written in a style that places the narrative in the same temporal timeframe as *Great Expectations*, the opening moments clearly stating that 'it was, to be precise, six of the clock on the fifteenth of April in the year of 1837 that those hooded eyes looked out the window of the Dover coach and beheld... the sign of his inn, the Golden Ox' (Carey 1). As with Carey's other neo-Victorian novel, *Oscar and Lucinda*, there is a conscious desire to emulate the writing style of the Victorian realist narrative through choice of vocabulary, sentence constructions and direct address to the reader. Though covering only three weeks here as opposed to the formative years of Pip's development, by employing a shifting narrative that moves between past, present and future, Carey unveils the life of his protagonist from childhood to adulthood and beyond without recourse to the canonical text's first person narration. Through the title of this adaptation, Carey signals from the outset that the narrative point of view is realigned: as with many Victorian novels (*Jane Eyre*, *Shirley* and *Villette* by Charlotte Brontë, or *David Copperfield*, *Oliver Twist* and *Nicholas Nickleby* by Dickens, for example) the naming of the protagonist in the title signals to the reader both the nature and the focus of the journey contained therein. However, whilst Dickens' *Great Expectations* presents us with a bildungsroman that progresses in the anticipated manner, mapping the protagonist's development from childhood innocence to adult self-knowledge, in *Jack Maggs* Carey subverts the traditional structure by beginning Maggs' journey from a position of adult naivety and ending at a point of self knowledge that is achieved by revisiting the realities of his past childhood and his past relationship with the country of his birth. It is a journey that leads him to the realization that his nostalgic perception of England and Empire is misguided, and it is through the act of writing that Maggs progresses from a position of adult misconception to one of clarity.

Whilst Dickens' tale is narrated by an adult Pip, capable of mature reflection, Carey's protagonist takes charge of the narrative only intermittently and initially with little capacity to assess and reflect upon his past. He is reluctant, guarded, but through his hesitant acts as a writer, with his albatross quill and his invisible ink, Maggs comes to terms with his past and records his version of events. He writes himself into existence – an existence that he learns is not dependent upon his relationship with his country of origin or his sense of himself as 'a fucking Englishman' (Carey 128). Just as Cuaron's Finn draws himself into existence, Maggs makes himself visible on the page, even though he does so without the kind of writerly conviction and assured manner of Dickens' protagonist. Through the vehicle of Maggs as writer, the novel engages in an intimate exploration of his life but the narrative is not restricted to matters known only by a first person narrator. Instead, the backstories of characters like Mercy Larkin and Percy Buckle form an intrinsic part of Carey's complex plot – a plot that involves a cast of characters as diverse and eccentric as those found in Dickens' novel.

However, each of Carey's characters is written from a position of historical hindsight, and his exploration of sexuality and class is informed by late twentieth-century perceptions and values. Carey is able to explore in a forthright manner the kind of sexual matters Dickens, as a Victorian writer, could not. Edward Constable's closeted homosexuality and his relationship with Henry Phipps (this adaptation's Pip, who functions as the novel's marginalized plot device, does not appear until page 227), and Percy Buckle's disturbing paedophilic relationship with Mercy Larkin take the story into territory that would have been beyond the scope of Victorian novelists, tethered to and reflective of the moral values of their contemporary scene. Carey also explores the underbelly of Victorian England, amplifying Dickens exposé of matters related to class, social injustice and the barbarity of transportation. Themes of social injustice explored in Dickens' novels in general are revisited here but Carey writes of such matters in a much more direct, disturbing manner. Buckle's arbitrary rise to the status of 'gentleman' is mapped out here, and the workings of the criminal underclass – from the raising of child thieves to the practices of ironically named backstreet abortionist Ma Britten – form an intrinsic part of the narrative and its plot complexities. Chapter Nineteen, dedicated to Mercy Larkin's story, provides a neatly structured vignette of Mercy's decline from a daughter of a working father to a child prostitute whose widowed mother serves as her 'pimp'. Dickens' preoccupation with the plight of the orphan becomes part of Carey's story as Maggs reflects upon his own upbringing as orphan child saved from the mud flats and put to work as a housebreaker's accomplice, alongside his 'first love' Sophina, but Carey's exploration of the plight of the abandoned child in Victorian times is much more disturbing and graphic.

Yet it is Carey's exploration of 'authorship' that provides both the structural and the ideological momentum underpinning this metafictional adaptation. Peter Ackroyd's biography of Dickens is employed here as an intertext, providing the adaptation with additional narrative complexity: Tobias Oates functions as the novel's pseudo Dickens. Biographical points of similarity abound, from Dickens' questionable interest in his sister-in-law, Mary Hogarth, and Oates' affair with his sister-in-law Lizzie Warriner, to their shared occupations as newspaper journalists, emerging authors and amateur mesmerists interested in particular in the criminal mind. By fictionalizing certain aspects of the life of Dickens, Carey is able to explore the relationship between the writer and his subject, the story that is told and the one that is not. During the course of this adaptation he asks readers to reverse their traditional view of writer and thief: Maggs the thief becomes the novel's writer, Oates the writer becomes its thief. When Maggs first arrives at the home of Oates, he is warned by the cook to beware the prying mind of her employer who will 'look at you like a blessed butterfly he has to pin down on his board' because he is 'an author who must know your whole life story or he will die of it' (42). Oates, as writer, preys upon the life stories of others – he is the 'cartographer' (92) who assumes the authority to map and bring into existence the narratives of others but Maggs vows he 'will not tolerate it, this feeling of being "burgled, plundered" by Oates, the story thief (32). Instead Maggs, as the much maligned subject of Oates' (and by inference Dickens') stories, learns to voice his own history, to be his own 'cartographer'.

Both of the re-visionist adaptations considered in this section 'tell the story' in a manner that suits the purpose of the adapter – not 'the way it happened' in Dickens' canonical text but in accordance with the agenda of the newly conceived story. Screen adaptations of *Great Expectations* invariably dwell upon the gothic, the visual potential of Miss Havisham and the romantic possibilities of the relationship between Pip and Estella, but Carey's novel returns to Dickens' overriding interest in his protagonist's relationship with the males in the text (Herbert Pocket, Wemmick, Drummle). The central concern in *Jack Maggs* is the relationship between Maggs and Oates, though his eventual union with Mercy provides a parallel point of romantic closure, giving Maggs the happy ending that his character is denied in Dickens' tale. Carey amplifies the realist aspect of his narrative: the fairy tale tropes of the novel with its witch-like Miss Havisham and the romanticized decay of Satis House are replaced by the horrors of the home of backstreet abortionist Ma Britten who, along with Silas, acts as 'benefactor' for orphaned children. Like Miss Havisham, Ma Britten manipulates her charges for her own ends but she does so in a more forthright manner with no less disturbing consequences: she is a lethal combination of the canonical text's Miss Havisham and Mrs Joe. There is no direct fictional parallel to Estella: Sophina serves as Maggs' initial love interest but it is the pragmatic Mercy Larkin who emerges ultimately as his wife and saviour. The novel ends on a note of optimism that goes beyond the confines of Maggs' story. Dickens closes with the moment of Pip and Estella's union, but Carey's story provides an epilogue of the kind employed in Brontë's *Jane Eyre*, purposely taking Maggs' narrative *to* the colonial outpost and illustrating the success of this protagonist in his new homeland – as a business man and as a family man, where his death is part of the natural course of life. He is no longer the marginalized 'other' who, functioning as plot device, is removed from the narrative when his purpose is served. Instead, argues Brian McFarlane, Maggs epitomizes 'valorized male hardihood' and 're-enshrin[es]' Australia's 'masculinist ethos' (*Relationship Text and Film* 46–47). Carey's metafiction, however, does not 'valor[ize]' or 're-enshrine' the canonical text in the way that screen adaptations traditionally do: rather, it challenges the colonial authority invested in it.

Great Expectations: A radical rethink (*Mr Pip* and *South Park's* 'Pip')

Adaptations that 'affect a more decisive journey away from the informing source' (Sanders 26), engage in an often radical repositioning of the chosen canonical text. Though *South Park* episode, 'Pip', and Lloyd Jones' novel, *Mr Pip*, signal immediately their relationship with Dickens' *Great Expectations* via their titles, neither of these texts meet preconceived expectations of what a story thus named may involve. The creators of *South Park* radically change the cultural positioning of Dickens' *Great Expectations* by appropriating the canonical text as a template for satirical intent within the format of an animated television series aimed at a teen audience. Yet, despite its radical repositioning of Dickens' narrative on a cultural level, from what has become the high art status of all things Dickensian to the realms of populist teen culture, there are more connections with and intriguing explorations of the ideas that circulate *Great Expectations* in particular and canonical works of literature in general in this short episode of *South Park* than in many adaptations that may be labelled 'classic' or 're-visionist'. Similarly, in *Mr Pip*, Lloyd Jones employs *Great Expectations* not as a story template but as an integral part of his own narrative: it is central to our understanding of the novel's protagonist and takes on an almost biblical status within the context of Jones' tale – a status that the reader is encouraged to question. Its function here is twofold: it serves as a narrative prop for the unfolding of Matilda's bildungsroman but, as with *South Park* and *Jack Maggs*, it also asks the reader to think about her/his position in relation to works of the English literary canon.

As a writer, Jones is preoccupied with finding the persuasive and credible 'voice' within his narrative rather than matters related to plot. He 'resists' plotlines in his work, and yet admits that *Mr Pip* is a novel that is 'all about story' (Random House). The initial seeds of the novel began not with anything related to Dickens' *Great Expectations* but with abstract ideas manifested in a concrete way within the confines of 'the spare room', now a sequence that does not enter the novel until page 153; its walls are plastered with the writing of Mr Watts and Grace as they scribe 'weird lists' noting their culturally oppositional viewpoints. However, abstraction evolved into an exploration of the act of storytelling, the 'oral competing with the Great Western Tradition' in a narrative that has what Jones terms 'tributaries' or 'discussion points' about what constitutes narrative: he asks: 'What is *story*? How does it grow?' (Random House). The answers are, in part, explored in *Mr Pip* through the funnel of Dickens' tale. Despite the temporal, geographical and cultural shift from mid-nineteenth-century England to late twentieth-century-war-torn Bouganville, *Great Expectations* offers parallels and points of recognition rather than any kind of narrative framework for the story that unfolds. From the perspective of the novel's child narrator, Matilda, it becomes emblematic of storytelling of almost biblical proportions, offering hope, continuity and the possibility of escape. Adapted into the current of Matilda's tale, it acts as a mechanism for survival, a humanizing tool employed by Mr Watts during inhumane times, and a visible, sacred property, guarded by Watts and the community. The canonical text is not present as adaptation proper, but its appropriation into the fabric of Jones' novel is of central importance to the evolution of Matilda's story. Though there are a number of eccentric characters in *Mr Pip*, there are no clear parallels between such figures and those found in Dickens' *Great Expectations*. Grace, as Queen of Sheba, wheeled around on a cart by her 'husband', Mr Watts, is Jones' most bizarre Havisham-like creation, and Dolores' certainly imbibes the qualities of both a caring Joe Gargery and the acerbic Mrs Joe, but there are no direct correlations here of the kind found in the classic adaptation. The anticipated landmarks are also absent: the marshes are replaced by the tropical topography of Bouganville and there is no direct equivalent of Satis House. Parallels can, however, be drawn between Satis House and the 'spare room' meant 'for th[e] coffee-coloured child' (Jones 153) of Grace and Watts; time stands still and the occupants of both 'rooms' dwell upon their respective loss of lover and child, and like the jilted Miss Havisham, child-less Grace becomes an eccentric figure within the community, 'mad as a goose' (2) Watts's 'Queen of Sheba' (168), carrying a parasol as he pulls her along on her cart.

The narrative follows the traditional coming of age story template employed in nineteenth-century realist novels like *Jane Eyre* and *Great*

Expectations, and a similar first person narration is used here, but whilst both Brontë and Dickens ensure from the outset that their narrator's commentaries are those of an adult looking back on the journey from childhood to adulthood, in *Mr Pip* the experiences are related through the eyes of child Matilda, and it is not until the novel's final section that the narrative voice shifts to Matilda's adult perspective. This narrative strategy maintains the childlike innocence of the protagonist; there is no sense of a self-reflective adult commentary, remarking on the naivety of the child at the centre of the story. Instead, we journey with Matilda through what for the overwhelming majority of readers will be the uncharted terrain of a childhood mapped out by the terrors of guerrilla warfare: the story emerges without recourse to adult considerations, allowing Jones to create the authentic 'voice' of his child narrator. When the child Matilda seeks solace in the tales of a nineteenth-century English orphan rather than the oral stories of her fellow islanders, there is no adult self-reflection upon the limitations of her perception nor commentary on some of her misconceptions about Pip's story at this stage. Instead, she aligns her own experiences firmly with those of Pip:

> At some point I entered the story. I hadn't been assigned a part – nothing like that, I was not identifiable on the page, but I was there, I was definitely there. (40)

As the narration passes to the adult Matilda, there is not only a decided shift in tone, but in the relationship between the novel's narrator and Dickens' tale. *Great Expectations* is no longer viewed as a totem for new beginnings; it becomes a redundant prop, in a cultural, literary and literal sense. The reverence afforded Dickens by the young Matilda is replaced by her realization that 'the man who writes so powerfully about orphans' (212) is not an exemplary father nor are his novels treated with the same kind of reverence in contemporary England where they are relentlessly commodified, becoming shop signs, café names, fruit and vegetable shops. She notes, 'everywhere you look, Dickens is a shopkeeper. A restaurateur, a merchant in secondhand goods' (217).

Matilda the PhD student realizes that her perception of the story has been predicated on a falsehood and unlike Dickens' Pip, she is able to return 'home'. Structurally, the two novels revolve around a similar moment of adult realization, but whereas Pip comes to know the true worth of a 'gentleman', Matilda comes to realize the true worth of her own cultural heritage, and she begins to write her version of events:

One morning I woke and threw back the covers.... I walked across to the desk. I was being urged to do something I had put aside for too long. I took the top sheet of paper from 'Dickens' Orphans', turned it over, and wrote, 'Everyone called him Pop Eye'. (216)

Both novels and their protagonists, however, share a preoccupation with questions of humanity and with flawed 'heroes': Mr Watts, Mr Dickens, Dolores. Jones uses his novel as a vehicle to explore the importance of storytelling and its humanizing potential, yet he also deals in the bleak and graphically portrayed horrors of war, with the deaths of Matilda's mother Dolores, and her teacher Mr Watts pushing into the narrative in stark contrast to the earlier scenes of a fragile yet more harmonious village life.

Due to the particulars of Matilda's tale, it may be seen as a kind of 'life writing' or what has come to be termed 'testimony' literature (Norridge 63) but this is a novel written by an adult white male from a western cultural background, and any claims for its legitimacy as testimony literature are confined to its use as literary conceit. As with Carey's *Jack Maggs*, Dickens the writer becomes a conscious presence within the tale; here, Mr Watts becomes a pseudo-Dickens, mirroring the writer's public readings, adapting and improvising in response to his audience. He edits, for example, the violent actions of Orlick since his listeners are already surrounded by violence, and it is not until later that Matilda realizes that lines from the text have been altered at will by Watts as keeper of the narrative. Through such interventions, Watts is set up initially as one who retains arbitrary control of language. Like Jones and Dickens, he is representative of white, male power. Jones asks his reader to question the validity of such ownership by highlighting the questionable, privileged position of Western Literature and its colonization of narrative. Despite the fact that Matilda claims 'you couldn't muck around with Dickens' (Jones 196), this is exactly what Mr Watts does. 'Mr Watts' claims Matilda 'had rewritten Mr Dickens' masterwork' (93). But Watts has finished reading *Great Expectations* to his students by page 79 of Jones' story and it is what Watts does with the text after it has been read and subsequently 'lost' that takes the reader into a different ideological space.

As Watts urges the children to remember fragments of the narrative, he hands control of language and story to its audience, inviting them to adapt it. Matilda has already acknowledged that as a listener she finds 'the trouble with Dickens is it's a one-way conversation' with 'no talking back' (39) but Watts asks Matilda and her peers to recreate it as a collective act of remembrance, scribing the name of each contributor to every recollected fragment, enabling them to 'talk back' to the canonical text and to assert their own authority onto it. Just as Finn, in Cuaron's 1998 film adaptation asserts his role as one who will recount the story not as it happened but 'as he remembers' it, Matilda and the villagers are encouraged to adapt on their own terms. Watts speaks of the importance of retaining the 'gist of what is meant' in the narrative when retelling it, but Matilda also notes that he has 'added a line or two of his own' (111), implying that all adaptations are selective versions of a given text, whether works of popular fiction or works deemed part of the canon. As the novel progresses Watts adapts his own life story, narrating what Matilda describes as his 'Pacific version of *Great Expectations*', his personal 'orphan narrative' designed to 'entertain the Rambos and keep the violence at bay'; he delivers this story over a series of evenings, thus delaying the inevitable violence and emulating Dickens' serialized storytelling mode of delivery (149), again reminding the reader of his status as a pseudo-Dickens embedded within Jones' text, but a 'Dickens' who is willing to hand back the narrative 'voice', unlike Carey's wilful 'cartographer', Tobias Oates. Norridge notes that Mr Watts 'adopts the culturally determined position of "colonial superior"' who asserts his 'right to speak' (Norridge 62); he does assume authority over the text as the lone white man able to mediate between the words of the canonical text and the community he shares it with, yet he passes on that authority to Matilda and her fellow islanders by encouraging them to remember the lost fragments of it, and he pens their name to each reclaimed and reworked segment. The narrative power also shifts to the villagers and their oral storytelling tradition at certain points in the tale, and the vitality of such passages within the text demonstrates the importance of other modes of storytelling, from other cultural positions. Everyone is invited to become a storyteller, from Gilbert's uncle or Mabel's aunt to a reluctant Dolores. Matilda remarks that, 'to the startled ears of all us kids, we began to hear all the fragments that our mums and uncles and aunts had brought along to Mr Watts' class' (Jones 154). Far from stifling the stories of the islanders, Watts serves as a catalyst to the telling of their tales, through the vehicle of their own oral tradition.

Norridge voices the concerns of numerous critics when she asks whether there is 'a form of incipient imperialism in Lloyd Jones narrative' – a sense that Jones is 'writing the white male gaze into the text through the very figure of the flawed Mr Watts' (62), but the text ends with a firm rejection of that mediatory 'gaze': Matilda is well aware of the flaws of her teacher and her literary 'hero', Dickens, both of whom are revealed as frauds by the end of the novel, when the story of Watts' legal wife, June, is uncovered, and Matilda's research unearths a less benevolent side to her literary hero. By finally writing her own story, Matlida learns to 'tal[k] back' to the canon, and the story ends with her firmly in control not only of the narrative voice but of language. There remain many parallels between the experiences of child Matilda and child Pip: they share an initial disdain for their respective carers, Dolores and Joe, and for the limitations of their cultural origins, and yet Matilda's close is one that places her in a more secure place than the culturally fractured Pip. 'Pip was my story', she concludes, 'even if I was a girl, and my face black as the shining night. Pip is my story, and the next day I would try where Pip had failed. I would try to return home (Jones 219)'. John Thieme argues that postcolonial texts 'engage in an interactive rather than a passive relationship with their intertexts, offering multiple narrative strands that destabilize the very basis of fictional authority' (2–3). Jones' *Mr Pip* models the process of such 'destabiliz[ation]', questioning 'fictional authority' and placing it ultimately in the hands of those whose experiences are being recounted. Its success as a work of literature in its own right is predicated on this rather than its association with the canonical text with which it engages.

Though not writing from a 'postcolonial' perspective, writers Trey Parker and Matt Stone also destabilize Dickens' *Great Expectations* in 'Pip' (Episode 5, Season 4, *South Park*) through their satirical treatment of this revered novel, prompting us to question the authority of authorship and the reverence afforded to the canon. They radically alter the cultural positioning of Dickens' *Great Expectations* by employing the canonical text as a template for satirical intent within the format of an animated television series. As may be anticipated, this particular episode of *South Park* proved unpopular with the show's fan base, placing fans in a far from 'interactive' relationship with the programme's content for most of its twenty-two minute duration and alienating them on a number of levels. Its fans do not tune in on a weekly basis to contemplate their relationship with western literature and in many respects writers Parker and Stone miscalculated the capacity for a show like *South Park* to accommodate this clever satirical treatment of a classic piece of literature. Unlike a television series such as *The Simpsons*, *South Park* attracts a one track audience of predominantly male teens for whom many of the satirical reference points in this episode do not have currency. The relationship between its audience and the text is neither 'interactive' nor 'multi-stranded' but rather a story of two parts: satirical yet fidelity-driven for the majority of the episode, its closing scene reverts to the traditional

South Park format, destabilizing narrative continuity and credibility as an inevitable consequence and ultimately returning viewers to the creative universe of the *South Park* series. It presents a purposely odd mix of 'classic adaptation' and 'radical rethink', and though 'Pip' does not offer the kind of complex 'talking back' to the canonical text that is achieved in Jones' adaptation, it does enact a rejection of narrative ownership through a return to its own storytelling roots in the closing scenes. Despite its lack of success with the core audience, writers Parker and Stone achieve with this episode an insightful, radical repositioning of Dickens' narrative on a cultural level, presenting a pop culture commentary on high art and our attitudes towards it. They incorporate into it more intriguing explorations of the ideas that circulate *Great Expectations* than many of the adaptations labelled 'classic' or 're-visionist'.

There are a number of ways in which a series like *South Park* connects to the writing of Dickens, not least in its attempt to highlight the shortcomings of cultural snobbery. Jeffrey Sconce notes that 'like all commercial artists working in popular media, Dickens was not above a few populist broadsides against the hypocrisy of aristocratic taste and refinement, even as he may have unwittingly contributed to the very ideology that maintained such class relations' (182). As a televised series, made up of numerous episodes, *South Park* mirrors the serialized release pattern of a Dickens novel, and its animated storytelling demonstrates a visual sensibility that can, to a certain extent, be identified in Dickens' tales with the use of illustration being part of initial publication practice. It also shares a similar degree of contemporary success; it is Comedy Central's highest rating, longest running series, and a winner of numerous Emmy awards. Despite its current positioning as 'high art' the work of Dickens, like that of Shakespeare and Austen, bridges the cultural divide, providing adapters with popular narrative templates that also have cultural currency; the adapters in this instance build upon the connections between their populist product and the populist roots of *Great Expectations* but turn the latter's cultural currency into the mainstay of its satirical intent. The satire employed targets several groups and assumptions. The opening speech from this episode's far from usual narrator voices many of its satirical preoccupations:

> Hello. I'm a British person. For years now, the character Pip has been featured prominently in the American show 'South Park'. However, many Americans don't realise where Pip came from. He's the prowling little adorable Englishman from Charles Dickens' timeless classic, 'Great Expectations'. And so, tonight, the makers of 'South Park' have agreed to take a break from

their regular show, and instead present the prestigious Dickens tale in its entirety from beginning to end. Indeed, after watching this show, you'll know the timeless classic as if you'd read the Cliff Notes themselves. (Episode 14, Season 4, *South Park*)

In its construction of the 'British person', authorized to act as mediator of the tale for a culturally ignorant American audience, the narrative satirizes not only American cultural redundancy and its stereo-typed view of 'Britishness' but also the misplaced cultural superiority of the British and by inference British literature. The reach of its satire does, however, extend beyond national boundaries: its commentary on the culturally reductive 'bite-size' mentality of postmodern society targets everyone. The reference to Cliff Notes as some kind of meaningful adage to an understanding of a 'timeless classic' echoes lines from Amy Heckerling's *Clueless* (1995) in which protagonist Cher demonstrates her superior knowledge of Shakespeare's *Hamlet*, gleaned not from study of the play but from 'remember[ing]' her 'Mel Gibson accurately'. It sets up a playful commentary on the very act of adaptation – one that invites us to rethink our relationship with and our evaluation of canonical source texts. The narrative structure of the episode is itself predicated on what *may* be termed a reductive or at least a filtered engagement with the canonical text, for it is as much an adaptation of Lean's 1946 film as it is an adaptation of Dickens' novel, and the knowledge many viewers have of *Great Expectations* comes from viewing Lean's film rather than from reading the weighty classic tome written by Dickens. Moreover, its claim to provide us with a definitive knowledge of the text in a condensed twenty-two minute format serves to undermine the prestige of Dickens' tale, though what follows is a surprisingly comprehensive coverage of the story's main narrative hinge points.

These main narrative reference points are, however, pared down to a bare minimum, and its set pieces are modelled on Lean's cinematic rendition of the tale in terms of narrative content and visual style. Both the initial meeting between Pip and Magwitch and the scene in which Herbert Pocket teaches Pip gentlemanly etiquette reference Lean's film, and though the vulgarity of the language that epitomizes the dialogue used in *South Park* jars with the visual echo of Lean's film, the latter's presence is visually foregrounded. The timeframe remains an odd mix of the Dickensian (as envisioned by Lean) and the contemporary. Pip is a *South Park* regular – a foreign exchange student who is habitually bullied and victimized within the context of the show: both his characterization and his costuming in this episode remain the same. However, this episode departs from the predictable *South Park* norm: it does not have its cast of regulars nor does it make reference to topical issues, and though the political incorrectness, vulgarities and violence characteristic of the show become part of the episode, they do so with less frequency. Visually, the episode maintains the pattern of representing its younger cast members in the recognized *South Park* style: Pip, Estella and Herbert look like *South Park* 'kids' while the adults are drawn in a more realistic, elongated fashion that resembles the casting and costuming found in Lean's film. The ethereal appearance of this Havisham, for example, echoes the crone-like appearance of Martitia Hunt, and though she is initially played as the traditionally grotesque fairy godmother, with lines of dialogue straight from Dickens' novel, she transforms into the mad scientist figure, who devises a Genesis machine to aid her in her pursuit of eternal youth, taking the narrative far from the realist tradition of its source texts and into the realms of sci-fi fantasy.

References to contemporary cultural preoccupations such as this do lend the episode a contemporary relevance, as does the depiction of a violent, emotionally redundant, bunny-killing Estella who serves as a parody of all things post-feminist. Through such representation, its writers also highlight the hypocrisy of the romantic endings inscribed in Dickens' amended close and in the majority of screen adaptations. Despite the unlikelihood of romantic closure, given Estella's character arc in this and all versions of the story, like its adaptive forerunners, the episode ends with Pip and Estella united; her earlier interest in Steve because 'he's seventeen and has a car' wanes and she is last seen sporting a wedding veil and holding hands with Pip. In a throwaway summation of plot, the narrator reinforces this 'happy ending':

> And they all lived happily ever after. Except for Pocket, who died of hepatitis B. [closes book and rests it on his lap] And so ends Charles Dickens 'Great Expectations'. We hope you now have a deeper appreciation for Pip, and indeed, [holds up the book] all masterpieces of literature like this one. [rests it again] until next time, I'm a British person. Good night. (Episode 14, Season 4, *South Park*)

The satirically loaded 'happy ever after' reference implies a highly unlikely fairy tale close that is immediately undercut by the casual reference to the death of Herbert Pocket, and the narrator's final emphasis returns once more to the 'masterpiece' he reads from. His South Park claim that 'so ends Charles Dickens' 'Great Expectations' delivers the final irony of the piece for those who are familiar with *Great Expectations*, but for *South Park* fans, it is a misjudged irony that is unlikely to be appreciated or acknowledged. Other *South Park* episodes reference literature through degrees of appropriation but none take the kind of aside that is experimented with in 'Pip'. 'The Return of the Fellowship of the Ring of the Two Towers' (6.13) spoofs J. R. Tolkien's *Lord of the Rings* classic through its titular link and contains scenes parodying *Harry Potter*; however, unlike *Great Expectations*, both would be familiar to the *South Park* fan-base, the former through its mainstream screen adaptations and the latter as children's literature that the audience would have grown up reading.

Whilst the episode still follows the journey of Pip, there is little sense of this being a bildungsroman since Pip's development during the course of the narrative is handled in a superficial and distanced manner. The novel's first person voice is replaced by the device of a narrator who exists both outside the Dickens text and the *South Park* universe, and any sense of a self-reflective Pip who learns what it means to be a gentleman is displaced. Instead, the 'gentleman' narrator becomes a parody of what the novel's Pip aspires to; he provides a distanced, intrusive commentary on the story's progress – one that purposely maintains the gulf between the *South Park* world and Dickens' text by constantly reminding the audience that this is not part of the series' usual fare in terms of content and visual style and condescendingly implies that a commentary is required if its audience is to understand the basics of its plotline. Contrary to the norms of the series, the narrator is not an animated figure; his appearance is alien to the *South Park* format as is his function. Via the mise en scène of the room in which the narrator sits, the sense of a forced, stereo-typical 'Britishness' is visually reinforced; the coat of arms, the brandy glass, the leather-buttoned arm chair establish the air of a gentleman's club. Similarly, repeated edits from the *South Park* visualization of the narrative to the canonical text, held and thus controlled by the narrator, serve as a cultural referent to high art that impinges on the animated telling of the tale and privileges the narrator and language over the adaptation's animated visuals. Like Jones' Mr Watts, British actor Malcolm McDowell serves as a symbol of white, male western power, manipulating and directing the story for the benefit of a less knowledgeable and thus less powerful audience; he too becomes a pseudo Dickens, authoring and performing the text. Both Watts and the narrator ultimately lose control of the narrative to their respective audience, and yet whilst Jones' character works to bring this about, the story in 'Pip' spirals unwittingly out of the narrator's control into the world of *South Park* robot monkeys, violence and mayhem. The prerequisite deaths of Havisham and Magwitch still take place but they do so within the parameters of the show's frame of reference rather than those of the revered text held by the narrator. His claim that 'so ends Charles Dickens' 'Great Expectations' is undermined by what has been presented on screen throughout. Even though he is handed the final summing up, the plot has escaped the confines of his narration and entered the identifiable realms of the adaptation's origins instead. The narrative power rests ultimately with this adaptation's pop culture roots.

Mr Pip and 'Pip' demonstrate the diversity of ways in which adaptations may engage with existing texts; their adapters' 'decisive journey away from the informing source' (Sanders 26) sets up a different kind of relationship between 'source' and adaptation but one that is no less valid, no less insightful than those journeys taken by the classic or the re-visionist adapter: some may even argue that these radical departures produce a more challenging and thus more engaging dialogue with the precursor text.

A creative practice-based approach: Exercises related to *Great Expectations*/adaptations of *Great Expectations*

From 'hypo' to 'hyper' text

Step one: The genetic model

Literary theorist Gerard Genette employs the fertile language of horticulture to explore the relationship between adaptation and source text; he speaks of the source text as the 'hypotext' and the adaptation (or appropriation) as the 'hypertext' which *grafts* itself onto its source text, imitating it and transforming it into different shapes and forms (Genette 5).

Take a look at the following diagram: the first figure shows the trunk (i.e. source text) with a branch (i.e. the adaptation) *grafted* in place; figure two shows each (trunk/source and branch/adaptation) as separate entities, prior to the act of grafting; figure three illustrates the end product of successful grafting.

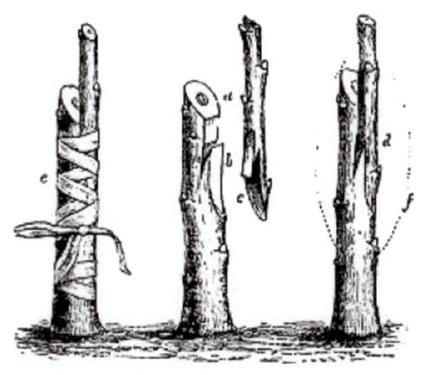

© The Florida Center for Instructional Technology

- What does each stage of the process suggest about the relationship between source and adaptation? Jot down some ideas for future reference.

Step two: Cardwell and cultural adaptation

In *Adaptation Revisited: Television and the Classic Novel*, Sarah Cardwell argues that this kind of genetic modelling helps us to see the interdependency of source and adaptation; as such, unlike some theorists, she advocates the importance of exploring that interdependency as part of the process of understanding how the new text evolves.

- What are the positives of seeing adaptations/hypertexts as an evolutionary extension of their source texts/hypotexts?

However, Cardwell also builds upon Genette's horticultural metaphor by comparing *cultural adaptation* (i.e. the focus of our studies) with the kind of *biological adaptation* illustrated above and finds perceptions of the latter far more positive than those associated with the former. She notes that the assumption of betterment and evolution that characterizes our study of genetics does not transfer to our assumptions about cultural adaptation. In cultural adaptation (which we may read here as the adaptation of narratives), she argues, the newly formed adaptation is seen not as a product of evolution and/or betterment but as an 'aid to the survival of the original' – a means merely to 'revitalize the source' – and this is a position Cardwell sees as a negative (2002 13).

- Why may an adaptations theorist like Cardwell see this notion of adaptation as 'aid to the survival of the original' as a negative?
- What are the problems associated with viewing the adaptation as an 'aid to survival'? What does such an approach suggest re the *function* of the adaptation?
- Biological adaptation presents a straight forward model, but what other factors come into play when we consider cultural adaptation? (Think of other factors that may influence the production of the adaptation.)

Cardwell is not suggesting that the source text/hypotext constitutes the 'major part of the adaptation's identity' (19–20). Instead she sees the adaptation as a new thing that takes its place within a different set of cultural referents that relate to its *own* era of production, its *own* industry structures, its *own* issues-based agenda.

Step three: Process

- Identify an existing narrative (from ANY medium) that you would like to adapt.
- How would you graft your ideas for adapting a story onto the existing narrative? (Think of the bandages on the above illustration as the ideas that hold it onto that existing narrative.)
- What would you identify as essential points of connection with the existing narrative? (e.g. what plot points/character constructs/thematic preoccupations would you retain?)
- How would your own agenda (related to, e.g., your gender, ethnicity, class) influence the choices that you make?
- What other cultural factors would come into play (i.e. factors beyond the simple 'biology' of grafting one thing onto another: e.g. would you, in an effort to ensure your adaptation is 'current', change the genre? e.g. would you change the protagonist's gender? sexuality? class? e.g. would you address a different target audience?)

Exploring story design

Storytellers construct their tales in different ways, though many adhere to a classical story template. Adapters, in turn, may choose to engage with the structural properties of their chosen story's design in a variety of ways; however, the skeleton of the story's narrative remains a given, whether reproduced in its entirety (so-called 'faithful' adaptation), in a selective manner (re-visioning from a different narrative perspective/focus on a particular moment), as a springboard for the telling of a different tale (prequel/sequel) or as textual allusion (appropriation).

Step one

One of the first and most essential steps in the process of adaptation involves identification of what Roland Barthes terms the 'narrative hinge points' of the tale. Brian McFarlane identifies fifty-four narrative hinge points in Dickens' *Great Expectations*. Draw up a list of what *you* feel are the narrative hinge points in this novel.

Step two

What points within that list of hinge points do you feel lend themselves to further creative exploration? Identify three areas for development and ask yourself:

- What characters are involved in each?
- What setting dominates each?
- What are the thematic preoccupations of each?
- How could the story points you've isolated be adapted and to what end?
- What medium would you choose to work in? Why?
- What would be your writerly intent? (e.g. to subvert the 'politics' of the moment? e.g. to offer a marginal character's perspective? e.g. to change the temporal/cultural parameters of that moment?)

Step three

It is through *narration* – the *how* as opposed to the *what* of storytelling – that the adapter can make significant changes to the ways in which we receive the story. Having identified moments of adaptive potential within the narrative framework of *Great Expectations*, select *one* of these moments for further exploration. Now think about *how* you will deal with that narrative moment given your chosen mode of expression (short story, screenplay, poetry, playscript ...)

How will you:

- Add to/work with the descriptive energies of the scene via language/visuals/aural properties?
- Add to or create a different kind of tone to the setting, embellishing or subverting what is a given in the adapted text?
- Create narrative 'voice'?
- Introduce sound qualities to the moment – and if so, for what purpose?
- Dwell on the physical aspects of characterization?
- Incorporate moments from earlier/later in this moment?
- Introduce a different focus to the scene?
- Handle the dialogue?

For each/any of the above, validate your choices:

- Why do you wish, for example, to pare down the dialogue to a minimum? Is it because you are writing a screenplay adaptation in which the actions of the characters can be communicated instead through actions seen on screen? Have you, perhaps, replaced a conversation and its purpose with use of a telling metaphor in the poetry sequence or short story adaptation you are writing? Can a song or musical score replace that dialogue when writing for a stage, TV or film adaptation?

The adaptation process

Step one

The following poem by Carol Ann Duffy adapts one character from Dickens' *Great Expectations*. As you read the poem, think about:

- the physical features of Miss Havisham that Duffy chooses to highlight
- the way Duffy presents Miss Havisham's state of mind
- the story content that she chooses to focus on
- the economical way she employs language to convey meaning

'Havisham'

Beloved sweetheart bastard. Not a day since then
I haven't wished him dead. Prayed for it
so hard I've dark green pebbles for eyes,
ropes on the back of my hands I could strangle with.

Spinster. I stink and remember. Whole days
in bed cawing Nooooo at the wall; the dress
yellowing, trembling if I open the wardrobe;
the slewed mirror, full-length, her, myself, who did this

to me? Puce curses that are sounds not words.
Some nights better, the lost body over me,
my fluent tongue in its mouth in its ear
then down till I suddenly bite awake. Love's

hate behind a white veil; a red balloon bursting
in my face. Bang. I stabbed at a wedding-cake.
Give me a male corpse for a long slow honeymoon.
Don't think it's only the heart that b-b-b-breaks.
(from *Meantime* Anvil Press: London 1993)

Step two

Linda Hutcheon argues that adaptations offer:

- 'An acknowledged transposition of recognizable other work or works;
- A creative and interpretive act of appropriation/salvaging; and
- An extended intertextual engagement with the adapted work' (8).

Consider 'Havisham' in light of these statements. Does it successfully:

- transpose in a recognizable form?
- appropriate or salvage the canonical text in some way?
- offer an intertextual engagement with the 'source' text?

Justify your responses.

Step three

Think about the taxonomies we have been considering. How would you classify an adaptation like 'Havisham' according to Geoffrey Wagner's classification system? Justify your choice.

- Transposition – text 'is given directly on screen with a minimum of interference' > text translated as directly as possible
- Commentary – 'where an original is taken and either purposely or inadvertently altered in some respect' > text amended to suit adapter's 'agenda'
- Analogy – 'which must represent a fairly considerable departure for the sake of making another work of art' > text as a point of departure?

(Geoffrey Wagner, *The Novel and the Cinema*.
Rutherford, NJ: Fairleigh Dickinson University Press, 1975)

Step four

Douglas Lanier proposes an alternative way of addressing the relationship between adaptation and source. He proposes the following narrative classifications based on treatment of narrative:

- The EXTRAPOLATED NARRATIVE > plot material is generated from the events mentioned but not developed in the 'master' narrative
- The INTERPOLATED NARRATIVE > new plot material dove-tailed with plot source
- The REMOTIVATED NARRATIVE > new narrative retains basic plot line/situation of source but changes the motivations of characters
- The RE-VISIONARY NARRATIVE > new narrative begins with character/situation of source but changes plot
- The REORIENTED NARRATIVE > narrative told from a different point of view
- The HYBRID NARRATIVE > narrative elements or characters from two or more [sources].

(Douglas Lanier's *Shakespeare and Modern Popular Culture*.
Oxford: Oxford University Press, 2002)

Now consider:

- Which of Lanier's narrative models do you feel best describes the relationship between 'Havisham' and *Great Expectations*? Why?
- Can it also be aligned with any of the other narrative models proposed by Lanier? Why? How?

Step five

Now choose a different character from *Great Expectations*, and devise your own adaptation. First, think about characters that you are drawn to and that present interesting avenues for further narrative development. Here are some suggestions:

- 'dark' female characters like Havisham (e.g. Molly, Estella, Mrs Joe)
- 'dark' male characters (e.g. Magwitch, Jaggers, Bentley Drummle)
- 'good' characters (e.g. Joe, Biddy, Herbert Pocket)
- marginal characters (e.g. Wemmick, the Aged P, Mr Pumblechook, Orlick)

Jot down your preliminary ideas about how you would create a different adaptation inspired by one of these characters. Think about:

- the narrative template you would employ (see Lanier);
- the narrative hinge points you would retain/excise;
- its temporal/cultural placement (i.e. different/same location? different/same era?);
- the medium you would choose (e.g. monologue for stage performance? comic book? Young Adult Fiction novel? short story? Screenplay? TV script?);
- the way your chosen medium will influence your decisions; and
- who your target audience would be/how that would influence your approach.

When time permits, return to your ideas, refine them, and WRITE at least the opening chapter/speech/scene etc. of your own adaptation!

References

Acker, Kathy. *Great Expectations*. New York: Grove Press, 1983. Print.

Ackroyd, Peter. *Dickens*. London: Minerva, 1990. Print.

Barreca, Regina. 'David Lean's *Great Expectations*'. *Dickens on Screen*. Ed. John Glavin. Cambridge: Cambridge University Press, 2003. 39–44. Print.

BBC TV blog: Gillian Anderson. '*Great Expectations*: Falling in Love with Miss Havisham'. *BBC. Co. UK*. 27 Dec. 2012. Web. 5 Jan. 2013.

Bonham-Carter, Helena. 'Helena Bonham-Carter Interview with Hilary Oliver – *Great Expectations*'. *YouTube*. YouTube, LCC, 26 Nov. 2102. Web. 3 Feb. 2013.

Brooks, Peter. *Reading for the Plot: Design and Intention in Narrative.* Cambridge: Harvard University Press, 1992. Print.

Cardwell, Sarah. *Adaptation Revisited: Television and the Classic Novel.* Manchester: Manchester University Press, 2002. Print.

Carey, Peter. *Jack Maggs.* London: Faber & Faber, 1997. Print.

Chang, Justin. 'Review: *Great Expectations*'. *Variety.* Variety Editions, 11 Sept. 2012. Web. 5 Nov. 2012.

Chatman, Seymour. *Coming to Terms: The Rhetoric of Narrative in Fiction and Film.* Ithaca, NY and London: Cornell University Press, 1990. Print.

Clayton, Jay. *Charles Dickens in Cyberspace: The Afterlife of the Nineteenth Century in Postmodern Culture.* Oxford: Oxford University Press, 2003. Print.

Collin, Robbie. 'Review: *Great Expectations*'. *The Telegraph.* 29 Nov. 2012: Film Reviews. Print.

Dickens, Charles. *Great Expectations.* Harmondsmith: Penguin, 1965 [1860]. Print.

Duffy, Carol Ann. *Mean Time.* London: Anvil Press Poetry, 1993. Print.

Eaton, Michael. 'Dickens on Film'. *bfiscreeenonline.org.uk.* Web. 9 Oct 2013.

Eisenstein, Sergei. 'Dickens, Griffith, and Film Today'. *Film and Literature: an Introduction and a Reader.* Ed. Timothy Corrigan. 2nd ed. London and New York: Routledge, 2012 [1999]. Print.

Elliott, Kamilla. 'Cinematic Dickens and Uncinematic Words'. *Dickens on Screen.* Ed. John Glavin. Cambridge: Cambridge University Press, 2003. 113–121. Print.

Fawcett, F. Dubrez. *Dickens the Dramatist.* London: W H Allen, 1952. Print.

Genette, Gérard. *Palimpsests: Literature in the Second Degree.* Trans. Channa Newman, and Claude Doubinsky. Lincoln: University of Nebraska Press, 1997 [1982]. Print.

Hassell, Anthony. 'A Tale of Two Countries: *Jack Maggs* and Peter Carey's Fiction'. *Australian Literary Studies* 18.2 (1997): 128–135. Print.

Hitfix. 'Alfonso Cuaron Remembers Lessons Learned on 1998 *Great Expectations*'. *Hitfix.* 18 Sept. 2014. Web. 28 Oct. 2013.

Hutcheon, Linda. *A Theory of Adaptation.* London: Routledge, 2006. Print.

Jacobson, Howard. '*Great Expectations* has been Ruined by the BBC'. *The Guardian.* 6 Jan. 2012: Culture. Print.

Johnson, Michael K. 'Not Telling the Story the Way It Happened: Alfonso Cuaron's *Great Expectations*'. *Literature Film Quarterly* 33.1 (2005): 62–78. Print.

Jones, Lloyd. *Mr Pip.* London: John Murray, 2008. Print.

Kaplan, Cora. *Victoriana: Histories, Fictions, Criticism.* Edinburgh: Edinburgh University Press, 2007. Print.

Katz, Pamela. 'Directing Dickens: Alfonso Cuaron's 1998 *Great Expectations*'. *Dickens on Screen.* Ed. John Glavin. Cambridge: Cambridge University Press, 2003. 95–103. Print.

Kermode, Mark. '*Great Expectations* Review/Interview: Mark Kermode and Simon Mayo'. *Radio 5 Live*. *YouTube*. YouTube, LCC, 30 Nov. 2012. Web. 17 Oct. 2013.

Klein, Michael and Gillian Parker. *The English Novel and the Movies*. New York: Ungar, 1981. 204–223. Print.

Landow, George P. 'Newman on the Gentleman'. *Victorian Web*. 19 Oct. 2009.

Lanier, Douglas. *Shakespeare and Modern Popular Culture*. Oxford: Oxford University Press, 2002. Print.

Letissier, Georges. 'The Havisham Affair or the Afterlife of a Memorable Fixture'. *Etudes Anglaises* 65.1 (2012): 30–42. Print.

Lott, Tim. 'A Prettified Pip, and a BBC That Wants to Condescend to the Past'. *The Independent*. 30 Dec. 2011: Independent Voices. Print.

Marsh, Joss. 'Dickens and Film'. *The Cambridge Companion to Charles Dickens*. Ed. John O. Jordan. Cambridge: Cambridge University Press, 2000. Print.

Maslin, Janet. '*Great Expectations* Film Review; Tale of Two Stories, This one with a Ms'. *The New York Times*. 30 Jan. 1998: Arts. Print.

McFarlane, Brian. *Novel to Film: An Introduction to the Theory of Adaptation*. Oxford: Oxford University Press, 1996. Print.

McFarlane, Brian. *Charles Dickens' Great Expectations: The Relationship Between Text and Film*. London: Methuen Drama, 2008. Print.

McKee, Robert. *Story: Substance, Structure, Style, and the Principles of Screenwriting*. London: Methuen, 1999 [1998].

Mukherjee, Ankhi. 'Missed Encounters: Repetition, Rewriting, and Contemporary Returns to Charles Dickens's *Great Expectations*'. *Contemporary Literature* 46.1 (2005): 108–133. Print.

Neill, Natalie. 'Adapting Dickens' "A Christmas Carol" in Prose'. *Victorian Literature & Film Adaptation*. Ed. Abigail Burnham Bloom and Mary Sanders Pollock. New York: Cambria, 2011. 71–88. Print.

Nicholls, David. 'Adapting *Great Expectations* for the Screen'. *The Guardian*. 17 Nov. 2012: Culture. Print.

Norridge, Zöe. 'From Wellington to Bougainville: Migrating Meanings and the Joys of Approximation in Lloyd Jones' *Mr Pip*'. *The Journal of Commonwealth Literature* 45.57 (2010): 57–74. Print.

Powell's Books Blog. 'Ink Q&A with Peter Carey'. *Powells Books.com*. 15 Feb. 2008. Web. 3 Jun. 2009.

Random House of Canada. 'Author Lloyd Jones on *Mr Pip*'. *YouTube*. YouTube, LCC, 7 Dec. 2007. Web. 5 Jan. 2009.

Regis, Amber K. and Deborah Wynne. 'Miss Havisham's Dress: Materializing Dickens in Film Adaptations of *Great Expectations*'. *Neo-Victorian Studies* 5:2 (2012): 35–58. Print.

Rich, Adrienne. 'When We Dead Awaken: Writing as Re-Vision'. *College English* 34.1 (1972): 18–30. Print.

Samuel, Raphael. 'Dickens on Stage and Screen'. *History Today* 39.12 (1989): 44–51. Print.

Sanders, Julie. *Adaptation and Appropriation*. Abingdon: Routledge, 2006. Print.

Sconce, Jeffrey. 'Dickens, Selznick and South Park'. *Dickens on Screen*. Ed. John Glavin. Cambridge: Cambridge University Press, 2003. Print. 171–187.

Shiller, Dana. 'The Pleasures and Limits of Dickensian Plot, or "I Have Met Mr. Dickens, and This Is Not Him"'. *Neo-Victorian Studies* 5:2 (2012): 84–103. Print.

Shoard, Catriona. '*Great Expectations* Film Review: 2012'. *The Guardian*. 12 Sept. 2012: Culture. Print.

Singh, Anita. 'BBC Left Out the Humour, Says Writer Andrew Davies'. *The Telegraph*. 31 Jan. 2012: Culture. Print.

Thieme, John. *Postcolonial Con-Texts*. London: Continuum, 2001.

Urban, Cinephile. 'So What'd You Expect: Dickens?' *Urban Cinephile*. 3 Jan. 1999. Web. 6 Jun. 2010.

Woodcock, Bruce. *Peter Carey: Contemporary World Writers*. Manchester: Manchester University Press, 1996.

Wollaston, Sam. 'TV Review: *Great Expectations*; Fast Freddie, the Widow, and Me'. *The Guardian*. 28 Dec. 2011: Culture. Print.

Filmography

Great Expectations. Dir. Robert G. Vignola, Paul West. 1912.

Great Expectations. Dir. Stuart Walker. 1934. VHS.

Great Expectations. Dir. David Lean. 1946. DVD.

Great Expectations. Prod. Dorothy Brooking. 1959. VHS.

Great Expectations. Dir. Alan Bridges. 1967. VHS.

Great Expectations. Dir. Joseph Hardy. 1974. DVD.

Great Expectations. Dir. Julian Amyes. 1981. DVD.

Great Expectations. Dir. Alfonso Cuaron. 1998. DVD.

Great Expectations. Dir. Julian Jarrold. 1999. DVD.

Great Expectations. Dir. Brian Kirk. BBC. 2011. DVD.

Great Expectations. Dir. Mike Newell. 2012. DVD.

Great Expectations: The Untold Story. Dir. Tim Burstall. 1986. DVD.

'Pip', *South Park*: Episode 14, Season 4. Dir. Eric Stough. DVD.

4

Adapting 'The Turn of the Screw': Drawing Parallels Across Texts

Henry James is a prolific writer whose work bridges the nineteenth and twentieth centuries, and in this section we will be looking at how the preoccupations of the canonical nineteenth-century texts we are exploring evolve over time. Though his early novels follow the nineteenth-century realist tradition, his later works move away from the form and content of the realist writing mode with its convoluted plotting and its conscious attempts to hold up a mirror to contemporary life. Instead James focuses on the psychology of his characters and their *perception* of events, pre-empting the stream-of-consciousness style of early twentieth-century Literary Modernism. Unlike Charles Dickens, whose work readily crosses over from its canonical platform to popular culture, James is a writer associated with a 'high art' aesthetic – a 'commodified … status symbol [of high culture]' (Rowe 205). So how does this influence the adapter's approach to his narratives? In one sense, James' status as a 'symbol' of a high art aesthetic constrains the adapter and can result in a particular kind of adaptive response: one that places undue emphasis on the aesthetic and nostalgic possibilities of his stories. The 'Merchant Ivory' cinematic treatment of works by writers like James (*The Europeans* 1979; *The Bostonians* 1984; *The Golden Bowl* 2001) and E. M. Forster (*A Room with a View* 1985; *Maurice* 1987; *Howard's End* 1992) for example, has led to a body of film texts that many academics argue wallows in a visual aesthetic at the expense of any kind of rigorous exploration of the narrative's loaded thematic concerns, despite the fact that both of these authors write challenging critiques of society rather than conservative period pieces. This costume period treatment is symptomatic of screen adaptations of James's work in general, though not all are overwhelmed by a preoccupation with period detail. Screen adaptations of 'The Turn of the Screw' present a much wider array of adaptive responses: it is the most often adapted of all James' stories, whether to screen or to other adaptive forms, and unlike the majority of his stories, it has mainstream, populist appeal.

'The Turn of the Screw' was one of two stories published in four parts in 1898; *The Two Magics* consisted of contrasting genre pieces – one a ghost story and the other a comedy titled 'Covering End'. However, it may be argued that their generic differences are not so sharply realized if we read 'The Turn of the Screw' as a parody of the gothic ghost story and sensationalist literature so popular at the time of its publication. James's intent here is purposefully ambiguous in every respect; he leaves the reader (and thus the would-be adapter) with a range of possible options: how reliable are its narrators? Is it serious or parodic? And how are we to 'read' the story's coded, potentially disturbing messages? His dismissive reference to it as 'essentially a pot-boiler and a *jeu d'esprit*' (Horne, Letters 9 Dec. 1898) belies the complexity of a tale that is still read and constantly recycled over a hundred years later. If it is, as he claims in the preface of a collection of his tales, 'a piece of ingenuity pure and simple, of cold, artistic calculation, an amusette to catch those not easily caught … the jaded, the disillusioned, the fastidious', then there is some credence to its definition as parody (VII *The Novels and Tales of Henry James*). Written with a more populist and American readership in mind, James sold the serialization of 'The Turn of the Screw' to *Collier's Magazine*. It was well received by both critics and the public (Wilson 104), whether read as a parodic tale by the knowing audience, able to connect with the writer's ironic treatment of the gothic ghost story and its sensationalist in its excesses, or as a tale of thrilling evil.

But there are such unsettling matters subtly coded by James into this tale that to read it as a simple 'pot boiler', an 'amusette', or a fear-inducing horror story is to side-step its capacity to address the fin de siècle anxieties of the Victorian age. James interrogates these anxieties through guarded allusion and carefully crafted ambiguity: he is at pains to distance himself from the more disturbing potentialities of his story – its critique of the dysfunctional Victorian family and Victorian morality, its inferred sexual transgressions and the deconstruction of the Victorian obsession with both childhood innocence and the period's oppressive construction of women as angels or demons. He states that, having established a 'portentous evil', it is for the *reader* to 'think the evil, think it for himself' in whatever guise such 'evil' may take (James qtd in Brown 61); thus it is for the reader to note (or *not*) references to homosexual and paedophilic relationships, to childhood sexuality or the sexual frustrations of his governess and her mental instability. It is 'the power to guess the unseen from the seen, to trace the implication of things' that 'constitutes experience' according to James (James, 'The Art of Fiction' 53), and in this tale, readers are encouraged to draw their own inferences. Under such a pretext, James is able to raise matters that could not have been addressed in any explicit manner given the context of the times.

'The Turn of the Screw' is itself a tapestry of existing narrative threads, appropriated and re-visioned by James within the framework of a typical ghost story. The seeds of the story come from the tale of Mary Ricketts (recounted to James by Edward White Benson, Archbishop of Canterbury). However, it also draws upon a number of established tropes, from popular sensationalist novels and governess narratives of the Victorian era, to ever-popular gothic stories, ghost stories and fairy tales. James' tale does not adapt a particular text but its content is mediated by stories that have gone before, and it functions as an historical marker of turn-of-the-century anxieties related to matters of sexuality and the moral ambiguities of Victorian society. The narrative (and James's treatment of that narrative) is also informed by emerging Freudian psychoanalytical studies and by a contemporary fascination with spiritualism. Though public interest in spiritualism was waning by the 1890s, James uses its notion that the living can communicate with the dead to explore taboo matters of transgressive sexuality and violence through the medium of ghostly apparitions who may or may not appear, who may or may not be a symptom of the protagonist's unstable state of mind or the anxieties of the times.

The narrative framework employed here also adds to the instability of its content. Events are filtered through several narrative voices. The story begins with an anonymous narrator of no specified gender who sets the scene for the delivery of a tale by Douglas, a fellow guest whose tale is so disturbing that it is kept 'in a locked drawer' and 'hasn't been out for years' ('Turn' 8). The story shifts to a reading of the governess's memoir, seemingly delivered by Douglas, though there is no sense of his voice within the recounted narrative. Instead, it is delivered to the reader in the first person voice of the governess and the narrative remains in her control to its closing moments. The anonymous narrator who directs the tale at its outset does not reappear to conclude it, leaving the governess as the authoritative narrative voice within the text. However, this same anonymous narrator has already advised that what we read is 'an exact transcript of [her/his] own made much later' (10–11) and titled by her/him (14), rather than the written account of the governess, so carefully guarded and locked away by her former charge, Douglas. This represents yet another layer of narrative intervention that brings with it the possibility of misinformation and misinterpretation. That the governess's written account is designated 'memoir' rather than autobiography is similarly indicative of narrative unreliability; though deemed fact rather than fiction, the memoir as a form lacks the literary kudos of the autobiography. Unlike *Great Expectations* and *Jane Eyre*, this is not a first person narration that plots the coming of age story of its protagonist: it shares with these bildungsroman narratives an intimate first person voice, but as memoir it deals in the psychology of a particular moment in time, and is delivered from an adult perspective throughout, mapping what appears to be its protagonist's descent rather than building to a moment of self awareness and personal growth. Jane Eyre and Pip are constructed as reliable, if initially naïve, narrators from the outset – they own and narrate their own stories. However, in 'The Turn of the Screw' the unnamed governess remains unfathomable, an enigma like the tale she relates. Given the open-ended possibilities of such a tale and such a protagonist, it presents a wealth of opportunities for the adapter.

Numerous gothic tropes and fairy tale references are employed in the construction of 'The Turn of the Screw' but James subtly subverts the features of these tropes. Bly provides the prerequisite isolated country mansion shrouded in secrecy, and symbolic of morally dubious colonial wealth, but it is not described in the usual gothic manner. His governess, informed by her reading of gothic texts like *The Mystery of Udolpho*, anticipates a place of fog-bound, 'dreaded melancholy' but what she finds, as she arrives on a 'lovely day' of 'summer sweetness', is a house with 'a broad, clear front', 'open windows', 'fresh curtains' and 'bright flowers', 'rooks circl[ing] and caw[ing] in the golden sky' ('Turn' 14–15).Unlike Thornfield House or Satis House, Bly is not a place of shadows and decay but its manicured appearance, at least from the increasingly disturbed governess's perspective, is a façade. The gothic romance's brooding male with a dark secret also appears briefly at the start of the tale; her employer is a Harley Street 'bachelor in his prime, such a figure as had never risen, save in a dream or an old novel, before a fluttered, anxious girl out of Hampshire' (11), and she imagines him to be her prince who will eventually come to claim her from the fairy tale turrets of Bly. However, the governess's attraction to her social superior is not mutual and the relationship no more than a romantic fantasy; the Cinderella-like narrative initially constructed by the governess becomes superseded by darker tales, as her employer becomes synonymous with the tyrannical and secretive Bluebeard, and she an ever more inquisitive 'wife', searching out the secrets of Bly. James refers to his story as 'a fairy tale pure and simple' and Quint and Jessel as 'goblins and elves, imps and demons, … wooing their victims forth to see them dance under the moon' (*The Novels and Tales*), but the story's devastating conclusion subverts its fairy tale elements. Quint and Jessel represent the demonized spectres of the gothic tale rather than the goblins and imps of fairy tale; yet, like the story's fantasized 'romance', their presence may be nothing more than a sign of the governess's mental instability. Jane Eyre's demonized spectre, Bertha Mason, exists but there is no way of knowing whether the governess's spectres are real: instead, she may be construed *as* the demonized spectre readily associated with insanity in gothic terms. The supernatural elements of the gothic become matters of the mind rather than matters related to spectres alone, and the genre's preoccupation with interiority and alter egos, with mirror images and doubles, is also explored through Jessel, the governess's Bertha Mason-like alter ego, who acts out the sexual desires of the sexually repressed governess.

James uses the ghost story template as a means to avoiding the marriage plot that dominates the realist nineteenth-century novel. Despite the fact that the first person narration of his young, vulnerable and impressionable governess is littered with her bold assertions of her own capabilities and courage, her use of overly dramatic language and the grandeur of her claims hint at both her increasing instability and her unreliability as narrator of this tale. Unlike the very calm, self-contained Jane Eyre, she is the stereo-typical, self-dramatizing, fainting heroine of gothic convention who displays an 'over-abundance of imaginative frenzy' (Botting 3). James exaggerates her emotional excesses and ensures she is the only one in the story who sees the ghosts of Jessel and Quint, thus implying that her 'imaginative frenzy' may be proof of her insanity. But it is in her role as governess in a house that functions without the hierarchical structures of Victorian society that James presents his most radical critique of Victorian values and attitudes. As a governess she has no fixed place; she becomes the ' "deviant" female', on a par with women who must earn their keep through labour or prostitution. She is paid to do what middle-class mothers who constitute the 'norm' do for free, bringing her 'perilously close to the figure of the prostitute' (Newman 51), and leaving her with an anxiety-inducing identity crisis, unsure of her position as 'angel of the house' or as 'fallen, demonic woman'. Jessel is the 'monstrously exaggerate[d]' realization of the governess's own 'social invisibility' (61), but like Jane Eyre's alter ego Bertha Mason, she also represents the dangers associated with sexual desire. She is the 'fallen woman' that the governess may become. Yet despite her social standing and her gender, James's governess is placed in the unusual position of being in control due to her employer's lack of interest in Bly and his extended family. She functions within the household as both surrogate 'mother' *and* patriarchal father figure, but the boundaries between the two roles blur and she is unable to fulfil the expectations of either. While Quint transgresses class boundaries by assuming the role of Master of Bly, her position as 'Master' is validated by her employer, but it constitutes a similarly, transgressive scenario: she lacks the social standing for the role *and* she is a Victorian woman. Though she sets herself up as the courageous guardian of moral virtue – the captain 'strangely at the helm' of 'the drifting ship' ('Turn' 18) – she becomes an over-protective, over-bearing, increasingly unhinged mother-figure, unsure of her own identity. The many parallels that can be drawn between *Jane Eyre* and 'The Turn of the Screw' add credence to assertions that James is writing a parody – one that is aimed at his contemporary society's fascination with governess narratives and all things gothic. Alice Hall Petry takes this assumption a step further, claiming that James's borrowings from *Jane Eyre* are an intentional 'undermining of the literary tradition of the plucky English governess' (61) and his governess 'a highly dramatic imitation of Jane Eyre' (74). The shared gothic features of each text – country mansions full of secrets with similarly secretive and desirable masters, hidden spectres who must be vanquished by the story's female protagonist – suggest that both texts are part of an ever-evolving narrative continuum. Whether or not Brontë's novel is intentionally appropriated by James is open to debate, but at some level it becomes yet another story thread within the fabric of his tale, one that is particularly significant for the reader who is familiar with *Jane Eyre*. Just as 'The Turn of the Screw' emerges from a textual web of existing tropes and narrative threads, the adaptations that circulate it, and to some extent adaptations of *Jane Eyre*, form part of its complex genesis. It is what Brian A. Rose terms a 'cultural text' – one that evolves *as* it is adapted, 'permit[ting] a redefinition of anxiety-provoking issues' (2). Since its publication, James' slim novella, with its coded messages and its subtextual energies, has maintained the interest of the reading public, academics and adapters. This 'internalized drama' is, according to Edward Recchia, 'based as much on nuances of the psyche as on external events, and James's method of developing that drama exists not so much in the story told as in the telling, not so much in what the narrator says as in the way she says it' (28). It is the *narration* (or the 'how' of storytelling) rather than the *narrative* (or the story events) that makes this such an intriguing and complex piece of writing, especially from an adapter's perspective. However, adapters may 'read' the ambiguities of James' prose in any number of ways, and though in its Jamesian form it is the psychological unravelling of the governess that drives the narrative, for many adapters it is its identity as a ghost story first and foremost that appeals.

Unlike other screen adaptations of James's work, 'The Turn of the Screw' is not given a Merchant Ivory makeover, but it is his most adapted story, with ten film and television adaptations produced since the late fifties and a number of films that appropriate it in part. While Dickens is lauded as a writer whose prose translates readily to the screen, James's work is considered by many to be 'unfilmable'. Director Jacques Rivette argues that his work is 'perhaps unfilmable' because his stories can be translated to screen 'diagonally … but never literally' (Rivette qtd in Mitchell 282). Yet despite the internalized nature of its prose and the difficulties of dealing with the representation of ghosts within a realist medium like cinema – ghosts perhaps seen only in the mind of the protagonist – 'The Turn of the Screw' has continued to attract the attention of filmmakers and TV producers who have dealt with such matters in a variety of ways, both 'literal' and 'diagonal'. Some screen adapters take the literal path, translating the complexities of the tale into a ghost narrative that fits the horror genre template; others explore the psychological complexities embedded in James's prose, though most retain its period detail. However, while televised adaptations of nineteenth century texts are usually presented in serialized form, 'The Turn of the Screw' is produced instead as TV movie, as part of a series like the *Nightmare Classics* (1989), or as a one off drama, which again emphasizes its difference, in terms of both content and style, from the sprawling, intricately plotted realist novels characteristic of its time of production. Marking its difference from the adaptive treatment of most nineteenth-century texts, its narrative when appropriated for televised serialization takes a very different form: *Dark Shadows* (1966–1971) presents pseudo-Quint, Quentin Collins, in the very different genre of gothic soap opera.

John Frankenheimer's live television play, starring Ingrid Bergman in 1959, is swiftly overshadowed by Jack Clayton's *The Innocents* (1961) – a film which, like David Lean's screen adaptation of *Great Expectations*, is now regarded as part of the cinematic canon. The post-censorship seventies saw a revival of interest in the novella due to the popularity of the horror genre at this time and the possibilities the text presented for the exploration of sexual transgression. The most infamous screen adaptation, Michael Winner's *The Nightcomers* (1971), starring Marlon Brando as Quint, serves as a prequel to the novella's storyline; it exploits the subtextual hints of sexual transgression, turning such ambiguities into acts of sado-masochistic violence, and the children into incestuous voyeurs. Marketed in the UK as a 'sexploitation' film with a 'sex-starved spinster' as its heroine (Raw *Adapting Henry James* 72), it achieved minimal success. Winner's adaptation was released shortly after the uber-violent *Straw Dogs* (1971), and though it reflects a similar seventies desire to push cinematic boundaries in this post-censorship era, it lacks the menace and the psychological edge of a film like *Straw Dogs* and remains a film that functions for many as pure voyeurism. Dan Curtis, creator of the soap opera *Dark Shadows*, went on to direct a TV movie adaptation of 'The Turn of the Screw' in 1974; like Winner's *The Nightcomers* it exploits the sexual ambiguities of the narrative, as does a French production (*Le Tour d'ecrou* by Raymond Rouleau) released in the same year. Subsequent screen adaptations continue to amplify these ambiguities. In Shelley Duvall's 1989 television adaptation, part of the *Nightmare Classics* series, the horror elements are foregrounded but the explicit nature of its many sex scenes suggest that the seventies preoccupation with the sexual undertones of the story persist into the eighties and beyond. In the nineties, there is a revived interest in adapting the narrative to screen, with two film and two TV productions released between 1994 and 1999. Rusty Lemorande's 1994 adaptation sees a temporal shift; set in the sixties in a psychiatric hospital, it constructs a backstory of childhood sexual abuse for its disturbed heroine and turns the novella's subtle references to the sexualization of childhood into an on-screen reality. Other nineties adaptations return to a more traditional costume drama rendition: television movies *The Haunting of Helen Walker* (1995) and Ben Bolt's *Turn of the Screw* (1999) focus on period detail while a Spanish film production, *Presence of Mind* (1999), also exaggerates the gothic horror elements of the text. Like Lemorande's film, the most recent screen adaptation, a BBC television production directed by Tim Fywell (2009), moves the narrative forward in time and initially infers that the governess is mentally unstable: here, the story begins in post First World War England, with the governess incarcerated in a psychiatric ward, and though its Edwardian period detail is a significant part of its look, Fywell challenges our expectations of televised costume drama by employing a surreal cinematic style which again echoes Lemorande's treatment of the narrative in his 1994 film.

There are also a number of films which, though not closely drawing upon 'The Turn of the Screw', appropriate certain elements of the tale. Maternal horror films *The Others* (2001), *In a Dark Place* (2006) and *The Orphanage* (2007) appropriate its treatment of female paranoia and its exploration of the over-protective mother figure, forging subtle connections with James's narrative. They become part of its narrative evolution from fin de siècle ghost story to contemporary horror film. If we identify 'The Turn of the Screw' as a 'cultural text' – that is, one that evolves *as* it is adapted, 'permit[ting] a redefinition of anxiety-provoking issues' (Rose 2) – it exists on a continuum alongside such films, in a relationship with them that is not defined as authoritative or primary and that transcends tired fidelity issues: it foregrounds instead the genesis of narrative across time, genre and media platforms. An Italian 3-D horror film adaptation from director Marcello Avallone, first proposed back in 2010, has yet to reach pre-production stage, but it is interesting to note that the subtleties of James' prose may be seen as material that translates to such a graphic cinematic treatment and demonstrates yet again its function as a 'cultural text' that redefines and responds to the contemporary moment.

'The Turn of the Screw' has also been adapted into what are considered 'high art' forms more readily aligned with James' so-called status as a 'symbol [of high culture]' (Rowe 205). Prior to a wealth of screen adaptations of the story dating from the late fifties to the present day, it was successfully adapted as an opera by Benjamin Britten (1954), and a German adaptation of this opera was later translated to the screen by Peter Weigl (1989). Most recently, William Tuckett's one act ballet adaptation of the novella was performed at Sadler's Wells (1999). In all three adaptations, the adapters present challenging interpretations of the text. Britten's opera, and its cinematic adaptation, foregrounds the homosexual, paedophilic relationship between a charismatic Quint and Miles, whilst Tucker's ballet explores the sexually transgressive nature of the novella's subtext by creating a ghostly transvestite Jessel. Tellingly, the novella's adaptation to these high art forms, even back in the fifties, is not constrained by the same kind of censorship exercised in its adaptation to screen. It has also been adapted regularly to stage and radio; the most famous stage adaptation, William Archibald's *The Innocents*, was first performed in 1950 and served as the adaptive template for Jack

Clayton's film in 1961, though Archibald's playscript is far more definitive in its approach to the narrative: here, the ghosts' existence is never in doubt, and the psychological subtleties of the governess's state of mind becomes of secondary importance. The story is regularly adapted to the stage; the most recent, a co-production from Rebecca Lenkiewicz and Hammer Theatre Horror, performed at London's Almeida Theatre in 2012, exaggerates the horror as may be expected from an adaptation that forms part of a revival of the well-known Hammer brand.

Contemporary novelists continue to re-vision the story in a number of ways. Graphic novelist Guido Crepax focuses on the erotic nature of the text in his *Giro Di Vite* (1989). Some writers, like Toby Litt ('Ghost Story' 2004) and Stephen Beachy ('Some Phantom' 2006), retain the novella's form but appropriate only elements of its narrative, whereas Joyce Carol Oates' short story, 'The Accursed Inhabitants of the House at Bly' (1994), is a prequel that establishes its close relationship with James's 'Turn of the Screw' and entails a detailed, graphic re-imagining of the story from Quint and Jessel's perspective. Adele Griffin's *Tighter* (2011), classified as Young Adult Fiction, is relocated to Little Bly, an idyllic New England island, where her protagonist unravels the mystery of what happened 'last summer', giving the narrative a more mainstream thriller treatment. John Harding's novel, *Florence & Giles* (2010) hands the narrative to the less substantially drawn Flora of James' story, investing her with the mental instabilities and complexities we associate with James' governess. Harding plays with the novella's notions of the innocent/evil child, mapping Florence's narrative onto James's story template, but like the maternal horror films of the early twenty-first century, his text moves beyond the parameters of the traditional ghost story into a very different psychological terrain.

James' 'Turn of the Screw' presents the adapter with endless possibilities; it is a slippery, ambiguous text that lends itself to a wide range of interpretations. However, unlike realist novels of the nineteenth century, a literal translation of its content presents the most problematic option. Are the ghosts real or imaginary? Is the governess the bastion of moral virtue or a psychologically disturbed hysteric? Are the children innocents or demons? James presents the conundrum without the solution, and in so doing leaves his readers and would-be adapters free to interpret his enigmatic tale as they see fit. Its one common and enduring feature is its capacity to disturb and disrupt, whether in a Victorian or a contemporary cultural context, and it is this thread that continues to unravel as the novella is reworked, re-imagined and revised.

'The Turn of the Screw': The 'classic' treatment (*The Innocents* and *The Turn of the Screw*, 2009)

A number of screen adaptations of this text frame the narrative within the historical moment of its production, paying attention to both its period detail and its ghost story template. However, matters of fidelity that figure so prominently in the adaptation of realist novels like *Great Expectations* and *Jane Eyre*, are not the primary concern of adapters approaching 'The Turn of the Screw'. To what is the adapter meant to be 'faithful'? James's text does not present an extractable 'essence' in quite the same way. Though there is an extractable storyline here, there is no clearly defined way of reading its textual ambiguities and its psychological complexities. It is open to interpretation: such is James' intent. While screen adaptations of *Jane Eyre* and *Great Expectations* invariably align themselves with the canonical text by retaining its title, screen adaptations of 'The Turn of the Screw' often begin with a conscious act of 'infidelity', renaming the narrative from the outset: from *The Others* (1957), *The Nightcomers*, *Otra Vuelta de Tuerca* (*Another Twist* 1985), *The Haunting of Helen Walker*, *Presence of Mind*, to the most cinematically revered adaptation of James' tale, *The Innocents*, all choose to establish a separate identity, regardless of how much they then choose to engage with the novella's malleable thematic preoccupations and its narrative threads.

What, then, constitutes the 'classic treatment' of a text like 'The Turn of the Screw'? If our assessment is measured against what has become its canonical cinematic equivalent, Jack Clayton's *The Innocents*, like David Lean's *Great Expectations*, emerges as the undisputed 'classic' rendition of the tale. Yet Clayton's film is as much an adaptation of William Archibald's stage play, from which it borrows its title, as it is an adaptation of James's novella. It engages with each text but it retains its own creative identity by generating *another* manifestation of a tale that is more a refraction of cultural anxieties than a 'faithful' adaptation of a particular writer's narrative. Moreover, Clayton's exploration of the cultural anxieties embedded within his narrative is realized in the very different medium of film and it is his manipulation of screen space that takes us into territories that expand rather than replicate the story. Lean's canonical screen adaptation of *Great Expectations* foregrounds its associations with Dickens' novel; here, Clayton's producer credit appears before the acknowledgement that this is 'based on the story of "The Turn of the Screw" by Henry James', and the final on-screen credit of these opening moments also goes to Clayton as producer-director. The collaborative nature of its genesis becomes a part of this film product from the outset, with James mentioned as one of the contributors rather than its primary originator. Archibald is credited with the writing of the screenplay, alongside Truman Capote, though there is no mention of the former stage play and no recognition here that the screenplay is predominantly the work of Capote, who makes significant amendments to Archibald's playscript. Even more telling is the film's opening reliance upon the powerful visual and aural signifiers of cinema; there is no attempt to lend cultural weight to this film product via its relationship with any literary 'source' text. Clayton does, however, choose to mirror the Jamesian ambiguities of the text; he exploits its uncertainties in a conscious effort to invite his audience to 'exercise its intelligence' (Clayton qtd in Recchia 29); like James, he leaves the reader/viewer to interpret the complexities of the governess's state of mind, to decide whether its ghosts are 'real' or imagined and to ponder (or not) the more disturbing aspects of the tale.

Clayton is a director who adapts: all of his films are adaptations of existing narratives, from his earliest short film, *The Bespoke Overcoat* (1955), to his most famous adaptation of Joe Orton's *Room at the Top* (1959), but in all of these film adaptations, Clayton establishes his own mark as director. Though distributed and financed by a major Hollywood studio, Twentieth Century Fox, *The Innocents* is an independent production, produced and directed by Clayton; contracted to working with the studio one last time, both Clayton and the film's star, Deborah Kerr, chose to work together on *The Innocents* as their final studio commitment. Despite Clayton's attempts to distance the film from the popular horror films of the fifties and early sixties the studio's investment in the project, with its relatively big budget of £1 million (Dyson *The Innocents* DVD extras) and the casting of an established female lead, resulted in a predictable marketing campaign aimed at harnessing the popularity of the horror genre. However, the film's initial reception was mixed: it was not well received by horror fans and the box-office take was underwhelming. The mainstream marketing campaign, with its repetitive tagline: 'Do they ever return to possess the living?', and the trailer's emphasis upon gothic horror tropes, amplifies the film's identity as horror, but while certain stock horror devices are employed in the film, it presents a more ambiguous, challenging viewing experience than the usual Hollywood fare. Its mysteries do not play to the strengths of classic story design, and its content has more in common with other disquieting films of the era – films with disturbing, 'perverse images of childhood', like *The Bad Seed* (1956), *The Village of the Damned* (1960) and later *Lolita* (1962) (Hanson 368) – than with the kind of Hammer horror films popular with mainstream audiences. Produced at a time when the constraints of the Hays Code were on the wane, Clayton could engage in a more open exploration of sexuality; treatment of matters related to the governess's latent sexual desires is central to the film, yet, like James, Clayton chooses to hint at possibilities rather than present an explicit reading of her psyche and her motivations. As with readers of 'The Turn of the Screw', viewers are left to interpret the film text in terms of their own engagement, seeing or not seeing such matters as its paedophilic subtext as well as seeing or not seeing its ghosts. If the term 'classic adaptation' relates to the adaptation's capacity to engage with another text's subtextual subtleties, then Clayton's *The Innocents* serves as a 'classic' exemplar of this classification.

Unlike the complicated, slowly unwinding bildungsroman format employed by Dickens and Brontë, James' novella is predicated as much on what does not happen, what is not seen, as it is on any kind of narrative momentum. Given the realist nature of cinema, the novella's emphasis on the narrational 'gaps' and its lack of narrative momentum, present specific challenges to the adapter. Moreover, James' protagonist is an adult, reflecting, via the literary vehicle of a fictitious memoir, on a specific period in time; her recollection does not follow a sequential coming of age narrative trajectory, and there is no cathartic moment of self-realization. Its ending is disturbingly inconclusive: it refuses to conform to the classic story design of the nineteenth-century realist novel and challenges its readers to project their own interpretation of its finale. Just as James rejects any sense of comforting closure, Clayton refuses to follow the uncomplicated classic story design of mainstream genre cinema, despite the wishes of Twentieth Century Fox. William Archibald's three act stage play, from which *The Innocents* takes its title, restructures the novella, employing a classic story design and leaving the audience in no doubt as to the existence of the tale's ghosts; it presents events in a linear fashion, and without ambiguity. However, though Archibald is retained as one of a number of writers involved in the writing of the screenplay, the re-visioning of the play and the novella into the narrative we see on screen falls to Truman Capote who claims:

> I got the shock of my life. Because Henry James had pulled a fantastic trick in this book: it doesn't stand up anywhere. It has no plot! …. I kept building up more plot more characters, mores scenes. In the entire book, there were only two scenes performable. (Stafford, *TCM*)

Despite his initial consternation, Capote works with the text's unseen and unknown moments, introducing a cinematic rendition of the novella's sexually loaded subtext through recurring visual motifs – of white roses and statues in particular – and the addition of several scenes which, when translated to screen by Clayton and his cinematographer, Freddy Francis, present a similarly ambiguous and ambivalent realization of the anxieties at the heart of this tale. Like the stage play, it limits the geographical confines of the narrative: apart from the early scene between Miss Giddings and her employer, all of the action takes place within Bly's grounds, and its gothic interiors (constructed for purpose at Shepperton Studios) create the same kind of intense and claustrophobic space provided on a stage set.

The decision to edit out the structural narrative framework provided by both James' anonymous narrator and Douglas is one taken by the majority of adapters re-visioning the tale for screen consumption. Its multiple narration is in cinematic terms a clunky story-telling device that serves to complicate what is already a difficult translation of first person narration to screen space. Capote's screenplay adopts a cyclical framework, ending where it begins: it amplifies the ambiguities of the novella's close, and places the governess centre screen at outset and finale, cleverly inferring that the whole narrative is playing on a continuous loop, over and over in the mind of the governess and suggesting that what we have experienced has been solely from her viewpoint. Just as the ambiguities of James' novella continue to draw us in to ponder its mysteries, it is what lies beyond the cinematic frame – beyond the control of the actor on screen – that continues to intrigue Clayton's audience. Its silences are as voluble as its destabilizing dialogue, and the possibilities that haunt the edges of the frame are as telling as what is constructed within it. The black screen of the opening moments is disorientating: we are presented with a blank space and the disembodied voice of a child singing of love and death as we wait for something to enter the screen void. This unnatural lack of cinematic vision continues and the sound of birdsong more readily associated with daybreak takes over, adding to the mismatch between sound and image. Hands clasped in prayer move up into the empty space, and the diegetic sound of whimpering hovers at the edges of the frame. The audience is left wondering what and who lies beyond the field of vision and as we hold on this image, a shrill orchestral soundtrack begins, amplifying the tension. It is not until … seconds into the film that a face appears, again tentatively moving into the static frame. We are, from the outset, positioned with the story's disturbed protagonist, unsure of where we are and of what is happening.

The film remains haunted by what lies at the edges of the frame. Alan Nadel notes that Clayton's film, like James's novella presents the same 'freedoms and limitations cogent to James' form of realism' by presenting the audience with a cinematic gaze that realizes on screen only 'fragments of an always partial world' – one that 'imp[lies] limitless absence' (194) and aligns the governess with that fragmentation and absence. Her first person narration is inscribed by cinematic means through editing and cinematography rather than through the more obvious and intrusive device of flashback. The narration shifts to flashback once only, after the destabilizing opening scene, and its return to that opening scene does not present anticipated closure. Earlier drafts of the screenplay employ a more traditional use of the flashback device as a means of situating the audience with the story's protagonist: it opens with an ostracized Miss Giddens in attendance at Miles' funeral and moves to the traditional flashback cue of letter-writing, as she reflects on events that have led to this moment in time, setting in motion a linear recount of her story. However, such an opening and linear storytelling mode would present the viewer with a different kind of story from a very different narrative viewpoint – one that is devoid of the intended narrative ambiguities and inherent instabilities of Clayton's opening scene. He places the narrative viewpoint in the hands of the tale's governess but he also infers, from the outset, the unreliability of her narration through the way in which the moment is shot. Though the narrative then moves in flashback to the clarity of the scene in which she is interviewed by her employer, the clarity and reliability of the narrative presented on screen is constantly undermined by the instabilities of its opening moments. Andrew Higson argues that, post flashback, the narration is passed on to an 'objective, clinical camera' that does not stay with or return to Miss Giddens narrative point of view (208). However, such an assertion fails to take into account either the adapter's final return not to the relative safety of the flashback but to its disturbing opening scenes, filtered so alarmingly through Miss Giddens' viewpoint or its constant alignment of the camera with *her* experience of its limited story events. As an adapter, Clayton successfully translates the novella's first person narration to screen space, maintaining a sense of its inherent unreliability through the manner in which the film is framed, shot and edited. Francis' cinematography amplifies the narrative's lack of clarity; shot in Cinemascope black and white on degraded film stock, with filters that illuminate only the centre of the shot, the edges of the screen are blurred and indefinable. The camera is neither 'objective' nor 'clinical'. When we edit between various scenes, images playing in Miss Giddens' mind merge into the next shot, seamlessly joining together selected moments of a narrative she constructs and presents.

However, despite Clayton's avowed intent to remain 'faithful' to what he reads as the unsolvable ambiguities of the novella, Deborah Kerr insists that, 'following Henry James' writing in the original story', she plays the governess 'as if she were perfectly sane' (Stafford, *TCM*). For Kerr as reader of the novella, the story presents a woman who, though 'deeply frustrated' and capable of having 'nurtured' the ghosts 'in her own imagination', remains sane, but Clayton's cinematic construction of Miss Giddens plays *against* his star's performance and results in an even more disturbing exploration of her psyche. The studio inevitably objected to the inclusion of sexually ambivalent scenes like those of the Miles/Giddens kiss and argued for their deletion, citing Kerr's star status as its main objection, but at Clayton's insistence these sexually disturbing, loaded scenes are retained. Similarly, Clayton's child actors are playing against any preconceived notions of their demonic potential; their performance is very much of the moment. They remain relative 'innocents' from a performative perspective, playing into the unknown spaces of the narrative, their knowledge of the storyline restricted to lines meted out as filming progresses (Dyson DVD extras), though the casting of Martin Stephens, one of the 'damned' children from *The Village of the Damned* (1960), as Miles does colour our perception of this character from the outset. As in the novella, the nature of the relationship between the governess and her charges, or between Quint, Jessel and the children, is never clearly outlined in this adaptation. Miss Giddens' opening voiceover suggests her overriding desire to love and protect the children: to 'save the children, not destroy them', but placed within the destabilizing context of the film's establishing shots, her protestations of 'love', of their 'need' of 'someone who will belong to them and to whom they will belong' suggest an unhealthy, over-protective kind of involvement, of the type Miss Giddens goes on to associate with her 'ghostly' antagonists, Quint and Jessel. Laurence Raw notes the film's distinct shift 'away from the narrative' to 'the characters and their reactions' (*Adapting* 98); it becomes a disquieting psychological thriller rather than a ghost story, its narrative momentum reliant upon the power of performances intriguingly and potently at odds with directorial intent.

Capote reintroduces the more disturbing possibilities of James' novella: the statues are 'erotic', the children play 'some monstrous game ... something secretive and whispery and indecent', (Archibald & Capote 88) and – like the actors involved – we are never sure whether Miss Giddens' relationship with the children, and with Miles in particular, is sexually motivated, even if only at a subconscious level. Added moments, like the passionate kiss initiated by Miles, disturb the narrative equilibrium, and it is via the reaction shots that the audience is invited to draw its own conclusions; the final kiss (again an addition to the narrative) between Miss Giddens and the dead Miles is equally open to interpretation. Similarly, the insertion of a dream sequence suggests through the cinematic merging of images, a latent sexual desire; Ellis Hanson notes the way in which 'the whispering children' are superimposed on 'the moaning face of the governess as she dreams', their 'moving lips seem[ing] always to caress a shifting body in an uncanny kiss' (384). This merging of images becomes part of the film's editing strategy – a strategy that constantly aligns what is seen on screen with the narrative viewpoint of the governess, presenting a shifting reality. Jessel's school-room visitation, for example, is realized on screen in what appears to be a concrete ghostly manifestation, as Miss Giddens touches the tear drop left where Jessel sits; however, despite the silence of this on-screen moment, Miss Giddens then goes on to recount to Mrs Grose a conversation with the ghostly Jessel, stating, 'She was here. She was waiting for me. She spoke', and thus undermining any faith we may have in the reliability of her narrative. Though the casting of Kerr, an established, older actor, ensures we are less likely to view the governess as the potentially unreliable, unstable, naïve and *young* protagonist of James' tale, Clayton's cinematic narration suggests otherwise; she is just as naïve, as vulnerable and as impressionable. Capote's screenplay visually aligns her with white roses from the outset: they become symbolic of both her innocence and her capacity to corrupt, visually signalling the inherent ambiguities of the heroine of James's tale. The white roses are synonymous with Miss Giddens and her romantic fantasies, and with the false beauty of an Edenic Bly, but Clayton constantly undermines such perceptions: rose petals fall at her touch, and it is as she cuts white roses in the garden that she unveils the disturbing image of a stone statue of a child, its hands joined to broken adult hands, a beetle protruding from its mouth. Clayton cuts from this sexually loaded image to Miss Giddens' horrified reaction, and the moment serves as a prelude to her first sighting of Quint as he appears to her on the tower in a haze of blinding sunlight at a point in time that aligns his appearance with her earlier romantic fantasies of a visit from her employer and thus suggests he is a figment of her imagination. Any inference that the ghosts materialize in the film is limited to one scene near its close, when we are momentarily positioned with Quint as he stands in the ring of stone statues.

Clayton's construction of the novella's orphaned children is, according to Hanson, 'bolder than the novella in courting sexual suspicions' (378): 'child-loving is', he claims, 'the bête-noire of this film', its implicit exploration of homosexuality, incest and sado-masochism serving to distract from its dalliance with the controversial matter of paedophilia (371). Whether this film text engages in a conscious exploration of paedophilia or presents it as one of numerous options is left (as in James' novella) to the audience's discretion, but in the aftermath of *The Innocents*, the 'gothic child' or 'modern sexual child' has become a more prominent motif in the horror film (368). In his novella, James constructs ambivalent images of childhood: Miles and Flora are described by the governess as being 'vision[s] of angelic beauty' ('Turn' 16), 'cherubs' (31), yet with 'false little lovely eyes', and an 'incomparable childish beauty' that 'suddenly failed … quite vanished' (101). In Clayton's film, moments when we feel confident that the children know nothing of ghostly matters, despite the protestations of Miss Giddens, are juxtaposed with scenes that may imply knowledge and evil intent. The governess's shifting, judgemental estimation of the children is realized on screen by the addition of moments that demonstrate their duality. Shots of Flora as she hovers over her sleeping governess are redolent with tension, and her childlike inquisitiveness as she watches a spider devour a butterfly takes on a more sinister intent within the context of the film. Capote introduces several scenes that hint at a similarly sinister side to Miles' character: the scene in which Miss Giddens finds a dead bird under Miles' pillow is initially framed as a moment that demonstrates his sensitivity but this impression is swiftly undermined when she finds the catapult that, presumably, has been used to kill it. During what begins as an innocent game of hide-and-seek, Miles' violent strangle-hold on the governess, couched as play, is constructed as a moment of intense anxiety. Are these the natural acts of inquisitive, over zealous children or signs of demonic possession? And even though seemingly motivated by a desire to protect the children, Miss Giddens' incessant questioning *is* menacing, and we are left to ponder the obsessive nature of her desire to protect. Clayton purposely constructs such ambiguity, leaving his viewers to decide for themselves. However, regardless of such ambiguities, unlike the orphaned child in *Great Expectations* and *Jane Eyre*, James' and Clayton's orphaned children are devoid of hope: they speak to the anxieties of their respective society – the last throes of a corrupt British Empire, a twentieth century still recovering from two world wars and the ever-present threat of nuclear annihilation.

Clayton is not averse to the use of stock horror devices, and there are some scenes in which the tropes of mainstream horror are employed to create the prerequisite tension. We move from the subtleties of inferred horror, in disturbing moments such as the dream sequence and the kiss, to purposely overloaded horror scenes depicting the mental disintegration of the governess as she becomes increasingly convinced that the children are possessed by the ghosts of Quint and Jessel. After Jessel's school-room visitation, she wanders the gothic corridors, candle in hand, seeking out the whispering voices; close up shots of gargoyles punctuated by reaction shots build to a high angle shot as the camera spins around with her, stopping at the moment she turns to a black, gleaming-eyed statue held in close up, as the sound of overbearing manic laughter dominates the screen space. Such moments are rare: Clayton prefers unnerving silences, the sound of incongruous birdsong in the dead of night, the flapping of birds' wings, the buzzing of flies or songs and poetry recitals about love and death delivered by children rather than traditional terror-inducing devices employed in the horror genre. Tellingly, the few stock horror moments employed by Clayton serve to visually signify Miss Giddens' increasingly unstable state of mind, placing his audience once more with her narrative point of view. Though it plays with the tropes of the ghost story and cinema's horror genre, *The Innocents* is a film that is primarily concerned with exploration of the psychosexual ambiguities embedded in James's novella.

The BBC television adaptation, *The Turn of the Screw*, broadcast on 30 December 2009, signals its relationship with James' canonical text from the outset. The title of the novella is retained, and it is marketed as the BBC's 2009 prestigious Christmas broadcast: Ben Stephenson, BBC Controller of Drama, states 'Christmas wouldn't be Christmas without a ghost story for adults to watch in front of the fire' (BBC Press Release). He identifies it, first and foremost, as a ghost story designed to strike fear in its audience though, as in James tale, from the relative safety of hearth and home; Stephenson presents potential viewers with a clichéd image that harks back to notions of the Victorian 'family', but where James' uses this as a starting point from which to undermine this cosy image, the BBC adaptation uses it as a means of further distancing its yuletide viewers from the narrative's subtext, presenting them with a story meant to provoke through its ghostly dimension rather than through any kind of coded critique of the modern family. The pre-release marketing strategy does not play upon the novella's potentially disturbing messages. However, despite a distinct emphasis upon the presence of supernatural evil in this adaptation, director Tim Fywell and scriptwriter Sandy Welch do attempt to retain a sense of the novella's capacity to address the unspoken fears and anxieties that permeate society, whether Victorian, Edwardian or contemporary. By introducing a temporal shift from the late 1890s to post First World War, the production aligns the fears and anxieties embedded in James' text – fears of sexual transgression and decaying Empire – to those of a society coming to terms with the horrors of war. What is inferred in James' novella and Clayton's film becomes part of a fixed geographical and temporal backdrop in Welch's televised adaptation. Similarly, its treatment of the relationship between this production's very real ghosts, and its children, hints at our modern-day malaise, our fear of paedophilia, but the subtleties of child sexuality and the complexities of adult desire are not explored here in the ambiguous and disturbing manner of the novella or *The Innocents*. The psychological dimension of the text is addressed in a far more forthright manner: the drama opens with the governess placed in the psychiatric wing of a hospital for returned war veterans in the early twenties and facilitates the inclusion of a Freudian psychiatrist whose observations of the governess provide, as part of the narrative, a more overt, clinical assessment of her psyche. We shift constantly from this present, to a past filtered through her troubled mind and often realized on screen via an overload of images, fast edits and handheld camera-work.

Although screenwriter Welch's previous televisual adaptations of canonical nineteenth-century literature (*Our Mutual Friend* 1998; *North and South* 2004; *Jane Eyre* 2006; *Emma* 2009) were well received, this adaptation of James's fin de siècle story attracted critical dismay. Writing in *The Independent*, Tom Sutcliffe claims it becomes a 'rebuke against psychiatry' that 'comprehensively vandali[zes]' the text, while critic Adrian Warren maintains director, Tim Fywell, is so sidetracked by the desire to 'crea[te] a visual sheen of "spooky cool"' that the production becomes 'slick beyond purpose, peppered with gloss and noise' (Warren). Where Clayton's film works through understatement, this production works through excess. However, to its credit, the production does attempt a level of visual sophistication that takes the televisual adaptation of the classic text beyond the predictable confines of costume drama. Its postmodern aesthetic provides what Cardwell terms the 'more visually sophisticated, intertextual, contemporaneous, performative, playful and internally reflexive' engagement with narrative characteristic of certain post-nineties televisual texts (206), and, though it extracts the traditional ghost story as the mainstay of its momentum, its onscreen realization comes through unconventional filming methods. It achieves a sense of separation from the classic television adaptation of canonical nineteenth-century texts – a separation that reflects James' move away from the realist prose and structural parameters of Victorian realism. The adaptation also establishes a playful intertextuality with Lemorande's 1994 adaptation: its temporal timeshift, its construction of a young governess undergoing psychiatric treatment and a similarly surreal use of cinematography demonstrate its appropriation of elements from Lemorande's film. There are, however, considerable differences in the way that each governess is constructed. We learn through flashback that they share an abusive childhood, but where Lemorande's governess remains the vulnerable victim haunted by her sexually abusive past, Fywell's Ann, emerges as a strong, rational, courageous woman convinced of the existence of evil and of ghosts she must defeat in order to save the souls of her charges. The ghosts are real, the children possessed, and where Clayton's *The Innocents* makes tentative connections with other disturbing films like *The Village of the Damned*, the intertextual nods here are to less subtle horror films of the seventies like *The Exorcist* (1973) and *The Omen* (1976). Maternal horror films like *The Others* and *The Orphanage*, peopled by ghosts and over-protective mother figures, also assert their presence in this adaptation. Yet again, James' story picks up on cultural anxieties, reworking ever-changing permutations of the same tale, and though the Edwardian costume drama elements of this BBC adaptation in one sense comply with what we see as 'classic adaptation', its cinematic slipperiness and its intertextualization of other adaptations, and other horror films, takes it into unexpected territory, subverting our expectations of the conservative costume drama adaptation.

Unlike most adaptations of 'The Turn of the Screw', this adaptation retains a sense of the novella's multiple narrative framework. By introducing Dr Fisher and his colleague, Welch engineers a structure that allows for periodic commentary on both story events and the governess's state of mind. It gives a clinical context to the psychological ambiguities found in James' text and places the governess initially in a position of relative dependency. Any sense of feminist agency is diluted: the control of the narrative is in male hands, her recount prompted and shaped by Dr Fisher's probing questions. There are also moments when the narrative is handed over to others within her story world: flashbacks from Carla and Mrs Grose as well as from Ann present a backstory that serves to explicate matters that in the novella are explored through ambiguity and inference. Once the governess's narration begins, we stay with her in James' novella, but here, additional scenes give us access to male deliberations of her state of mind, and the inclusion of a new ending in which the doctor's shift from man of science to one who sees her ghosts places him at the centre of the drama, governess Ann having already been taken away for execution as a child killer. The story returns momentarily, however, to Bly and the arrival of the next governess and to the inference that the same events will be played out, this time with a different and yet equally naïve female keeper of the keys. As in Amenabar's *The Others*, the story is set to begin again. The intimacy of the viewer's relationship with the governess is compromised by the addition of other narrative voices, even if those of Carla and Mrs Grose are filtered through Ann's recollections. Fywell's Bly is staffed solely by women who seem to be implicated in the evil that surrounds it, whether through the resistance of Carla, or by the inferred collusion of the silent driver and this adaptation's housekeeper. There are echoes here of the ghostly servants found in *The Others*: we are never quite sure of the status of Sarah Grose and the servants at Bly, and Fywell's production plays on this ghostly ambiguity – an ambiguity that is lacking in most respects throughout this production. On first meeting Mrs Grose, Ann declares: 'I thought you were a ghost', and though assured there are 'no ghosts here', the housekeeper's knowledge of all matters related to Quint and Jessel indicate at least a measure of collusion. Carla's flashback recount of the violence and sexual debauchery of not only Quint but the master of Bly spells out the very real evil that is merely hinted at in both the novella and Clayton's *The Innocents*. Sarah's flashback also spells out the backstory of Jessel: she is presented as a heavily pregnant woman, an Ophelia-like suicide drowned in the lake at Bly. While the latter two renditions of this tale work through understatement, their audience being invited to read into the gaps and listen to the silences, in Fywell's directorial hands most matters are explicated to the point of overload.

Despite the casting of a youthful protagonist, initially presented as a disturbed and incarcerated mental patient, Docherty's governess emerges as an incredibly strong, self-assured individual who has 'decided [she is] in charge'; she is 'the captain of the ship' in 'a world of women cast adrift' by the horrors of the First World War, and it is her duty 'to watch and wait', to 'protect the children' (transcript). She is devoid of the self-dramatizing traits of James' heroine and of the self-doubt that characterizes Deborah Kerr's governess. Even when incarcerated, and as we later learn, in this adaptation condemned to death for the murder of Miles, she asserts her belief in the existence of pure evil, and in her role as moral arbiter, lone saviour. She pitches herself and her story against the edicts of science, openly challenging the traditional Freudian reading of her character, telling Dr Fisher, who is synonymous with male power and calm, rational thought, that '[she] is not some hysterical female who only thinks of men'. She questions his inability to acknowledge the existence of 'evil – evil that endures', and her final warning – 'If you don't believe in evil, evil throughout the Ages, if you don't believe in Quint he will keep coming back for you' – proves true as Quint's ghost invades Dr Fisher's world, firstly as ghostly whisperer, then as a figure in the photographs of Bly and finally as he morphs into one of the prison guards who take Ann away for execution. The ghosts in this adaptation are seen by others, and certain points in the narrative are shown directly from their point of view. Their concrete representation on screen and in photographs undermines the realism of each medium, and serves to question the scientific certainties of its Edwardian context. It is Ann's world view that dominates at the close of Welch's narrative: despite the early twentieth century's faith in science, evil prevails. In this sense, it has more in common with William Friedkin's *The Exorcist* than with *The Innocents*, suggesting that contemporary audiences are still torn between religious belief and scientific certainty.

However, the credibility of this governess is undermined at times by the production's visual and aural overload. The establishing shot positions Ann in the drab confines of a cell-like room, her face half in shadow, in a visual echo of the opening shot of Clayton's governess; yet here, the focus is much clearer and the light more naturalistic. And in stark contrast to the prolonged, disturbing inertia of Clayton's opening moments, Fywell edits at speed to garishly bright green countryside and a handheld point of view shot as the camera tracks down a tree-lined avenue, shifting from fast paced edit to slow motion, to the sound of flapping bird's wings and a bell-like soundtrack accompanied by children singing, creating the desired audience disorientation. What follows is a further series of confusing split second edits to various objects that later figure in events at Bly – the doll Miles gives to Flora, the rocking horse in the attic, specimens in glass domes, a graveyard – and to distorted shots of sky or canted close up shots of a blond haired boy, as the camera speeds up again, culminating in a close up shot of rotting meat riddled with maggots. The frantic edits and the unsteady camerawork communicate a sense of Ann's psychological distress, but this montage overload, delivered at high speed, serves to confuse rather than create tension. Where Clayton asks us to consider not only what is in the frame but what lies beyond it, Fywell's mise en scène is so cluttered and his cinematography so overpowering that we scarcely have time to take in what *is* already in each frame. The production does revel in Edwardian period detail, but it also employs stock horror devices that undercut the splendour of scenic shots of boating and picnicking in the grounds of a stately country mansion, shot for the main part in warm, bright daylight rather than gothic shadow. The stock horror treatment of the arrival of Miles at the station, shrouded in fog, jars with the naturalistic filming of most daylight scenes, and the Exorcist-like voices of the possessed children as the story draws to a close are similarly unconvincing. Here, Flora and Miles are played without the kind of ambivalence and complexity of the child actors from *The Innocents*, and this is in part due to the way Welch has constructed her much more self-assured governess who calmly declares 'I am staying...I will do whatever it takes' in her final confrontation with Quint. They are the angelic-looking children of James' tale, but their relationship with their governess is less complex. The sexual dimension between Miles and his governess is lacking, and the children seem far more open to the idea of being 'saved'. As with many of the novella's open-ended story threads, Miles' expulsion from school is explained: we hear the off-screen voices of boys declaring 'he's evil'.

The 'classic' screen adaptations of 'The Turn of the Screw' considered in this section stand out from the usual heritage fare. Fywell's televisual adaptation is inevitably judged against Clayton's *The Innocents* – an adaptation that, like Lean's *Great Expectations*, is now regarded as part of a growing canon of classic adaptations on screen – but both of these adaptations present a medium-specific response to the text: one that works through an exploitation of the visual and aural signifiers that define the chosen medium. While Clayton's adaptation has become synonymous with cinematic 'high art', Fywell's televised adaptation is much more difficult to place. Its identity as a work produced for television immediately defines it as 'mainstream' costume drama, though its experimental cinematography challenges expectation and pushes the boundaries of the genre. Each text exists on a continuum that builds on the anxieties at the centre of James' narrative; each recycles and intertextualizes permutations of this narrative ad infinitum. However, only Clayton's 'classic' adaptation realizes on screen the same level of moral malaise embedded in the novella, 'The Turn of the Screw'.

'The Turn of the Screw': Re-visioning the text (*Florence & Giles*, 'Accursed Inhabitants of the House of Bly', and Britten's *The Turn of the Screw*)

Re-visionary adaptations seek to redefine the source text's dominant discourse. They bring to the fore matters that have thus far lain dormant and present the expectant reader/viewer with alternative ways of engaging with both the originary canonical text and its adaptive offspring. The three adaptations that form the focus of this section explore 'The Turn of the Screw' from the point of view of those consigned to the margins of the text: in Benjamin Britten's opera and Joyce Carol Oates' short story, ghosts Quint and Jessel take centre stage; in John Harding's *Florence & Giles*, it is child Florence who colonizes the narrative. In each of these adaptations, the subtextual ambiguities embedded in James' gothic tale are dealt with in explicit terms. Both its sexual and moral transgressions are 'normalized' to disturbing effect, and preconceived notions of childhood innocence are challenged. These stories are peopled by charismatic, arguably paedophilic ghosts, and children who murder or seduce: they employ new and challenging ways of engaging with the canonical text and its coded messages.

In *Florence & Giles*, John Harding takes James' tentative deconstruction of the romantic Victorian image of childhood and constructs instead a complex portrait of a psychologically disturbed child whose lack of agency and visibility align her with the narrator of 'The Turn of the Screw'. Harding gives his reader access to the troubled mind of a child capable of calculated murderous acts, bringing to the fore the cultural anxieties of our contemporary times and indicating that romanticized Victorian notions of childhood innocence have no currency in a post-Bulger cultural climate. What we have thus far read as either a ghost story or psychosexual study of a troubled female becomes a narrative that has another dimension of an even more disturbing nature. The homosexual undertones embedded in James' tale are no longer seen as transgressive, but like the paedophilic inferences coded into the subtext of the novella, films like *The Innocents* or Benjamin Britten's opera, the notion of the 'evil' murderous child remains inherently unnerving and serves not only to present hitherto unnamed fears but to reshape our perception of the canonical text's Flora and Miles.

Our way into the story comes via the first person narration of the novel's Florence. Though writing from the perspective of a 24-year-old about events that happened when she was 11/12, this first person narrator does not mirror the self-critical and self-reflective voice of the adult first person narrators of other canonical texts like *Great Expectations* or *Jane Eyre*. Harding sets up a bildungsroman structure of sorts – one in which his protagonist recollects her past, but there is little indication that Florence experiences the kind of moral growth or maturity that typifies the narrative momentum of the classic bildungsroman and no sign of her capacity to weigh the consequences of her misdeeds. There is no instructive moment of catharsis. Its focus on a specific period suggests instead that it mirrors the memoir structure of James' novella, and one senses that Florence's narration, like the memoir form, is riddled with misinformation and misinterpretation. Florence, unlike the governess, is the sole narrator of her tale, yet it is a tale ventriloquized through two distinct language systems – one public, the other private. Her private voice is loaded with captivating neologisms that establish a bond between reader and narrator. We are given access to her private world, and the inventiveness of the neologisms that characterize her speech is indicative of her intelligence. They have the power to detract from the abnormality of her thoughts and actions. Moreover, her private language system gives her agency and control in a situation where, as female orphan child, she has none. Like *The Piano's* Ada, her rejection of patriarchal language is in part a rejection of patriarchal control, and like Ada, she remains an enigma, despite her position as the novel's first person narrator.

Florence notes that 'were[she] to speak as [she] thinks, it would be obvious [she]'d been at the books' (Harding 5); hiding her private language system is not only a mode of control but a matter of survival since knowledge and education are construed as dangerous and out of bounds for women within the context of Harding's tale. The compulsion to hide this language from all but the reader also adds to the intimacy of the relationship with Florence. However, she emerges as an unreliable narrator, often unable to see what her reader and others in her tale can and disturbingly unaware of both her own psychological instability and the evil nature of her acts. Such acts are reported rather than pondered; as with other literary child narrators like Patrick McCabe's *The Butcher Boy* or Iain Banks Frank Cauldhame of *The Wasp Factory*, she is devoid of conscience, devoid of moral compass. At a certain point in the narrative she becomes for the reader the 'almost ugly' Flora of James' novella, whose 'very presence could make [the governess] quail' ('Turn' 99–101). Knowledge of her deeds and of her thought processes inevitably keep the reader at a distance despite the intimacy of her first person address; her status as unloved, psychologically unhinged orphan, who 'phanto[ms] a whole family' to alleviate her loneliness, and whose only sense of identity comes through her role as sister to the fragile Giles, invites reader sympathy though not empathy. Moreover, the voice of Florence remains that of a child who has yet to attain anticipated levels of maturity; despite the fact that she is recollecting from the adult perspective of a 24-year-old woman, her voice remains that of her 11-/12-year-old self and thus retains a childlike dimension.

Harding repositions the narrative's cultural framework by relocating the tale from Victorian England to late nineteenth-century America and an equivalent country mansion situated 100 miles north of New York. Where James' governess initially perceives Bly House as a place of sunshine and promise, Blithe House is from the outset 'a crusty mansion ... uncomfortabled and shabbied by prudence, a neglect of a place, tightly pursed', a 'place ghosts love' (Harding 5). Building on the fairy tales and gothic allusions of the novella, Harding's re-visionary novel demonstrates yet again, the manner in which adaptations circulate the canonical text, along with sister texts that occupy a similar narrative space and explore similar thematic threads. Though ostensibly a reconfiguration of James' Flora, transformed here from the less central child figure to the novel's protagonist, Florence is by inference also aligned with the intelligent, orphaned Jane Eyre who seeks solace in books. As an avid reader of gothic stories – The Mysteries of Udolpho, The Monk, The Woman in White, the works of Radcliffe and Poe – Florence imbibes the dark mysteries of her reading material and begins to weave it into her own solitary, mundane existence as a means of intellectual sustenance. Like James' governess, she self-dramatizes, and the boundaries between reality and constructed fantasy become increasingly blurred. Where child Jane grows out of her imaginings, Florence grows into them with ever-increasing surety. Her constant allusions to fairy tales build on those embedded in James' novella and reinscribe the notion that Florence is creating her own fictions. This purposeful narrative strategy reminds us of Florence's childlike state of mind: her thoughts are peopled by the ghosts of the gothic and the morally good characters of fairy tales, but her recasting of the two results in a disturbing amalgamation of good and evil – an amalgamation that reminds the reader of her incapacity to differentiate between the two. Much like James' governess, her storytelling becomes a form of female agency: we sense that she is devising her own gothic tale, her own 'happy ever after' that ends not in the romance the besotted Theo craves but in a Hansel and

Grettel style close. Though she plays with the idea of being the damsel in distress, 'princessed in the tower' as Theo 'knight-in-shining-armoured up the drive' (155), she ultimately casts herself as a heroic Grettel, saving Hansel from the wicked witch, Miss Taylor, who she 'Hansel and Grettelled with a magnificent blow' (234) to the head. In Harding's warped take on the story of Rapunzel, Theo, unlike the prince who loses then regains his sight after throwing himself from the tower to save his damsel, dies as a consequence of seeing clearly at last; gaining his 'sight' – ergo the realization that Florence is unhinged – he loses his life.

Sensitive Giles is presented as the antithesis of his intelligent, forceful sister; unlike the complex, potentially evil Miles of James' novella and Clayton's film, he personifies the romanticized image of the innocent Victorian child, whilst Florence represents the child as dangerous 'other'. The Victorian preoccupation with the sexual transgressions of dangerous, unstable women of no fixed identity, found in *Jane Eyre* and 'The Turn of the Screw', are replaced here by the dangerous potentialities of the murderous child. Rather than becoming James' angelic Flora, Florence is constructed as being more like his self-dramatizing governess, a pseudo Bertha Mason who views her tower as a refuge. Her tower is her 'secret kingdom' (228) in which she is able to educate herself, safe from the interventions of her absent yet controlling uncle for whom the education of women is taboo. As with the novella's governess, her only emotional outlet comes in the form of Giles: she becomes a self-appointed, over-protective, over-bearing surrogate mother within the dysfunctional family structure of Blithe House, akin to James' governess and Clayton's Miss Giddens. All three use Miles/Giles to define themselves within a societal structure that reinscribes their invisibility. All three place themselves at the centre of a fantastic tale of their own devising – one that defines their efforts to protect as courageous acts of stoic endurance. Florence recalls that she 'had not let Miss Whitaker drive [her] to despair when she'd been alive', and she would not 'crumple and give in' to Miss Taylor now either; 'if [Miss Taylor] wanted a fight she should have one, no matter what dark powers she had at her beck and call...' (175). She describes in dramatic terms their final showdown as they 'fac[e] one another. Two beasts in mortal combat' (177). Miss Taylor should be her natural ally since she too seeks knowledge beyond that deemed appropriate for women, but Florence constructs her as the novella's ghostly, predatory Quint, whose aim is to steal away her innocent charge. The figure of the wolf in *Little Red Riding Hood*, traditionally conceived as male, becomes Miss Taylor, and her motherly crooning is redefined in sinister terms by Florence who describes her 'vulturing over [Giles], almost licking her lips' (150). By placing Miss Taylor inside the mirror – 'her reflection trapped in the glass, head back, laughing a terrible, silent laugh' (146) – Harding, like Brontë, reiterates notions of gothic doubling and alter egos, but here it is his protagonist, not Miss Taylor, who emerges as the dark 'Other' akin to Bertha Mason. Though Florence is at pains to construct Miss Taylor as the Jessel-like 'witch, striding over the water' (119), who 'sni[ffs] the air like a predator seeking its prey' (81), the reader, like Giles has no faith in her claims, despite the fact that she is in control of the narrative. Instead, her behaviour aligns her not with acts of stoic self-sacrifice but with a morbid obsession that shifts from the psychological to the physical, resulting in the murder of women who seek to usurp her role as surrogate mother.

In Harding's novel, the potentially psychotic governess of James' novella and Clayton's *The Innocents* becomes the psychotic child, but Florence *and* the governesses of her tale share traits with these forerunners, creating a disorientating mix of persona. Various signature moments from Clayton's film are referenced here: Florence becomes the crazed Miss Giddens, forcing Giles (rather than the film's resistant Flora) into a false admission that he sees the ghost of Miss Taylor standing in the lake (118). Yet just as *The Innocents'* Miss Giddens is synonymous with white roses, it is Miss Taylor who becomes synonymous with scented white lilies that, according to Florence, align her with death and decay. Similarly, the 'besotted' (70) Miss Whitaker shares the romantic delusions of both Miss Giddens and the unnamed narrator of 'The Turn of the Screw'. One thing that translates directly from Clayton's film, though, is the construction of moments that suggest the evil propensity of the narrative's children. Just as Flora speaks of watching with interest as a spider eats a butterfly and Miles sleeps with a dead bird under his pillow – a bird he has probably killed – Florence talks of a mouse 'skewered with an ice pick' (133) and fish 'gasp[ing] for air until expired' (237), picking up on the darker undertones of the film text's construction of Flora and Miles. The striking difference here, though, is that whilst the evil propensity of the children of the novella and the film remains ambiguous, in *Florence & Giles*, the reader is left in no doubt as to Giles' position as the innocent, and his sister's as the evil child of the horror narrative, realized not through gothic tropes but through a complex psychological study.

As with many of the cinematic adaptations of the novella, this narrative adopts a cyclical structure. Florence remarks: 'We were history repeating itself, the three of us, Mrs Grouse, Giles, and I, lined up to welcome the new governess just as we'd done for poor Miss Whitaker what seemed like a lifetime ago' (75). She later speaks of two dead governesses, and of a third yet to be appointed, inferring that the story she has related to us will play out again and again, each curious governess being disposed of by the Bluebeardesque Florence. James' novella and the numerous cinematic and televisual adaptations treat the story as either a ghost story or a psychosexual study, but Harding's novel defines Florence's ghosts as part of her psychosis: even as she narrates them into existence, it is clear that they are a symptom of her paranoia as evidenced by her belief in mirrors that perform acts of ghostly surveillance. It remains a psychological study that focuses on the protagonist's self-induced belief in ghosts, and it plays with the gothic tropes embedded in James' novella; however, it also adopts the strategies of the populist mystery thriller, refocusing the narrative lens on matters that are not necessarily morally ambiguous but structurally mystifying.

Its ambiguities come through plot points rather than through the prose or the cinematography. Harding asks us to ponder who Miss Taylor really is – Giles' mother and Florence's stepmother? Their father's second wife? Or their uncle's disgraced fiancée? – and why Miss Taylor left Giles, only to return for him at this point in the story. Through viewing the hidden family photographs, Florence becomes aware of discrepancies in the family history but she fails to make the connections that her distanced knowing reader can. There are hints that Hadleigh (and the reader) suspects her of being at least culpable in the death of former governess Miss Whitaker, though narrator Florence artfully circumvents questions of her own guilt through evasion and half-truths. It may not deal in mainstream mystery tropes of the kind explored in Adele Griffin's Young Adult Fiction novel, *Tighter*, itself an adaptation of 'The Turn of the Screw' set in a contemporary New England United States, but it draws upon its mysteries in concrete ways that signal a different approach to the story's genre identity to that of the canonical text and screen adaptations like *The Innocents*. Florence notes that this story is 'more like a fairy tale than a proper mystery' (129), but if so, it is a macabre one with disturbing implications. The reader of 'The Turn of the Screw' and the viewer of *The Innocents* is left to decide whether Flora and Miles are evil or innocent and to what degree. In *Florence & Giles*, Florence *is* guilty of committing evil acts. However, by giving his reader access to the amoral workings of her childlike state of mind, Harding encourages his reader to ponder what brings her to a point where she is unable to differentiate between good and evil. His is a more direct indictment of society, both in the narrative's contemporaneous times and our own, and the cultural anxieties coded into James' novella are given another disturbing twist as Florence presents the very real figure of the child murderer.

Victorian ghost stories are, Joyce Carol Oates argues, far too 'ladylike', James' prose 'too genteel' (Afterword 306). 'Accursed Inhabitants of the House of Bly', a postmodern gothic spin on James' 'The Turn of the Screw' which appears in a collection titled *Haunted: Tales of the Grotesque*, is a prequel that, like Britten's opera, treats the canonical text's coded exploration of repressed sexual desire in a much more open and disturbing manner. Taking as her starting point the bold assertion that 'evil is not always repellant but frequently attractive', she deals in 'unspeakable taboos' that make of her ghostly protagonists and their charges not 'victims' but 'active accomplices' (305–306). As in Jean Rhys's *Wide Sargasso Sea*, the story's temporal and narrational shifts refocus the lens: ghosts Quint and Jessel become its protagonists, and events unfold from their perspective, prior to the arrival of the novella's governess – a figure whose function in this adaptation is reduced to the level of plot mechanism. Oates builds on the novella's ambiguities, fleshing out its inferred critique of a morally corrupt Victorian society, by acknowledging the disquieting, 'aesthetically erotic appeal' of child love (306) and by deconstructing the romantic Victorian image of the innocent child.

The story's title provides cues for readers already familiar with James' novella and the many adaptations that circulate this canonical text, though even for the uninitiated, its appearance in a collection of macabre ghost stories and its reference to 'accursed inhabitants' foregrounds its generic identity as a horror narrative. However this short story, unlike some other adaptations of 'The Turn of the Screw', is not simply a ghost story; nor is it a psychosexual study of the novella's protagonist. Instead, it is a compelling study of the psychosexual mindset of the novella's lovelorn ghosts. Oates' prose is devoid of what she terms the gentility of James' ghost story (306): it is blunt, bloody and erotically charged, and there are other layers of generic complexity at play that take the tale beyond the parameters of horror. Initially, we enter the tale at a point where Quint and Jessel have 'crossed' to the world of ghosts and await the arrival of their beloved Flora and Miles, but the story moves back to recount events that have led to their current existence and on to its own very ambiguous close as the battle for the children concludes. Oates introduces plot points from the novella: the sightings of the ghosts, the governess's response to these sightings and her determination to 'save' the children all form part of the narrative's momentum as the climatic showdown between the pious governess and the eroticized ghosts draws to a close. Oates also references other adaptations: the schoolroom scene between Jessel and the governess introduced in Clayton's *The Innocents*, for example, becomes part of Oates narrative. However, James' governess is not at the centre of Oates' tale, and the ghosts' are not manifestations of her mental instability. Nor does Miles die as a result of the final battle for his soul.

The tale revolves around a similarly specific period in time but the convoluted first person narrational shifts employed in the novella are abandoned in favour of an omniscient third person narrator whose recount of events is aligned with Jessel and Quint. Unlike canonical texts explored thus far, this is neither memoir nor bildungsroman. There are, instead, disjointed moments that sit outside the overarching narration; set apart via the use of italics, such moments ask the reader to ponder events from the perspective of characters who exist on the margins of the story:

> Are the children watching from the house? Are their small, pale, eager faces pressed to the glass? What do little Flora and little Miles see, that the accursed lovers themselves cannot see? ('Haunted' 255)

Oates also shifts to random lines of first person narration from Quint and Jessel, delivered in a similar italicized form and providing telling insights into their troubled states of mind. Jessel's thoughts, in particular, play out across the narrative, mapping her realization that some force, whether good or evil, *'whose face [they] cannot see and whose voice [they] cannot hear, except as it echoes in [their] own thoughts'* (274) guides their actions. Her lines hijack the narrative without warning, haunting its prose and reminding us of her constant presence as she ponders the consequences of her actions. An elusive voice offers a closing philosophical comment – *'We must have imagined that, if Evil could be made to exist, Good might exist as rightfully'* (282) – but the identity of the speaker remains consciously ambiguous. Within Oates post-gothic world, the boundaries between good and evil are constantly blurred, and her narrational strategies serve to disorientate, at times aligning the reader with the disturbing perversities of the narrative's ghosts.

Though positioned as a post-gothic horror prequel that adapts 'The Turn of the Screw', the story also intertextualizes not only other adaptations that circulate the canonical text, *The Innocents*, and Britten's opera in particular, but also other canonical nineteenth-century texts. As in James' novella, thematic preoccupations explored in *Jane Eyre* become part of the fabric of 'Accursed Inhabitants of the House of Bly', but Oates' exploration of gothic romance moves beyond that to engage with the darker, ghostly undertones of possessive-obsessive love synonymous with Emily Brontë's *Wuthering Heights*. Jessel and Quint become a pseudo Cathy and Heathcliff, wandering the confines of Bly rather than the moors but held by a similarly obsessive desire; however, in this tale, romantic desire transgresses the 'norm' as lovers Quint and Jessel await the crossing of Flora and Miles, set up here as objects of equal sexual desire. It becomes a story of eroticized romance that explores taboo areas of sexual transgression, foregrounding the dangerous desires James' novella ambiguously hints at. Oates treatment of paedophilia challenges her reader: the behaviour of Quint and Jessel is normalized in ways that destabilize accepted codes of morality, both Victorian *and* contemporary.

Like James' governess, Jessel is initially constructed as a sensible, modest young woman, but whilst the instabilities of the former are slowly revealed, Jessel's conversion from a virginally 'good pious scared-giggly Christian girl' (256) to object of horror is dealt with swiftly, and the story dwells on her erotic melancholia. Both women harbour unfulfilled romantic fantasies of liaisons with their employer; 'like every other young governess in England, Miss Jessel had avidly read her *Jane Eyre*' (260). Similarly, like every other governess, both women are placed in a precarious class position, neither angel of the house nor yet whore, despite the fact that they are paid for their services and fulfil the problematic role of surrogate 'mother' within the Victorian household. But in Oates' tale, Jessel's romantic desires are realized; the ghostly apparition that accosts James' governess is presented here as flesh and blood, and the mutual sexual desire of a living Quint and Jessel is acted upon as a natural consequence. The early days of their relationship are 'flooded with sunshine!' and 'the very air pulse[s] with their love' (277): Jessel's sexual awakening is initially constructed as energizing. However, Oates soon undermines the nostalgia of such moments equating sex, in Jessel's mind, with insanity and loss of self, aligning her as much with James' mentally unstable governess as with her named counterpart from the canonical text. Her sexual experiences also align her not with the heroine of Brontë's *Jane Eyre* but with Eyre's alter ego, Bertha Mason. She becomes, like Bertha, 'a beast' who feels 'the sharp tug of a chain fixed to a collar tight around her neck' (255). Oates' description of Jessel echoes Brontë's description of the bestial Bertha; but at a subtextual level, it also echoes the language used to describe Jane Eyre's distressed emotional response to being shackled to Rochester through the gifts he bestows on her prior to their wedding day, mirroring the *Eyre* text's notions of gothic doubling.

Here, as in *Jane Eyre*, sex and patriarchal control equate with a loss of self and descent into madness. The catacombs become Jessel's 'tower' where she exists in a vampiric 'blood-trance', her mouth 'a wound' that for Quint becomes synonymous with sexual arousal (268). She is a 'ruined woman, a despoiled woman, a humiliated woman, a fallen woman, a woman made incontrovertibly a *woman*' (264) through the act of sexual intercourse – the Victorian 'whore' whose death is an inevitable consequence of her pregnancy outside marriage. She is the antithesis of her replacement, the puritanical governess who, 'dun-coloured, and so plain!' with her 'small, pale, homely face' (266) bears a striking resemblance to Brontë's Jane Eyre, yet 'hates and fears life...hates and fears joy, passion, love. All that [Jessel] and [Quint] ha[ve]' (267) and that Jane Eyre seeks.

Oates initially builds an image of an appealing, sexually magnetic Quint, inviting her readers to empathize with the plight of these trapped lovers whose desire to be reunited with the children is driven by affection. She constructs a charismatic Quint whose sexual potency is initially aligned with openness and freedom: he is the irresistible seducer to whom many of Bly's female servants have succumbed, including its housekeeper. Yet his relationship with Jessel is seemingly one of mutual love and desire; he 'feels a husband's loss: half his soul torn from him' with the passing of Jessel and claims they are ' "both accursed by love" ' (279). Jessel hints that his death, rather than being accidental is, like her own, a premeditated act designed to reunite them in much the same way as their ghostly predecessors, Cathy and Heathcliff, but here the lovers lurk 'unromantically, their place of refuge a corner...in the cellar of the great ugly House of Bly' (252) rather than the open moors of Brontë's tale. Free-spirited Quint is also drawn initially as a man of some moral virtue whose love of Flora and Miles is engendered by a desire to provide them with the family they are denied by their guardian; he sees his attachment to Jessel and the children as 'that of a man blessed (some might say accursed) by his love of family' (258). However, Oates introduces an ironic twist to this concept of 'family' as the story progresses, and cosy family fantasies are undercut as disturbing hints that the 'accursed love' Quint refers to relates to his love of Miles rather than the fallen Jessel.

Oates builds on James' exploration of the dysfunctional Victorian family through her depiction of servants Jessel and Quint's relationship with the wards of Bly, and through her equally disturbing study of Bly's absent patriarch, adding class issues to the thematic mix. 'Family' is intertwined with transgressive notions of 'love' of children: both Quint and Jessel are unable to see the boundaries between erotic obsessive love of their charges and their desire to be reunited with them as a family. As the story unfolds, the darker edge to this love becomes ever more apparent, and yet Oates denies us unequivocal moral positions. Her more direct exploration of the sexual freedoms afforded Quint builds on James' ambiguous critique of sexually repressive, class-bound Victorian morality. On the surface, Bly becomes synonymous with Christian morality but Oates undermines the Christian stance of Bly's master by presenting him as man of repressed sexual desires who uses his upper class status as a justification for his voyeuristic and homophobic passions. In his lewd directive to his valet – ' "Quint, my man, you must do my living for me, eh?" ' (Oates 257) – he sanctions the sexual excesses from which he gleans vicarious pleasure. Oates purposely contrasts Quint's dawning realization of the erotic appeal of his relationship with Miles to the unnatural, controlling behaviour of Miles' uncle, whose loaded homophobic decrees suggest not only his own latent homosexual desires but his suppressed sexual interest in Miles. Couched as a desire to protect the children's ' "moral Christian selves" ', he presents Quint with the task of making the 10-year-old Miles ' "not a boy" ' and is at pains to stress his vitriolic hatred of homosexuality and homosexuals – ' "degenerates [who] will be the death of England, if we do not stop them in the cradle" '. He would, he asserts, rather Miles were ' "dead, than *unmanly*" '. And yet his 'choked anger' and the 'rather ghastly slackening of [his] mouth' at 'the very prospect' of homosexual acts (261) speak of fearful, repressed desires that may provide a rationale for his unexplained absence from Bly and for his neglect of his wards. Indeed, Quint wonders whether his master knew of the sexual nature of the relationship not only between himself and Jessel but between them and 'the children' too (267).

Working-class Quint views the behaviour of his master, and by inference the wealthy upper classes, as 'savage' and is dismissive of the Christian piety that characterizes his master and the new governess. He is instead a man of primal urges, surprised by the nature of the feelings aroused in him by Miles – by 'that startled breathlessness that [he] found so appealing – finds appealing still' (272). He is at first 'astonish[ed]' by Miles' affectionate advances and would 'push him away in a nervous reflex' (262). However, even before Quint's paedophilic relationship with Miles is confirmed, his desire to retain sexual agency colours our perception of him: in his quest to maintain possession of his sexual potency, he becomes a ghostly rapist 'insinuating himself into ... the governess's bed, and despite her faint flailing protests into her very body' (271). He revels in the fear he evokes and recalls the moment of her 'naked terror' in 'a golden erotic glow' (268–269). Oates explores the complex psychology of transgressive sexual positioning – Quint as rapist, Quint as unwitting paedophile – but the distance that traditionally characterizes such representation is purposely lacking here, and the response of the reader is conditioned accordingly. Furthermore, the morally impeachable characters are either driven by ulterior motives or remain two dimensional. The Master's hidden agenda undermines his moral position and the new governess, who enters at a much later stage in the narrative, is unable to function at more than the level of plot device, despite taking the traditional stoic stand against what is defined as evil.

Oates' comments as to the shared love between Quint and Miles leave the reader unsure of the true nature of their relationship, but as the story reaches its closing stages, what may at first be construed as innocent takes on a decidedly sexual dimension. Whilst Clayton's Miss Giddens subconsciously toys with the idea of sexual interest in her charges in a dreamscape added to the narrative by Capote, Oates draws out the novella's paedophilic undertones to graphic effect. Quint ultimately 'recalls with a swoon in the loins, poor Miles hugging him about the knees, mashing his heated face against him' and at this point there can be no doubt as to the sexual nature of their love, but Oates tellingly concludes the passage with a provocative rhetorical question, asking 'How is it evil, to give, as to receive, love's comforts?' (280), forcing her reader to consider a disquieting alternative viewpoint. Whilst Michael Winner's *The Nighcomers*, also a prequel, evokes a sensationalistic engagement with the sexual transgressions embedded in 'The Turn of the Screw', Oates explores the complex moral dilemmas attached to the kind of sexual transgressions that are ambiguously coded within the novella. Furthermore, unlike other adapters of this tale, Oates presents Miles as the sexually aware seducer: he is neither synonymous with 'good' or 'evil'; he is instead aware of and in control of his own sexuality. The relationship between Flora and Jessel is not, however, construed in the same overtly sexual manner. Jessel's passionate desire is to become Flora's surrogate mother. This aligns her with James' governess and her various adaptive reincarnations, but Oates also provides a psychological rationale for Jessel's obsession with the living Flora: Flora becomes Jessel's 'own little girl, the babe cruelly drowned in her womb, hers and Quint's, in this very pond' (275), and she haunts Bly, a 'woman sighing for her lost child' (277). Whether there is a sexual dimension to the relationship between Jessel and Flora is debatable; Diane Hoeveler argues that both Miles and Flora 'are active participants with their parent-substitutes in sexual acts' (363), citing the following passage from the story:

> It had been Miles habit, charming, and touching, perhaps a bit pitiful, to seek out the lovers Quint and Miss Jessel in just such trysting places, if he could find them; then, silky hair disheveled and eyes dilated as with an opiate, he would hug, burrow, twist, groan with yearning and delight – who could resist him, who could send him away? And little Flora too. (Oates 273)

Miles' 'disheveled' hair and 'dilated' eyes are suggestive of his sexual arousal, but the inference is that Flora is also engaged in this sexual tryst, even though there has been little commentary on the sexual dimension of the relationship between Flora and Jessel thus far. The sexual implications here are even more disturbing; Jessel's mothering becomes part of an incestuous as well as a paedophilic desire.

James' tale connects through subtextual subtlety and ambiguity: as readers, we are never sure of his position as to the evil or innocence of its children, just as we are never sure of the real or fictitious nature of its ghosts or of its governess's state of mind. Oates takes a less ambiguous approach to the story: she challenges the reader's moral position and the moral codes of both Victorian and contemporary society. Her ghosts are real, her adults and her children are culpable, and the novella's 'unspeakable taboos' become disquietingly 'normalized'. In the re-visionist adaptations of Joyce Carol Oates and Benjamin Britten, James' 'The Turn of the Screw' becomes a narrative devoid of moral absolutes in which the coded transgressive sexual desires embedded in the text are foregrounded. Despite their very different adaptive modes – one prose, the other a performative piece – they share a preoccupation with the novella's sexual ambiguities and a desire to give voice to its marginalized ghosts. However, whilst the novella's subtle content lends itself to the short story format in which Oates writes, its translation to operatic form is more problematic. Henry James is a writer associated with a 'high art' aesthetic, and his focus is on the psychology of his characters; opera, though considered 'high art', is associated with melodrama and as such it does not, in general, deal in subtleties of a Jamesian type.

Yet Martin Halliwell argues that in 'The Turn of the Screw', James' 'synthesis of melodrama and psychological ambiguity' ensures its 'amenab[ility] to operatic form' (33). Lucile Desblache sees its inherent ambiguities, its 'communication of silence and other non-verbal elements' as a 'powerful agent' that can be utilized when translating his prose to opera (106–107). But whether Britten saw the novella as a tale that would translate to staged operatic space with ease or not, his determination to explore its textual ambiguities has resulted in the creation of an opera that, like James' tale, is constantly revisited and performed. Britten's chamber opera, with his musical score and a libretto written by Myfanwy Piper, was commissioned by the Venice Biennial and opened to critical acclaim when it premiered on 14 September 1954 at Teatro La Fenice, and it has been frequently revived and performed worldwide, each staged performance with its own particular signature. As a chamber piece, written for a small cast and accompanied by an ensemble orchestra, Britten's opera attains what Halliwell terms a 'complex synthesis of text and music' that is 'analogous to James' use of a centre of consciousness' (25): Britten's musical choices are conditioned by his adaptive intent. He employs a limited voice range of tenor, soprano and treble and affords the traditionally heroic tenor role to Quint, his anti-heroic protagonist, thus shifting musical expectation. The opera's musical interludes provide narrative duality, functioning as 'omniscient or implied narrator' or 'interven[ing] in the action to give a different perspective to that of the characters' (Halliwell 25).

Opera, like film and other dramatic stage productions, employs a range of semiotic systems with which to narrate its tale. Its visual signification comes from lighting, set design, costuming and the movements and gestures of those performing on stage as well as from its auditory signification. Though ostensibly dependent upon the auditory – the instrumental score and the voices scribed by the composer, the lines written by the librettist – opera shares with other performative modes collaborative work practices dependent upon collective creative input from a diverse range of disciplines. The musical score and its libretto are the most significant codes and signifiers at work in the production of operatic staged performance, but many other visual and auditory components contribute to each production's final realization. Piper's words and Britten's notes are scribed on the page and form the focus for the performance, yet the score and the libretto are not of a fixed or stable nature: the opera remains a work in progress, shaped by each director's agenda – an agenda that is *realized* through *performance*. Variations from one performance to another are inevitable, even within the same production employing the same conductor and orchestra, the same cast, production crew and design team. In recent years, for example, this opera has been set in the fifties (Glyndebourne 2006 and 2014 revival) and in the twenties (Opera North 2010). Its relationship with the adaptive text shifts in a way that screen or prose adaptation does not; like all staged performances, it is constantly engaged in the act of adaptation, changing and transforming according to directorial intent and the collaborative energies of all involved.

Valentine Cunningham credits Britten's attraction to this particular narrative to his desire to engage with challenging moral dilemmas; he is, he argues, intrigued by this ' "queer" ' story's 'question[ing] of the sexual corruption of children' (3) and his adaptive agenda is fuelled by his rejection of institutionalized moral codes. It is by giving voice to the narrative's silenced ghosts that Britten explores their position as characters marginalized by more than their incorporeality and their class. Though not afforded a backstory of the kind written into Oates' prequel, the relationship between the story's ghosts is central to Britten's adaptation, as are the homo-erotic desires of its male lead. Exploration of transgressive sexual behaviours forms part of the opera's coded subtext, but its god-like Quint is even more disturbing than Oates' charismatic yet more openly paedophilic ghost. Britten's questioning of moral codes in general and of attitudes towards homosexuality (and what Cunningham terms the 'love of young boys' in particular) is inevitably constrained by the fifties context of his opera's production era, when homosexuality was deemed a crime. Oates, writing in contemporary times, explores homosexuality without impunity and leads her reader to ponder the 'normalization' of sexual behaviours deemed transgressive, but cultural anxieties surrounding paedophilia continue to circulate, and representation of such behaviours remains challenging, whether in prose form or on stage and screen.

Desblache notes that Piper's libretto condenses James' 42,000 word novella into a very succinct 7,000 words (106). Its two act, sixteen scene structure follows the narrative hinge points of James' novella and employs a series of shorthand scene headings that foreground specific dramatic moments from the canonical source text – 'The Letter', 'The Tower', 'The Window' and so on. In this respect, Britten's opera is a model of fidelity. Piper's libretto is from the outset an exemplar of poetic brevity, its opening lines: 'It is a curious story', later echoed in John Harding's *Florence & Giles*. It opens with a prologue voiced by an extra-diegetic narrator (who may or may not be the canonical text's Douglas) and it closes, as does the novella, without a return to the opening narration. However, events are then filtered through several narrative voices – the governess, Mrs Grose, the children, Jessel and Quint – which adds to the instability of its content and shifts the adaptation away from the structural fidelity adhered to in its story design. Unlike the governess or Mrs Grose, Britten's ghosts speak in poetic verse that, when coupled with their physical on-stage presence, affords them a different kind of status. Quint's voice, silenced in the source text, emerges as the most dominant, both lyrically and musically. First sighted by the governess in Act 1, Scene 5, his appearance is delayed, but he dominates in every sense from Act 1, Scene 8 onwards, and in this, despite its structural similarities with James' tale, Britten's opera enacts a bold departure.

In Britten's adaptation, the ghosts are seen and heard by all, and though he does not appear until Act 1, Scene 5 and is not afforded any backstory of the kind written into the narrative by Oates, Quint emerges as its central figure, seen and heard by all. He is judged by the governess and Mrs Grose to be 'handsome/But a horror!', a seducer who 'made free with everyone-with/little Master Miles' and 'with the lovely Miss Jessel' despite her status as 'a lady so far above him' (1.5). In this adaptation, however, Quint constructs a very different image of himself: he is the rebellious 'hero highwayman', a god-like, mythical 'King Midas with gold in his hand' (1.8) whom Miles worships and who dominates both musically and in terms of stage presence from Act 1 Scene 8 onwards, even in his ghostly form. His relationship with Jessel is less central to the narrative than in Oates' adaptation: the gothic romance underscored in Oates' short story is undermined here by Quint's preoccupation not with Jessel but with Miles. Britten's tale has a distinctly male focus, and the nuances of the female gothic, explored in other adaptations, are not part of his re-visionary agenda. Quint's veiled, sexually loaded references to 'secrets and half-formed desires', to 'the hidden life that stirs/When the candle is out … The unknown gesture, and the soft, persistent word,/The long sighing flight of the night-winged bird' (8.1) relate not to his relationship with Jessel but with Miles. He rejects Jessel's heterosexual love, arguing instead that he seeks 'a friend-/Obedient to follow where [he lead[s]' and who will 'feed/[His] mounting power' (2.1). Interpretation of the sexually transgressive potential of Britten's opera varies in performance: some productions, like the 2014 revival of the Glyndebourne Opera's *The Turn of the Screw*, define Quint's relationship with Miles as overtly paedophilic: here, Quint delivers the disturbing, sexually loaded line 'I am King Midas with gold in his hands' whilst lifting a naked Miles from his bath.

Jessel – 'Despised, betrayed, unwanted' – emerges as Quint's needy accomplice, a 'self-deceiver' whose 'beating heart to [her] own passions lied' (2.1), and though she too is given a voice and a stage presence in this adaptation, she emerges as a less sympathetic character whose tragedy is swiftly converted to a revenge quest. Her litany of fairy tales and mythical stories are employed to lure in their child prey, and in the opening scene of

Act 2, their voices are united in their shared quest to steal the children away from 'careful watching eyes' (2.1). Despite Quint's stance as the charismatic anti hero, there is a disturbing Hindley-Brady type quality to their relationship as they work together to steal away the souls of the children. The beauty of the verse and the musical energy of their shared litany at the end of Act 2, Scene 1 establishes the narrative's chilling trajectory as Quint and Jessel vow to 'break the love' that secures Miles and Flora in their earthly bodies and to ensure that ' "The ceremony of innocence is drowned" ' (2.1). James' complex governess becomes a similarly naïve, romantically deluded, courageous figure in this adaptation, but the psycho-sexual dimension to her characterization is sacrificed. She is more than a plot mechanism but, despite her dominant presence in Act 1, her quest to save the children is secondary to that of the ghosts who seek to reclaim them. She may ultimately 'save' the children from the abusive clutches of the ghosts, but as in James' novella, this is achieved at the expense of exile for Flora and death for Miles. In the closing moments, her obsessive desire to own the children matches that of Quint as she cries 'You shall be mine', and the libretto ends with her disquieting acknowledgement that she too is culpable in Miles' death.

In Britten's adaptation, notions of childhood 'innocence' and 'evil' are blurred, leaving the audience unsure as to whether Miles embraces the love of the charismatic Quint, or becomes his manipulated victim. For the governess, the beauty of Bly and the excitable behaviour of Miles and Flora is swiftly redefined: the 'house is poisoned, the children mad', their 'false little lovely eyes' a deceit (2.2). Though initially aligned with childhood innocence through their games and their frequent singing of nursery rhymes, the children's allegiance to Jessel and Quint colours our perception of them and of their actions. As in the canonical text and most of the adaptations inspired by it, the relationship between Flora and Jessel is secondary to that of Miles and Quint. The latter becomes, according to Cunningham, synonymous with Britten's challenge to 'the rule-making heterosexual world of governess, school and church' that seeks to stifle and to define 'boyish same sex yearnings and adult gay male desires' as 'aberrant and heterodox': Miles functions here as 'compliant boyish other', a 'gender-crossed Eve' and a sexually knowing child who seduces Adam/Quint in the Edenic gardens of Bly (2–3). Whether, at Britten's insistence, the insertion of a sexually loaded Latin recitation by Miles during his lessons with the governess serves only as his means of intimidation and covert rebellion or as something more revealing is open to debate. His litany of these masculine, Latinate verbs of double meaning – 'clunis'/anus; 'caulis'/penis, and so on (2.6) – may be seen as simply a school boy prank, but such interjections afford Miles a certain level of sexual knowledge – a knowledge that invites us to question his position as innocent child. And yet, at earlier points in the narrative, Miles self-questioning tone – 'You see, I am bad, I am bad, aren't I?' (1.8) – speaks of his uncertainty, his vulnerability. The god-like status of Quint and the relentless pressure he exerts on Miles in Act 2, Scenes 4, 5 and 8 further suggest that Miles is more coerced victim of abuse than the sexually aware seducer of Oates' re-visionist adaptation. The sexual tension mounts as Quint warns Miles 'not to betray [their] secrets' (2.8), but in this adaptation the level of Miles' collusion remains an unknown. Even his closing line is tantalizingly ambiguous: he appears to be naming Quint as the 'devil' he has been forced to contend with, but he is just as likely to be naming his coercive governess.

In each of the re-visionist adaptations under consideration in this section, the audience is asked to confront what James merely hints at in 'The Turn of the Screw'. Our ongoing cultural anxieties related to matters of paedophilia are brought to the fore in both Oates' short story and Britten's opera, and each adaptation's disquieting deconstruction of the innocence of childhood continues to inform our relationship with the canonical text. By the time James was writing his gothic tale, romantic perceptions of childhood innocence were on the wane, but many of James' contemporary reviewers continued to 'wrestl[e] uncomfortably with the scandalous implication of child sexuality' (McCollum 39–40); the moral panic surrounding such matters persists well into the twenty-first century, making James tale and its moral dilemmas as current for today's audience as it was for his Victorian readership.

'The Turn of the Screw': A radical rethink (*The Others* and *The Orphanage*)

Unlike classic adaptations which signal their relationship with a precursor text or re-visionist adaptations that seek to redefine the source text's dominant discourse, works like *The Others* and *The Orphanage* establish a far more tangential relationship with Henry James' 'The Turn of the Screw'.

These films function as subconscious 'appropriation' rather than affirmed 'adaptation' and their engagement with James' novella takes us to the limits of what may be defined as adaptation. Like Sandra Goldbacher (*The Governess*), Alejandro Amenábar, screenwriter-director of *The Others*, and J. A. Bayona, director of *The Orphanage*, offer no definitive statement of adaptive intent. However, as with the re-visionist adaptations of Harding, Oates and Britten, these films present their audiences with alternative ways of engaging with 'The Turn of the Screw', refracting and doubling its gothic tropes and exploring once more the cultural anxieties embedded in it. Here, the focus shifts from sexual transgression, inferred in the novella and fleshed out in Oates' story and Britten's opera, to maternal transgression: James' psychologically disturbed mother-surrogate governess and the female protagonists of these films present us with haunted (and haunting) mother figures, taking us further into the disquieting territory of infanticide and suicide and adding to the critique of the 'innocent' child. Each text's mother figure traverses a similar generic landscape on a dubious quest to 'save' the children, and each text unpicks the threads of obsession. Most importantly they explore our unspeakable primal fear of children, not as demons but as achingly vulnerable individuals who bring with them a burden of care that evokes parental anxiety, a dread of loss, feelings of inadequacy, of guilt. These protagonists enact the unthinkable, subverting the role of nurturing mother and becoming instead (whether directly or indirectly) agents of their children's demise. The shared narrative connections here are tentative, but there is a mutual synergy of ideas and positions: each film text's debt to James is less obvious yet no less resonant than that of many adaptations of James' enigmatic tale.

'The Turn of the Screw' forms one of a number of intertextual references at work in both films. Amenábar and Bayona make no direct claim for their films' relationship with James' tale, though both directors have spoken of its influence. Bayona cites it as a text that informs his desire to produce a narrative full of ambiguity that can be 'read' as fantasy or in realist mode as 'a portrait of a woman who loses her mind' (femail.com.au), while Amenábar acknowledges his film's debt to Clayton's *The Innocents* (Tobias) and thus by inference James' novella. The literary gothic tropes of James' story have been translated to the genre of cinematic horror in numerous period costume dramatizations since the fifties but like Clayton, Amenábar and Bayona adopt a decidedly subtle approach to the horror genre. Despite being marketed as mainstream horror in their theatrical trailers, *The Others* and *The Orphanage* are decidedly understated, slow burn psychological horror films that reference the style of classic films of Hollywood's Golden Age rather than the schlock horror films of contemporary cinema. Amenábar's cinematic treatment of his horror screenplay incorporates a gothic, noir-like atmosphere and is influenced by forties B horror films from the RKO stable, while Bayona aims for a more realist, 'classic' style, reminiscent of sixties horror films, *The Innocents* and Robert Wise's *The Haunting* (1963) (femail. com.au). Both films, however, connect with the RKO films of the forties in terms of their treatment of the problematic female. RKO films bring us into what Barry Langford terms an 'unsettling proximity with the limits of this rational "civilized" world's ability to tame and control the irrational', (163) and herein lies the point of contact between 'The Turn of the Screw', *The Orphanage* and *The Others*: both are 'unsettling' horror narratives that explore, through their psychologically unhinged protagonists, our inablility to 'tame and control the irrational', whether related to matters of sexual transgression, infanticide, suicide or fantastical 'sightings' of ghosts.

Literary gothic fantasy is a site for exploration of all that remains unspoken – 'the forbidden, the repressed, imagination and desire' (Higson 205) and the female gothic deals specifically in fears of entrapment within the domestic confines of 'home' and the female body (Smith and Wallace quoting Ellen Moer 1). Like the literary gothic, horror cinema explores repressed desire, especially within the patriarchal institution of the 'nuclear family' (Barry Keith Grant 4). It invariably occupies domestic spaces and defines 'home' as a place of horror, where threats abound, not only from the institution of 'family' but from the psyche of those bound by its constraints (Langford 168). If cinematic horror is about the exploration of the 'boundaries of sanity and madness, of the conscious and the unconscious', 'the boundaries' between 'life and death' (158), then during the course of *The Others* and *The Orphanage*, protagonists Grace and Laura are precariously positioned at the precipice of all three. Grace is synonymous with those females who people nineteenth-century female gothic tales. She is placed at the centre of a dysfunctional family, trapped by her domestic situation and marooned in a country house of Bly-like proportions with children who are unable to surface in daylight and a husband who has abandoned her for the heroics of war. At the film's closing reveal we learn that her repressed desire to escape surfaces in acts of infanticide and suicide, but the ironic twist (or 'turn of the screw') in this tale is that Grace remains trapped in her incorporeal body. Just as Bly becomes the site of Victorian moral decay, synonymous with the dysfunctional family, where spectres may or may not haunt the living, the dysfunctional homes at the centre of these film narratives become horror cinema's abject space, full of dangerous uncertainty (England 355). In *The Others*, the gothic fog that surrounds this space is, we later learn, part of Grace's psychosis, a shield to protect her from the truth of her now incorporeal existence until the film's final reveal. However, while this Bly-like 'home' is a place of entrapment for Grace, for Laura the 'home' she returns to is associated with her past, and it becomes the place she chooses to remain in. Notions of 'home' are complicated and multi-layered in *The Orphanage*; 'home', asserts Bayona becomes synonymous with 'the trauma of separation' in the past, and with the 'threat of an imminent separation' (femail.com.au). Though her initial fears align her with the protagonists of the female gothic and entrapment, fairy tale allusions to Peter Pan, to Neverland and to her role as the narrative's 'Wendy yearning for her Lost Boy' (IndieLONDON) position her in the final moments with idyllic, eternal images of mothering and 'home', subverting expectation and taking us beyond the boundaries of horror and into the realms of maternal melodrama.

Both mothers are to a certain extent constructed as the 'over-possessive mother' of gothic literature, 'not trapped but entrapping' (Higson 210). Yet they are not unequivocally 'monstrous' mothers, despite the consequences of their zeal, the excesses of their 'protection' and their role in the deaths of children. Their desire to protect children in their care at all cost constructs each as the nurturing 'angel in the house'. Grace, as excessively possessive mother, conforms to Barbara Creed's notions of the abject 'monstrous feminine' of the horror genre, but her behaviour, and that of Laura, may also be defined as normative. They are portrayed as caring mothers who evoke audience empathy. As with other maternal horror films like *Beloved* (1998), there is no 'demonization' of the mother figure; instead, in keeping with a move away from the classic representation of ghosts as objects of fear, they are set up as women for whom we should 'grieve' (Bruce 23). Laura's all consuming love leads to her mental instability and ultimately to her act of suicide but it is constructed as an empowering act that in her mind reunites her with her son and with the orphans of her past. Grace becomes a less punitive mother in the final screen text; scenes from the original screenplay in which she relentlessly beats her disobedient daughter are cut, and Anne's lone bible recitation punishment for being a wilful child is curtailed from a month to a matter of days (though there remains here a disturbing echo of Jane Eyre's Lowood moment when punished by the hypocritical Brocklehurst). Here, as in *Beloved*, the kind of body horror associated with Creed's monstrous feminine is projected onto the figure of the child rather than the mother: Anne's bodily transformation into a wrinkled old woman who speaks with a child's voice provides the film's only moment of terrifying horror, and it is child ghost Tomas in his disturbing sackcloth mask that provokes a stock horror response in *The Orphanage*.

Surveillance of others and each protagonists' search for visibility form another crucial point of contact between *The Others*, *The Orphanage* and 'The Turn of the Screw'. The title of Amenabar's film echoes the novella's reference to 'the others' and relates to both the story's newly dead, the long term dead and the living intruders, all of whom are engaged in acts of surveillance. Servants Lydia, Mr Tuttle and Bertha Mills (who resides in the attic and whose name resonates with that of Bertha Mason) become watchers of ambivalent intent, only later revealed as benevolent ghosts, sent to help Grace on her journey towards self-knowledge; the intruders watch from a distance, through acts of mesmerism and séances that connect the film text to the nineteenth century's fascination with spiritualism; Grace, unaware of her status as newly dead and much to the chagrin of daughter Anne, watches over her children with obsessive care, as if her existence as well as theirs depended on it. Her visibility, however, comes only through her ghostly presence: like James' Quint and Jessel, she is a ghost, herself an object of surveillance whose exorcism is desired by the living within the narrative. In *The Orphanage*, Laura enacts a similarly obsessive surveillance of her AIDS afflicted adopted son, Simon, and she too becomes the object of surveillance, watched by the ghostly inhabitants of the home she has returned to at the start of the film [female.com.au interview], but whereas Grace resists her liminal visibility Laura embraces it as a way to reunite with her son and with the orphans she left behind. She instigates contact with the ghosts who haunt the house, she learns how to play their games once more as a means to finding her son, of healing the separation from him and from her past, and as advised by the medium, she learns that she must 'believe' in the presence of ghosts before she can 'see' them.

Bayona's film follows Laura firstly on her journey towards a realization that her son is dead, and secondly on her quest to be reunited with him. Amenábar's film is a 'journey for Grace and her children toward light as a form of knowledge' and it is this premise that shapes the narrative (Amenábar in Fuchs). Journeying towards the light becomes a visual, metaphorical conceit around which *The Others* is designed. It is a film that is about not 'what happens but how it happens' (Amenábar in Fuchs): from its opening moments, the story builds to the point where Grace can acknowledge not only her earlier acts of infanticide and suicide but also the fact that *they* are the ghostly spectres who haunt this tale. Ostensibly, the films present reality as Grace and Laura experience it, but as in James' novella, the text is littered with clues as to the unreliability of these female protagonists. Like the governess, Grace and Laura conform to the template of 'quest heroine': they have a 'burden'; they are 'tested' and forced to do 'battle' with the forces of evil; they face 'defeat in victory, and victory in defeat' (Namwali Serpell 228). However, the quests of Grace and Laura focus indirectly on a search for meaning. All are fantasists but in *The Others* and *The Orphanage* the riddles of each narrative are solved, and the solutions become part of each story's design. Despite the initial possibility that the belligerent, wilful, mischievous Anne is the narrative's 'evil' child – aligned with the evil potential of the novella's Miles rather than Flora – eventually, it is her 'truth' that is affirmed. Our faith in the veracity of the adult at the centre of the tale is undermined at the climactic moment of the story's disturbing reveal. Amenábar sets up a series of puzzles and loaded cues along the narrative path, placing his audience in the role of detective, especially on second viewing, and in this sense he emulates James' penchant for ambiguity. The ambiguities found in the film are far more pronounced than those found in Amenábar's original screenplay: many scenes are cut, much of the dialogue is excised, backstory and exegesis are removed. Like James' novella, the final film exploits the gaps and the silences, leaving the viewer to ponder its narrative possibilities. Similarly, in *The Orphanage*, we are positioned with Laura, whose psychological regression into the past is a form of ambivalent escapism as she creates a fantasy world in which she lives happily ever after, reunited with Simon and her former playmates, and functioning as an eternal mother figure. We follow her psychological 'truth' rather than the 'reality' presented by the detective, by Carlos, or by her realization that Simon's death is caused in part by her own inability to pay heed to *his* stories. Bayona's treatment of the scene in which Laura commits suicide, with its soft focus on a smiling Laura surrounded by children, is constructed as a wish fulfilment fantasy rather than as the conclusion to a horror story.

The camera positions us with Grace in a direct manner, inferring from the outset that the narrative will be filtered through her experiences. We hear her comforting voice playing over sepia-tinted sketches; her opening lines – 'Now children, are you sitting comfortably? Then I'll begin ... ' – reference the iconic BBC children's story time broadcast *Listen with Mother* (and by inference *Watch with Mother*) and function as a loaded cultural signifier of all things motherly and reassuring. However, what she relates is the biblical creation myth rather than the anticipated fairy tale, and the telling mismatch between narration and images – images which reference moments from the story we are about to see unfold on screen as well as the creation story – immediately raises questions about truth-telling and fantasy. Whilst this opening aligns Grace with all things motherly, it also aligns her with make-believe, and with biblical fantasies that we later see Grace holds as biblical truth. She is constructed as religiously devout, but here she aligns her biblical truths with 'a beautiful story' and the images scribe her children into that story in Hansel and Gretel mode, holding hands as they walk through the woods. The distinction between narratives based on truth and those based on fantasy becomes of central concern to this film and to *The Orphanage*. At a later point, when storytelling agency passes to Anne, whose sketches of 'the intruders' tell a different tale to that of her mother, the audience becomes increasingly aware of Grace as flawed storyteller. In this, she mirrors James' governess: the dubious authority of the memoir through which the governess tells her tale, and the many problems associated with first person narration in the medium of cinema become part of the conundrum in each. However, here we enter a story which is already in progress, its narrative momentum actively encouraged by the interventions of the newly arrived servants, and daughter Anne. There are three distinct realities at work in *The Others*: 'living, dead, newly dead' (Burkholder-Mosco and Wendy Carse 220) and though the story is filtered in the main through Grace, its other dead characters are instrumental in moving the story on. As with Oates short story and Britten's opera, we are positioned in this tale with its ghosts, even if unwittingly so until its final reveal.

The Others cuts swiftly from its reassuring opening moments to a canted close up of Grace's face as she lets out a blood-curdling scream on waking from a nightmare into what we assume is 'reality'. It is not until the closing moments of the film that we learn that this is, instead, her point of return to the moment she has killed her children, committed suicide, and entered the afterlife. From here onwards, Grace journeys back towards the metaphorical light of self-knowledge and truth. The audience is able to gather clues littered within the narrative, as the servants steadfastly lead a reluctant Grace to a point of recognition. The fog-bound Bly-like house and its gardens are devoid of light, and the children's light sensitivity becomes a rationale for keeping it at bay. Grace claims that 'The only thing that moves here is the light. But it changes everything', and this visual conceit plays out across the narrative, as chinks of light invade the space both literally, and metaphorically. Her obsession with shutting out the light becomes part of her quest, and as the light begins to physically enter the house, Grace, her children and the audience experience a growing realization of what she has done. There are more obvious clues as to what has happened in the screenplay; Anne, for example, asks her mother directly if she would ever contemplate killing them, and Grace forces Anne to learn by rote the biblical story of Abraham's infanticide, but such loaded inclusions are edited out of the film, leaving much of the storytelling to plot points in which the light literally enters screen space.

The closing of curtains, the locking of doors, the noir-like atmosphere that pervades the house all serve to create a fortress-like feel to this carefully, obsessively preserved environment – an environment that is ultimately challenged by the living who take down the curtains and literally let in the light, but more importantly by moments within the narrative that bring Grace closer to a psychological unveiling of her past. We are never sure, for example, whether the children's light-sensitivity is a reality or a metaphorical sign of Grace's state of mind: as Grace draws closer to the truth, Mrs Mills suggests the children may no longer be affected by the light, either because they are dead, or because their 'condition' has always been symptomatic of their mother's delusions. There are also distressing scenes which allude to Grace's acts of infanticide; on separate occasions both Grace and Anne re-enact the command to 'stop breathing', foreshadowing the revelations of the séance as the film draws to its close. Grace is unwilling to confront her transgressions but at such moments the metaphorical light that has been employed as a construct throughout the telling of this tale seeps into her psyche. The metaphorical dawning of the light becomes literal during the final confrontation between the living and the dead, as we witness pages torn and cast into the air by an invisible force where seconds before we see Grace. Whilst James' tale ends on an ambiguous note, *The Others* presents a resolution that is part of the story's design.

Where 'The Turn of the Screw' ends at the discomforting point of Miles' death, both Amenabar and Bayona introduce a structural and generic detour from Gothic Horror to Maternal Melodrama – in a style again reminiscent of *Beloved* – in the closing moments of each film. In *The Others* the fog dissipates and the screen is saturated with colour and natural light, signifying the end of Grace's journey – an end that works in contradiction to her avowed quest to protect her children yet serves to reaffirm their reintegration as 'family' (albeit a ghostly family) in a decidedly melodramatic mode. It functions as a moment of release for Grace and her children, and the closing mantra – 'This house is ours. This house is ours' – brings us full circle to the comforting 'Listen with Mother' scenario that forms our point of entry into this tale. The final shot of Grace and the children framed by a window and the closing shot of a 'For Sale' sign, suggest they will remain indefinitely, and that the 'intruders' will continue to arrive, lending the narrative a cyclical dimension of the kind so often employed in adaptations of 'The Turn of the Screw'. The closing moments of *The Orphanage* resemble the opening overtures of *The Others* with Laura as Wendy-like storyteller, surrounded by her Neverland children.

The ghostly mothers of Amenábar's *The Others* and Bayona's *The Orphanage* are haunted by and in turn haunt James' gothic horror story, refracting and re-visioning its thematic concerns through the creative prism of adaptation. Just as Sandra Goldbacher's *The Governess* (1998) has a tenuous relationship with Charlotte Brontë's novel, signalled by the ways in which it explores issues of female identity and class rather than by any overt identification as a film text that 'adapts' *Jane Eyre*, these film narratives play with the story's horror tropes by exploring our unspeakable primal fear of children, not as demons but as disquietingly fragile dependents who bring with them an unbearable duty of care, and an all consuming dread of loss.

Drawing parallels across texts: Exercises related to 'The Turn of the Screw', *Great Expectations*, *Jane Eyre* and adaptations of these canonical works

Drawing in the threads

Part one

Our exercises in this section focus on the ways in which texts (both 'source' and adaptation) feed into and off of each other within a wider cultural context, creating webs of meaning across a body of work.

Step one

Cora Kaplan argues that certain Victorian texts have acquired a mythic status in contemporary society: such texts are said to provide a fertile site for further exploration of ongoing cultural anxieties related to matters of sexuality, identity, scientific progress, religious belief, urban growth, and so on (133).

Consider the following:

- To what extent can we define *Jane Eyre*, *Great Expectations* and 'The Turn of the Screw' as Victorian texts of 'mythic status'?
- What 'ongoing cultural anxieties' do these texts explore?

Step two

Texts that evolve as they are adapted 'permit a redefinition of anxiety-provoking issues' related to matters of class, race, sexuality, gendered identity, social justice/injustice and so on. Across all three of our canonical 'source' texts and their adaptive counterparts, there are 'anxiety-provoking issues' of a similar nature: all three serve as what Brian A. Rose terms 'cultural text[s]' – texts that evolve *as* they are adapted (2), and all three share certain thematic preoccupations, certain character types, and tropes we can identify as 'gothic'.

- Try to identify at least three features shared by *Jane Eyre*, *Great Expectations* and 'The Turn of the Screw' (e.g. the 'mad' woman, the gothic house, class).
- Now select ONE of the features, and map out the way that feature is translated in at least ONE adaptation of each canonical text (e.g. the 'mad' woman in *Wide Sargasso Sea*, in Alfonso Cuaron's *Great Expectations* and in 'Accursed Inhabitants of the House of Bly', *The Others* or *Florence & Giles*).

Step three

Susana Onega and Christian Gutleben argue that canonical texts from the Victorian era and their adaptive counterparts are engaged in a two-way process (or dialogue) termed 'refraction'. They assume that there is 'a dialectic relation' between the canonical text and the adaptations it 'inspir[es]'; 'reflections of a previous text' are present in the adaptation, but the adaptation also serves to shed 'new light on the original work by its rewriting' (7–8). By urging us to place the emphasis on the way in which *each* text 'sheds light on the other', Onega and Gutleben are inviting us to view neither as the 'source' text (9).

Now go back to Step two and your chosen canonical text/adaptation/shared feature, and think about the following:

- How does the treatment of that shared feature differ when adapted? In what ways does its treatment remain the same?
- Does the medium into which it is adapted have any influence here?
- Does the cultural/temporal/geographical placement of the narrative influence the treatment of that shared feature?
- How does its treatment in the adaptation 'refract' and 'shed light upon' the 'source' text?

Finally, try to develop a substantial response to issues raised by the following questions:

- To what extent do you agree with Onega and Gutleben's assertion that the adaptation serves to shed 'new light on the original work'?
- To what extent does the adaptation serve as a 'cultural text' that 'permit[s] a redefinition of anxiety-provoking issues'?

Part two

In this part of the exercise we are widening out our field of enquiry in an effort to examine how shared traits are adapted across a body of work (i.e. our three canonical texts/their collective adaptations).

Step one

We have noted in Part one some of the ways in which all three of the canonical texts we are studying connect, and you may have already identified one or more of the following points of contact, but highlight those you have yet to consider in close detail:

- The orphaned child
- The brooding, male romance figure
- Patriarchal figureheads
- Housekeepers
- The 'mad' woman
- The sexually repressed female
- The gothic country mansion

- Transgressive sexuality
- Present/absent father figures
- Towers within gothic houses
- The housekeeper
- Class and social mobility
- Fairy tale tropes

Now select ONE of the above (making sure you choose a different feature from the one you have worked with in Part one), and this time, trace the ways in which that feature has a presence in a range of adaptive types from EACH of the canonical texts. (Try to explore at least THREE adaptations per canonical text.)

Step two

Think about that feature and its treatment across your selected range of adaptations:

- In what ways does its treatment remain the same across this body of work?
- How does the treatment of that shared feature differ when translated across this body of work?
- Does the cultural/temporal/geographical placement of the narrative influence the treatment of that shared feature?
- Does the medium into which it is adapted have any influence here?
- Does its new audience influence its treatment?
- Does its treatment here invite us to re-engage with the canonical text in a different way?

Step three

As you have worked your way through these exercises, you have been gathering lots of ideas and illustrations that will help you to approach the writing of an essay related to adaptation studies. One of the best ways of coming to terms with what essay questions are actually asking of you, is to engage in the process of devising them.

Drawing on the above and on your wider knowledge of the theories that underpin adaptation studies:

- devise at least THREE essay titles that focus on the shared feature you have been exploring and
- plan a response to ONE of your essay questions.

Part three

When we study a body of texts and their adaptations, certain commonalities emerge as demonstrated in Parts one and two. The gothic/pseudo gothic house emerges as one of the most enduring motifs employed across the texts studied thus far.

Step one

You may have already identified a number of the following, but highlight those you have yet to consider:

- Satis House (in *Great Expectations* and 1946, 1999, 2011, 2012 screen adaptations)
- Paradise Perduto
- Thornfield Hall (in *Jane Eyre* and 1944, 2006, 2011 screen adaptations)
- Manderley
- Holland's plantation house
- Wilkinson's Isle of Skye mansion
- House of Bly (in 'The Turn of the Screw', Oates short story, Britten's opera, *The Innocents*, 2009 TV movie adaptations)
- Blithe House (*Florence & Giles*)
- Stewart mansion (*The Others*)
- The orphanage (*The Orphanage*)

Is there anything else that some of these texts share in common in terms of their architecture? (Think of the symbolic as well as the literal implications.)

Step two

If we consider the gothic spaces within these gothic houses, many employ the gothic tower that we most readily associate with Brontë's *Jane Eyre*. Many also associate the narrative's female protagonist with this tower, though its symbolic resonances vary from text to text. For some it remains symbolic of incarceration at a literal/metaphorical/psychological level; for others it becomes a haven, a refuge, a place that challenges the norm, and opens up other possibilities.

How is the relationship between women and the gothic tower constructed in each of the following instances:

- Rebecca's West Wing at Manderley in *Rebecca* (novel and forties film)
- Cavendish's tower in *The Governess*
- Jessica's tower in *I Walked with a Zombie*

- Miss Giddens and the tower at Bly in *The Innocents*
- Florence's secret tower in *Florence & Giles*
- Miss Havisham's rooms in Satis House (1946, 1999, 2011, 2012 screen adaptations)

Now consider:

- To what extent does each permutation of towers and women play with the gothic genre?
- To what extent does each permutation of towers and women address the politics of sexuality and gender?
- What cultural anxieties are being constantly revisited and revised across this body of work?

Step three

Plan and write a 3,000 word response to the following essay question, drawing on your notes from the above exercises, and/or from exercises undertaken in Parts one and two:

By studying a *body* of work rather than an individual 'source' text and its various adaptations, we open up new ways of exploring the complex relationships that underpin the practice of adaptation. To what extent do you agree with this assertion?

Make sure that you contextualize your discussion by:

- engaging with a range of theories that support and/or refute the above statement;
- demonstrate your knowledge and understanding of a body of work and the connections between the texts you are grouping together; and
- employ specific illustrations to support your line of argument.

References

Amenábar, Alejandro. Draft Screenplay of *The Others*. Trans. Walter Leonard. Sept. 1998. *Screenplay Explorer*. 2 Nov. 2010. Web. 15 May 2012. 3–118.

Archibald, William and Truman Capote. Draft Screenplay of *The Innocents*. London: Achilles Film Productions, 1961. Print.

BBC Press Office. 'Press Release: The Turn on the Screw on BBC One'. *BBC*. 17 Aug. 2009. Web. 10 Jan. 2010.

Botting, Fred. *Gothic*. London and New York: Routledge, 1996. Print.

Brown, Monika. 'Film Music as Sister Art: Adaptations of "The Turn of the Screw"'. *Mosaic: A Journal of Interdisciplinary Study* 31.1 (1998): 61–81. Print.

Bruce, Susan. 'Sympathy for the Dead: [G]hosts, Hostilities and Mediums in Alejandro Amenábar's *The Others* and Postmortem Photography'. Discourse 27.2/3 (2005): 23–40. Print.

Burkeholder-Mosco, Nicole and Wendy Carse. '"Wondrous Material to Play On": Children as Sites of Gothic Liminality in "The Turn of the Screw", *The Innocents*, and *The Others*'. *Studies in Humanities* 32.2 (2005): 201–220. Print.

Cardwell, Sarah. *Adaptation Revisited: Television and the Classic Novel*. Manchester: Manchester University Press, 2002. Print.

Creed, Barbara. *The Monstrous Feminine: Film, Feminism, Psychoanalysis*. London and New York: Routledge, 1993. Print.

Cunningham, Valerie. 'Filthy Britten'. *The Guardian*. 5 Jan. 2002: Culture. Print.

Desblache, Lucille. 'The Turn of the Text? Opera Libretto and Translation: Appropriation, Adaptation and Transcoding in Benjamin Britten's *The Turn of the Screw* and *Owen Wingrave*'. *Quaderns de Filologia, Estudis Literaris* 13 (2008): 105–123. Print.

England, Marcia. 'Breached Bodies and Home Invasions: Horrific Representations of the Feminized Body and Home'. *Gender, Place and Culture: A Journal of Feminist Geography* 13.4 (2006): 353–363. Print.

femail.com.au. 'Juan Antono Batona *The Orphanage* Interview'. *femail.com.au*. 2008. Web. 8 Jul. 2012.

Fuchs, Cynthia. 'Interview with Alejandro Amenábar, Director of *The Others*'. *PopMatters*. Web. 20 Jun. 2012.

Grant, Barry Keith. *The Dread of Difference: Gender and the Horror Film*. Austin, TX: University of Texas Press. 1996. Print.

Halliwell, M. 'The Master's Voice: Henry James and Opera'. *Henry James on Stage and Screen*. Ed. John R Bradley. New York: Palgrave, 2000. 23–34. Print.

Hanson, Ellis. 'Screwing with Children in Henry James'. *GLQ* 9.3 (2003): 367–391. Print.

Harding, John. *Florence & Giles*. London: Blue Door, 2010. Print.

Higson, Andrew. 'Gothic Fantasy as Art Cinema: The Secret of Female Desire in The Innocents'. *Gothick Origins and Innovations*. Eds. Allan Lloyd Smith and Victor Sage. Amsterdam: Rodopi, 1994. 204–216. Print.

Hoeveler, Diane. 'Postgothic Fiction: Joyce Carol Oates Turns the Screw on Henry James'. *Studies in Short Fiction* 35.4 (1998): 355–371. Print.

Horne, P., ed. *Henry James: A Life in Letters*. Harmondsworth: Penguin Press, 1999. Print.

IndieLONDON. Web. 28 Jun. 2012.

James, Henry. 'The Art of Fiction'. *Longman's Magazine* 4 (September 1884). Print.

James, Henry. *The Novels and Tales of Henry James.* Vol. 12. London: C. Scribner & Sons. 1908.

James, Henry. *The Turn of the Screw.* London: Penguin Books, 1994 [1898]. Print.

Kaplan, Cora. *Victoriana: Histories, Fictions, Criticism.* Edinburgh: Edinburgh University Press, 2007. Print.

Langford, Barry. *Film Genre: Hollywood and Beyond.* Edinburgh: Edinburgh University Press, 2005. Print.

McCollum, Jenn. 'The Romance of Henry James's Female Pedophile'. *MP An Online Feminist Journal* 3.1 (2010): 39–56. Print.

Mitchell, Lee Clark. 'Based on the Novel by Henry James'. *Henry James Goes to the Movies.* Ed. Susan Griffin. Kentucky: University of Kentucky Press, 2002. 281–304. Print.

Nadel, Alan. 'Ambassadors, from an Imaginary "Elsewhere": Cinematic Convention and the Jamesian Sensibility'. *Henry James Goes to the Movies.* Ed. Susan Griffin. Lexington, KY: University of Kentucky Press, 2002. 193–209. Print.

Namwali Serpell, C. 'Mutual Exclusion, Oscillation, and Ethical Projection in The Crying Lot 49 and "The Turn of the Screw": Uncertainty, Affordance, Modes'. *Narrative* 16.3 (2008): 221–255. Print.

Newman, Beth. 'Getting Fixed: Feminine Identity and Scopic Crisis in "The Turn of the Screw"'. *Novel: A Forum on Fiction* 26.1 (1992): 43–63. Print.

Oates, Joyce Carol. *Haunted: Tales of the Grotesque.* New York and London: Plume, 1995. Print.

Onega, Susana and Christian Gutleben, eds. *Refracting the Canon in Contemporary British Literature and Film.* Amsterdam and New York: Rodopi, 2004. Print.

Petry, Alice Hall. 'Jamesian Parody, *Jane Eyre* and "The Turn of the Screw"'. *Modern Language Studies* 13.4 (1983): 61–78. Print.

Piper, Myfanwy. *The Turn of the Screw: Libretto.* London: Boosey and Hawkes, 1955. Print.

Raw, Laurence. 'Hollywoodizing Henry James: Jack Clayton's *The Innocents'*. *The Henry James Review* 25.1 (2004): 97–108. Print.

Raw, Laurence. *Adapting Henry James to the Screen: Gender, Fiction, and Film.* Lanham, MD, Toronto and Oxford: Scarecrow Press, 2006. Print.

Recchia, Edward. 'An Eye for an Eye: Adapting Henry James's "The Turn of the Screw" to the Screen'. *Literature Film Quarterly* 5.1 (1987): 28–35. Print.

Rose, Brian A. *Jekyll and Hyde Adapted: Dramatizations of Cultural Anxiety.* Westport, CT: Greenwood, 1996. Print.

Rowe, John Carlos. 'Henry James and Globalisation'. *The Henry James Review* 24 (2003): 205–214. Print.

Smith, Andrew and Diana Wallace, 'The Female Gothic: Then and Now'. *Gothic Studies* 6.1 (2004): 1–7. Print.

Stafford, Jeff. 'The Innocents (1961)'. TCM (*Turner Classic Movies*). n.d. Web. 3 Jun. 2012.

Sutcliffe, Tom. 'Last Night's TV'. *The Independent*. 31 Dec. 2009. Web. 30 Jan. 2010.

Tobias, Scott. 'Alejandro Amenábar Interview'. *A. V. Club*. 8 Aug. 2001. Web. 21 Jun. 2010.

Warren, Adrian. 'Things That Go Clunk in the Night'. *PopMatters*. 28 Mar. 2010 Web. 20 Jun. 2010.

Wilson, Val. 'Black and White and Shades of Grey: Ambiguity in *The Innocents*'. *Henry James on Stage and Screen*. Ed. John R Bradley. Houndsmill: Palgrave, 2000. 103–118.

Filmography

The Haunting of Helen Walker. Dir. Tom McLoughlin. 1995. DVD.

The Innocents. Dir. Jack Clayton. 1961. DVD.

Le Tour D'Ecrou. Dir. Raymond Rouleau. 1974. DVD.

The Nightcomers. Dir. Michael Winner. 1971. DVD.

The Orphanage. Dir. J. A. Bayona. 2007. DVD.

The Others. Dir. Alejandro Amenábar. 2007. DVD.

Presence of Mind. Dir. Antoni Aloy. 1999. DVD.

The Turn of the Screw. Dir. Dan Curtis. 1974. DVD.

The Turn of the Screw. Dir. Rusty Lemorande. 1992. DVD.

The Turn of the Screw. Dir. Ben Bolt. 1999. DVD.

The Turn of the Screw. Dir. Katie Mitchell. 2004. DVD.

The Turn of the Screw. Dir. Tim Fywell. 2009. DVD.

5

Adapting *The Great Gatsby*: Contesting the Boundaries of Classification

Like the realist texts of the nineteenth century studied thus far, F. Scott Fitzgerald's *The Great Gatsby* preserves a moment in time that is contemporaneous to its author. It encapsulates the hedonistic Roaring Twenties of America, shifting from a nineteenth-century preoccupation with empire building to a decidedly twentieth-century sensibility, fuelled by consumerist mass culture, immigrant social mobility and the elusive pursuit of the American dream. It also shares with the realist texts we have been focusing on, not only its canonical status but its desire to explore notions of seemingly doomed love across an insurmountable class divide. Yet, as with his compatriot, Henry James, Fitzgerald's writing style moves away from nineteenth-century realism and the weighty tomes produced by its authors to a Modernist mode of storytelling, replete with fragmentary images and dislocated narrative trajectories.

Though now considered an 'aesthetically authoritative' and 'canonically "modernist" text' (Porter 143), *The Great Gatsby*'s promotion to the canon of American literature was not instantly attained. Fitzgerald's earlier works (*This Side of Paradise* 1919; *The Beautiful and the Damned* 1921) were considered far too sentimental. On the advice of his literary peers, he adopted a more controlled, distanced approach to the writing of *The Great Gatsby*, and while not a commercial success initially, it was heralded by poet T. S. Eliot as 'the first step forward American fiction [had] taken since Henry James' (Eliot qtd in Kerr 424). By the mid-forties, after Fitzgerald's death, the novel had gained not only canonical status but a sustained reputation as the quintessential American novel. Like Herman Melville's nineteenth-century classic, *Moby Dick*, it is afforded an almost mythical status in the canon of American literature, and its thematic concerns explore ongoing cultural anxieties that relate to matters of class, social mobility and identity. Fitzgerald and fellow Modernist writers of the era (Ernest Hemingway, Eliot, Ezra Pound, Edmund Wilson) viewed popular culture as a threat to serious 'high art' forms; yet Fitzgerald's work, unlike that of many Modernist writers of the early twentieth century, crosses over from 'high art' to the populist mainstream and has been adapted on a scale akin to the realist novelists of the nineteenth century. *The Great Gatsby*, published in 1925, remains his most (posthumously) successful novel and has been prescribed reading within the American education system for decades.

Still read by scholars and mainstream audiences alike, it captures the spirit of a specific era in American history – an era of excess characterized by modernity and energized by consumerism that prophetically foreshadows the Great Depression of the late twenties. Fitzgerald's pointed inclusion of the symbolic Dr T. J. Eckleburg advertising billboard signals the spiritual vacuity and materialism at the heart of American society prior to Black Tuesday and the Wall Street Crash of 29 October 1929; god-like, it watches over the valley of ashes, a place that presents a stark contrast to the glitz and glamour of carefree high society life depicted in the mansions of West Egg and its genteel East Egg counterpart. Through his narrator's account of the rise and fall of Jay Gatsby (aka James Gatz), Fitzgerald ponders his contemporary United States, and critiques the illusory idealism enshrined in the American dream. Gatsby's rags to riches story builds upon the Horatio Alger myth, presenting us with a warped American fairy tale that ends in tragedy rather than the traditional 'happy ever after'. Alger's populist boys' own adventure stories follow an established narrative pattern: poor, rural farm boy moves to the 'city' where, through hard work, perseverance, righteous good fortune and the aid of a mentor, he attains the wealth and happiness seen as a central tenet of the American dream – a dream seemingly accessible to all. Gatsby's rise and his role as the orchestrator of grand parties designed to showcase his accumulated wealth is further invested with the weight of myth through allusions to Trimalchio, another self-made man of humble origins. These idealistic tales of upward mobility speak to notions of the United States as the land of opportunity and equality; however, in Fitzgerald's hands, they provide the template for a story of disillusionment in which the dream is exposed as nothing *more* than a fairy tale, anchored not in reality but in myth and ending in tragedy for his Alger 'hero'. By inverting the myth, Fitzgerald presents a critique of it, demonstrating its inherent flaws and revealing the class-based prejudices at the heart of American society. Gatsby is ultimately unable to transcend his humble origins, and his quest for self re-invention fails, despite his amassed wealth.

In the spirit of the consumerist age that Fitzgerald writes about, his Gatsby is an exercise in rebranding, from his mansion, a 'factual imitation of some Hotel de ville in Normandy' (Fitzgerald 5) to his wardrobe acquired by his 'man in England who buys [him] clothes' (59) that purposely set him apart – silver shirts, gold ties, pink suits – and the constructed photographic images of a Gatsby posing in exotic locales as he 'liv[es] like a rajah in all the capitals of Europe' (42). He courts a 'notoriety' of the kind that attaches to 'contemporary legends', creating a self-image 'that a seventeen year old' Jay Gatz 'would be likely to invent, and to this conception he [is] faithful to the end' (63), but Gatsby's innate, charming naivety is ultimately his downfall. In his carefully manufactured 'enchanted life' (42), Gatsby emerges anew from his humble origins, and though he has seemingly followed the Alger path to wealth, his 'poor boy made good' image is tainted by hints that his social mobility is the result of his criminal activities during this Prohibition era. Moreover, his ultimate goal remains unattainable without the final possession: Daisy Buchanan. She becomes his 'grail' (95), the fairy tale 'golden girl', a 'king's daughter' in a 'white palace' (127), whose love, and above all whose approval, is a prerequisite to Gatsby's successful transition from Gatz to Gatsby. Daisy holds the key to 'some idea of himself that had gone into loving [her]' (71), and all that follows becomes a regressive journey back to a nostalgic past that, like his image, has only an illusory currency. Central to Gatsby's realization of his newly constructed self, is the attainment of upper-class Daisy, as the prize possession that completes his re-invention: couched in narrative terms as a romance quest, the 'romance' is revealed instead as an integral part of his identity quest – an essential component in his rise from immigrant farm boy to accepted member of American society.

The illusory nature of the tale is further inscribed by its mode of delivery. Though divided into nine chapters and neatly contained within a three month timeframe, the narrative trajectory that begins with the wealthy, enigmatic Gatsby's appearance on the West Egg scene, and follows his doomed quest to become reunited with his lost love, Daisy, remains fragmentary, revolving as much around the disjointed reveals about Gatsby's past as the events of the moment. Meredith Goldsmith likens *The Great Gatsby* to the bildungsroman literature of the Harlem Renaissance and its preoccupation with ethnic migration (443) but while the novel has a similar vested interest in stories of the immigrant quest, its narration is filtered from a very different place – from the voice of an established Mid-Western man whose capacity to relate the rise and fall of Gatsby is influenced by his class position and, possibly, his sexuality. Events are filtered through the unreliable first person narrator, Nick Carraway, whose recount is inevitably coloured by his *own* nostalgic perception of them; what we are presented with is Carraway's own 're-invention' of Gatsby. Academic debate surrounding Carraway's infatuation with Gatsby abounds. For some, he is the disinterested observer, more witness than participant in the narrative he relates (Giltrow and Stouk 488); for others his 'public reserve hides private desires' of a homosexual nature (Kerr 412). The text is littered with lines that suggest Carraway's interest in his subject is more than that of distant observer: 'there was' he declares, 'something gorgeous about [Gatsby], some heightened sensitivity to the promises of life' (Fitzgerald 34), something that evoked 'the loud beating of [his] own heart' as he 'pulled the door against the incoming rain' (55). Adaptations construct the narrator in various ways, some giving greater prominence to his presence and persona, others maintaining that more observational stance, but with few exceptions, they focus on Gatsby as the tale's enigmatic romance figure, and it is his dream that fuels these narratives, though it is Nick Carraway's lyrical first person narration that transforms this 'devastated con man with romantic dreams into a mythic American hero' (Kerr 423).

Since its publication back in 1925, the novel has continued to attract the attention of adapters. For some, it remains in its adapted form a critique of American society and its counterfeit identity as the land of opportunity; for others, it is the novel's romance quest that takes centre stage; and for yet others, it is the lyricism of Fitzgerald's prose that is foregrounded in different and unexpected ways. As with many works of literary fiction, the novel was first adapted to the stage. One year after its release, playwright Owen Davis scripted a successful Broadway version that also prompted a silent film adaptation of the novel in the same year; directed by Howard Brennon from a screenplay by Elizabeth Meehan and Becky Gardiner, only one minute of sample scenes footage from the film remains. The recent rash of *Gatsby* adaptations suggests that its thematic preoccupations continue to speak to the cultural anxieties of our contemporary scene, but the hype surrounding the much anticipated 3D cinematic extravaganza from Baz Luhrmann in 2013 has fuelled its revival across a range of adaptive media. Despite the lyrical, illusory quality of Fitzgerald's imagistic prose and the difficulties posed by staging of some of its extravagant key scenes, there have been several stage productions of various types. Its adaptation to stage has also been stymied due to the proprietorial rights exercised by the Fitzgerald Estate: in recent years, only one stage production, directed by David Esbjornson and written by Simon Levy (first staged in 2006 and recently revived in 2012) was granted production rights in the United States. However, smaller contemporary productions have emerged, from a musical titled *The Great Gatsby* (2012), to an innovative and risky eight hour long production (The Electric Repair Service's *Gatz*) that stages every word from every scene of the novel. Though a stage play of such length seems doomed to failure, director John Collins' faith in the power of Fitzgerald's language and in the aptness of its content for our contemporary society proved well founded. First work-shopped back in 1999, *Gatz* was initially forced to tour abroad due to the Fitzgerald Estate's refusal to allow its production in the United States, but it was granted full performance rights in the United States in 2010 and opened in London to critical acclaim in 2012.

The Great Gatsby as musical theatre sounds a more likely prospect given that the Jazz Age is such an integral part of Fitzgerald's Roaring Twenties. Critical reception of Joe Evans' music and lyrics proved positive yet the show's production at the King's Head Theatre in London was inevitably constrained by the limitations of budget and stage space afforded by this small venue: perhaps a bigger, more extravagant stage production that fully exploits the musical potential through song *and* dance may prove a greater success. The popularity of the Gatsby narrative also extends specifically to choreographed adaptations: as with stage plays and musical renditions, the story does present a challenge to the adapter due to the complexities of its imagistic prose, but it also lends itself to a performative mode of expression, through its musical referencing of The Jazz Age, its hedonistic party scenes, its emphasis on costuming, celebrity culture and romance. Taking a lead from these aspects of the novel, as with its stage play adaptations, there have been numerous *Gatsby* ballets in recent years (Washington Ballet 2010, Northern Ballet 2013, Sacramento Ballet 2014 and Denis Matvienko's *Great Gatsby* in 2014). A BBC Radio Four broadcast of the novel in 2012 and a revival of John Harbison's 1999 Met opera production in 2012 again highlight not only the current interest in all things Gatsbyesque but its capacity to remain relevant in the similarly consumer-driven twenty-first century.

For some academics, the adaptation of *The Great Gatsby* to screen is 'an exercise in futility' since the 'multiple possibilities' opened up by Fitzgerald's prose are closed down by the realist mode of cinema: Sarah Churchwell argues that film can only offer us black or white – 'classy' Gatsby or 'gauche' Gatsby, 'charming' or 'repellant' Daisy, and so on (Churchwell qtd in Needham). For others, the cinematic quality of Fitzgerald's prose lends itself to visualization on screen. There is a rhythm to the sequencing of his scenes and a visual immediacy of almost photographic intent. Daisy's first introduction takes place in a staged white space of 'rippling, fluttering white' (Fitzgerald 8); we then cut to Daisy and Jordan, 'preced[ing] us out onto a rosy-colored porch, open towards the sunset, where four candles flick[er] on the table in the diminished wind' (9). Fitzgerald, like protagonist Gatsby, stage manages not only the visual content but the shifts from scene to scene with a directorial eye for detail. Enamoured of the burgeoning film industry, and employed as a screenwriter for Metro-Goldwyn Mayer in 1937, Fitzgerald's flirtation with Hollywood lasted for only one year. However, his works have been adapted to screen by others on a regular basis – *The Beautiful and the Damned* 1922, 2010; *Tender is the Night* 1962; *The Curious Case of Benjamin Button* 2008 – and *The Great Gatsby* has been adapted to screen a further four times. The 1949 film, in which the inferred gangster properties of the narrative are foregrounded, functions primarily as a star vehicle for Alan Ladd.

In the 1974 film adaptation, though both its marketing materials and the casting of screen idol Robert Redford foreground the story's central romance quest, director Jack Clayton and screenwriter Frances Ford Coppola seek fidelity to the canonical text and its critique of the American dream. Similarly, despite the dangers of losing any sense of the thematic concerns at the heart of the text in its overload of 3D extravagance and excess, Baz Luhrmann's 2013 adaptation remains a 'faithful' translation of Fitzgerald's text to screen. Both of these film texts reproduce on screen the hedonistic days of the twenties Jazz Age, paying meticulous attention to the story's period detail. While Clayton's thorough research into the music of the Jazz Age informs the historical moment being nostalgically recreated on screen, Luhrmann adopts a more eclectic yet no less informed approach to the music of the era, taking us back to the roots of the Jazz Age and its Tin Pan Alley origins and projecting forward to its hip hop future. However, the centrality of the romance quest is, in general, foregrounded in all screen adaptations of the novel: A & E's telemovie, *The Great Gatsby*, broadcast in 2000 on American cable television and on Granada television in the UK, constructs a far more sympathetic Daisy, and the romantic relationship between Daisy and Gatsby dominates. In the manner of Shakespeare's tale of doomed lovers Romeo and Juliet, it opens with what amounts to a prologue, foregrounding the climactic shooting of Gatsby in his swimming pool, leaving us from the outset with a sense of the narrative's tragic trajectory.

Christopher Scott Cherot's *G* (2002) relocates the novel in a temporal and geographical sense, setting up an exploration of class and social mobility within the world of African American hip hop culture but, rather than presenting an incisive interrogation of the story within a very different cultural milieu, it too plays the romance card giving the novel, above all else, a soap opera spin. Perhaps the most inventive re-visioning of the novel comes from Ernesto Quiñonez whose novel, *Bodega Dreams*, explores the American dream from the perspective of contemporary Latino immigrants of Spanish Harlem. His Gatsbyesque hero, Willie Bodega, seeks to realize the illusory 'dream' not for himself alone but for his immigrant Puerto Rican community. However, his altruistic motives are no less naïve than those of Fitzgerald's Gatsby, suggesting that ethnic and/or immigrant self-invention is yet another illusory dream in the United States past and present. As with Henry James' 'The Turn of the Screw', there are a number of prose adaptations, some of which target a much younger audience: Sara Benincasa's Young Adult Fiction novel, *Great* (2014), is set in the similarly affluent, class-conscious Hamptons and constructs a contemporary female teen Gatsby and a story of lesbian obsession. Like Quiñonez' Bodega Dreams, it takes the narrative to a different time, place and audience.

The story has also attracted the attention of adapters working in the graphic medium; Nicki Greenburg's lyrically beautiful graphic novel adaptation and Korean comic book series *The Great Catsby* offer two very different visualizations of Fitzgerald's novel, turning his cast of characters into bestial forms. *The Great Catsby* is a popular Korean comic book series currently in its sixth volume. Despite its comic book format, it too shares with *The Great Gatsby* a poetic use of language. As we follow the life of the youthful, angst-ridden Catsby, the series appropriates certain elements of Fitzgerald's novel, from referential plot points (his girlfriend Persu ditches him for an older, wealthy man) to loose character parallels (devoted best friend Houndu guides him through life's difficulties). This popular comic book, first published on the internet but now available in print too, has attracted the attention of its own body of adapters: it has thus far spawned a television drama, a musical and an animated film. *The Great Gatsby* has also been adapted into the unlikely realm of computer gaming; designed by Charlie Hoey and Peter Malamud Smith, *The Great Gatsby* NES free online retro Nintendo game harks back to the days of Super Mario and takes a tongue-in cheek journey through the novel's iconic scenes and plot points, shooting waiters and dodging through party scenes on route, leaving us on completion with the witty line 'Game over, old sport'. Its creators acknowledge its limitations: it functions as a nostalgic nod to gaming of the eighties and nineties rather than as a high-minded appropriation of the novel, but as with other adaptations that have emerged around the hype of the release of Luhrmann's 2013 3D film adaptation, it has garnered new fans to add to its established cult fan base.

Fitzgerald pondered several titles for his novel – from his working title, *Under the Red, White and Blue*, to *On the Road to West Egg, Gold-Hatted Gatsby, The High Bouncing Lover* and *Trimalchio* – before eventually settling on the name of his narrative's elusive central character, and adding the appendage 'great' as a multi-layered, loaded signifier, the meanings of which are revealed as the story unfolds. We enter the narrative at a point when Gatsby has attained his empire: he is the Trimalchio of West Egg, the modern embodiment of the nineteenth-century Alger hero, but his nostalgic desires outweigh any sense of personal fulfillment, suggesting that entry into the higher strata of society is always going to remain out of his reach. For Daisy, who is synonymous with the inherited wealth of East Egg and the class status that Gatsby aspires to, Gatsby's West Egg domain can never be anything more than a 'place that Broadway had begotten upon a Long Island fishing village': she and her ilk are 'appalled by its raw vigour' (Fitzgerald 69). With her disapproval comes the collapse of his empire – 'the whole caravansary … fallen in like a house of cards at the disapproval in her eyes' (72) – and with it his pursuit of the illusive American dream.

The Great Gatsby: The 'classic' treatment (screen adaptations of *The Great Gatsby*: 1974, 2013)

The declared intent of Jack Clayton, director of the 1974 film adaptation of *The Great Gatsby*, is to seek fidelity to Fitzgerald's novel. 'We've made', he boldly claims, 'the book' (Clayton in Atkins 221). The screenplay, first written by Truman Capote but much revised and credited to Frances Ford Coppola, functions almost as a transcript, with much of the dialogue transposed from novel to screenplay, and few additions or omissions to the story template. Clayton, an established auteur with a pedigree as a receptive, sensitive cinematic adapter of literature (*Room at the Top* 1959; *The Innocents* 1961; *The Pumpkin Eaters* 1964; *Our Mother's House* 1967), sought to bring to the screen the critique of American society embedded in Fitzgerald's prose. However, he acknowledges that his vision for the film was compromised from the outset by the 'blockbuster' approach of its production company, Paramount Pictures: it became for Clayton 'a violently over-publicized film, and a film which was never intended…to be anything like this' (Clayton qtd in Rosen 49). Its pre-release success immediately undermined Clayton's ideological intent, transforming it from the originally envisioned identity quest and complex critique of the American dream and American society, into a period piece that foregrounds its allegiance to mass culture and matters of style. The film's romance driven tagline and theatrical trailer belie the complex thematic concerns explored in the novel and in the film Clayton hoped to produce.

Marketed as a glossy romance, its tagline, 'Gone is the romance that was so divine', is derived from the sentimental lyrics of Irving Berlin's 'What'll I do?', a song employed throughout the film as a nostalgic signifier of the Gatsby – Daisy relationship; its theatrical trailer consists of scenes that focus on the latter and on the depiction of the glamorous Jazz Age. According to contemporary critic Irene Kahn Atkins it was 'the most publicized and ambitious remake in motion picture memory', on a par with other Paramount productions like *Love Story* (1970) and *The Godfather* (1972) (216). Made for 6.5 million dollars, it realized a pre-release profit of over 16 million dollars, attained through product placement deals that, incepted here by Paramount's Frank Yablans, have since become a common feature of the film industry landscape (Giannetti 13). Building on the narrative's alignment with glamour, Yablans exploited 'the Gatsby look', Redford serving almost as a mannequin for the fledgeling Ralph Lauren fashion house, whilst the production of a range of Gatsby-connected goods such as Gatsby Teflon cookware drew upon the text's preoccupation with consumerism and modernity, even if not in the critical manner Fitzgerald or Clayton intended. Joss Lutz Marsh argues that Hollywood's affiliation with glamour and its fans' desire to buy into 'Cinema Fashions' and 'Studio Styles' makes Gatsby 'the true Hollywood idol of consumption' (10) – a marketer's dream product and one fully exploited by Paramount but condemned by Clayton's contemporary critics for what is perceived as its crass marketing coup (Giannetti 13).

The debates surrounding its pre-release success become paratextual properties that enter critical discourse to the detriment of a more objective assessment of the film. Its fidelity is also cited as a weakness in so far as it follows the source text's narrative trajectory and recreates the glamour of the era yet fails, in the estimation of many contemporary reviewers, to capture the elusive essence of Fitzgerald's prose. *New York Times* reviewer, Vincent Canby sees it as 'all too reverential in attitude' while Roger Ebert claims it is 'faithful with a vengeance' and yet has 'nothing much in common with the spirit of Fitzgerald's novel' (*Gatsby* 1974). Though what is meant by the 'spirit' or 'essence' of any text remains indefinable, such responses indicate a general lack of enthusiasm for the film, despite its marketing triumph and relative box office success. It is seen first and foremost as a period piece, more concerned with its Roaring Twenties Jazz Age 'look' and sound than with the ideological substance of Fitzgerald's novel. Oscars awarded in 1975 for Best Costume Design (Theoni Aldredge) and Best Musical Score (Nelson Riddle) and BAFTAs in 1975 for Best Cinematography (Douglas Slocombe), Art Direction (John Box), and again for Costume Design, underline the success of the film in terms of its cinematic style. For many, though, this 'style' is all-consuming: it hijacks the thematic concerns Clayton strives to explore here. Despite Nelson's meticulously researched soundtrack, and the visual beauty of the film's set and costume design, Clayton achieves the desired cinematic rendition of Fitzgerald's lyrical, imagistic prose only occasionally.

The opening moments of the film, in which Clayton steps away from direct engagement with Fitzgerald's prose, create an equally haunting and fragmentary mode of expression through the medium of cinema. Shots of objects – from Gatsby's mansion and its opulent interiors to his car and the shrine-like array of photographic images of Daisy Buchanan – are accompanied by a distanced, echoing soundtrack, that establishes a sense of inertia, of insubstantiality and absence. Clayton introduces us to a narrative that foregrounds possessions rather than people as its primary focus, its protagonists present only through objects: Gatsby via the monographed objects and medals that adorn his dresser; Daisy through photographs and clippings from high society magazines detailing from afar her life as a minor celebrity up to the point at which Gatsby resumes his romantic pursuit of her. Here, Clayton reconfigures the illusory nature of their romance and of Gatsby's transitory wealth by exploiting the novel's critique of consumerism and mass culture, exposing both as shallow and ephemeral. The sound of laughter on the edges of the frame as the camera sweeps through the empty spaces of Gatsby's mansion again underscores the redundancy of material wealth. The final, drawn out shot of this sequence focuses on a disturbing, incongruous image of a fly as it hovers over a half-eaten sandwich, resting on Gatsby's dresser, undercutting the glamourous slideshow of wealth showcased thus far. It is not until the closing moments of the film that we return to this image to find that what we have witnessed is the novel's ending rather than its beginning. The visual complexities of the opening moments serve as prologue (and in part epilogue) to Fitzgerald's narrative: they demonstrate Clayton's capacity to adapt the novel's so called 'essence' but what follows on from this is, on the whole, a series of sequences that attempt to adapt its prose into cinematic form with limited success.

Clayton returns to the source text's narrative template in a much more literal manner from this point onwards, and despite his avowed disapproval of the way in which the film was marketed, any additions or omissions to that narrative template are engineered to amplify its romance plot. Fitzgerald voices his concerns about the absence of romantic moments within the novel, citing this as a flaw in its overall structure (Fitzgerald qtd in Bahrenburg 219), and so Clayton's decisions are perhaps informed by a similar desire for narrative cohesion. However, the addition of love scenes to a first person narration delivered by one who functions outside that relationship is in itself problematic: what access, other than that of voyeur, could such a character have to moments of romantic intimacy? The bounds of credibility are already tested in the novel during those moments that border on such intimacy. The cinematic medium has no direct equivalent to first person narration; its lens is given the freedom to see from multiple perspectives, and Clayton capitalizes on this, introducing private 'love' scenes between Daisy and Gatsby. For example, Clayton introduces a long, drawn out dance sequence in which Gatsby wears his army uniform and Daisy whispers into his ear: 'Kiss me. Be my lover. Stay my lover. Husband and lover.' Such moments redefine the relationship between Daisy and Gatsby: the possibility of a lasting romantic reunion is foregrounded here, even though Daisy's later actions suggest that for her this is merely a dangerous flirtation. Daisy, rather than Jordan, delivers her own version of events leading up to her marriage to Tom Buchanan, again adding a romantic emphasis to the narrative with lines like 'You broke my heart with your impossible love.' We are closer to the dialogue of Paramount's populist *Love Story* than the elegant prose of Fitzgerald's novel. Despite the long running time of the film, other romantic possibilities are excised: there is no exploration of the relationship between Nick Carraway and Jordan Baker, no subtextual hint of Nick's homosexual desire for Gatsby or of young James Gatz's relationship with his elderly mentor, Cody. Other potential love angles are forfeited in pursuit of the romance between Gatsby and Daisy.

The use of voiceover as a cinematic device that equates with *The Great Gatsby's* first person narration further adds to the problematic relationship between film text and novel. Nick Carraway's voiceover directs our film viewing at certain strategic plot points, but where the voiceover device is often used sparingly in cinema, as a means to entering the past or providing essential exposition, here it is employed as an addition to the onscreen narrative, commenting on events in the manner of Fitzgerald's narrator and using its lyrical, writerly prose. The opening lines of the novel play over the image of Nick clumsily navigating his way across the waters separating East and West Egg, his small rowing boat offering a visual contrast to the expensive yachts that circle the East Egg shoreline. In one sense, the prosaic voiceover is misplaced: it is not naturalistic spoken language, and it hijacks the visual medium to a certain extent. In another sense, as script doctor Robert McKee points out, if used sparingly, voiceover of this type offers a worthwhile counterpoint to the story unfolding on screen, providing insights that cannot be communicated by any other means (344). But what role does the film's Nick Carraway fulfil? Is he a distant observer offering this kind of candid, reflective commentary throughout or is he a central player with a vested interest in the events of the narrative? Clayton's Carraway hovers between the two functions. Since the film's focus is on the romance between Gatsby and Daisy, we learn little of his life past, present or future in this adaptation, despite the fact that Clayton claims Carraway 'has to be the single character in the story who actually develops as a human being' (Clayton qtd in Rosen 51). Though central to narrative momentum and serving as occasional reflective commentator, he remains a peripheral character whose presence at certain moments becomes awkward when Fitzgerald's lyrical prose becomes a concrete reality on screen. During the marital showdown at The Plaza Hotel, for instance, the presence of both Nick and Jordan seems odd: the scene takes on the quality of stage space rather than cinematic space. Similarly, the contrived nature of the reunion of Daisy and Gatsby at Carraway's house, when stripped of Fitzgerald's writerly wit, seems unnatural and forced, Carraway's presence incongruous. The film's incapacity to communicate to its audience the difference between reality and differing perceptions of Daisy, of Gatsby and of his 'dream' means that it lacks the capacity to recreate the 'tensions' that form an essential part of the novel (Marsh 300). Further edits and structural changes exacerbate this problem. Clayton chooses not to show the moment of Myrtle's death, not to show Tom and Daisy colluding after that death whilst Gatsby stands guard outside under the misconception that Daisy is in danger and worthy of his protection.

Much of the story is filtered through Carraway's subjective perception of characters in general and of Gatsby in particular, and in both novel and film the story's romantic hero does not make an appearance until a quarter of the narrative has unfolded. Marsh sees Gatsby as the novel's 'star' and Carraway as his 'inbuilt unconscious "fan" as well as a built-in conscious critic', who 'ideali[zes] Gatsby even while he is aware that his star is a manufactured fake' (103). Gatsby the star stage manages his life, changing his name from James Gatz to the more glamourous Jay Gatsby, manufacturing his consciously enigmatic star persona. His transition to screen star comes with relative ease, especially when played by an actor of Robert Redford's star status. Gatsby on screen, according to Marsh, should be modern cinema's equivalent to silent cinema's Valentino, a similar 'construction of star glamour' (6), and in this regard the casting of Redford is a master stroke. However, for many it is Redford's star status that makes him an unsuitable Gatsby. Suave, sophisticated and calm, this Gatsby displays none of the naiveties or vulnerabilities of the canonical text's Gatsby. In his Ralph Lauren suits and his gold tie, he is the 'classy' Gatsby of Churchwell's disdain (Needham); he remains unfamiliar, unreachable in a way that Fitzgerald's Gatsby and those of the 1949 and 2013 film adaptations are not. Though the 1949 film functions as a star vehicle for studio favourite Alan Ladd, his 'boy next door' image offers a sharp contrast to that of Redford. We do not sense in Redford's performance, the 'embarrassment', the 'unreasoning joy he was consumed with', his 'wonder at [Daisy's] presence' (Fitzgerald 59); there is nothing of the 'Jay Gatsby that a 17 year old boy would be likely to invent'. Redford's Gatsby is far too self-aware for that, and consequently he lacks the 'gorgeous' vulnerability of Fitzgerald's rags to riches protagonist. What is required in the role, according to Giannetti, 'is a mere mortal – an "ordinary actor", not a Robert Redford' who fails to see that it is Gatsby's 'romantic foolishness' that makes him 'so tragically poignant and universally appealing' (21–22). He becomes instead just another romantic hero whose fall from grace is inevitable. This in itself is not a negative: the romance genre is an ever popular mode of cinematic storytelling, but for Clayton, its reception as romance does not align with his adaptive intent.

For readers who are already familiar with Fitzgerald's canonical text the 'cinematic vision[s]' provided by Clayton and by Baz Luhrmann may 'colonize' the reading experience (Hutcheon). Just as our reading of *Jane Eyre* is coloured post reading of Jean Rhys's re-visionist text, *Wide Sargasso Sea*, our perception of the novel's enigmatic yet vulnerable Gatsby is shaped by his on-screen realization in films that adapt the story into this very different medium. However, as Hutcheon notes, our *first* experience of the narrative may come through viewing the film adaptation rather than reading the canonical text it engages with, situating the novel for some as the 'secondary' work. For many contemporary viewers, of Clayton's seventies *Gatsby* or Luhrmann's twenty-first century 3D extravaganza, Gatsby's story may be received as film before it is experienced as prose. As such, our perception of the tale and its protagonists shifts accordingly: despite an avowed intent on the part of both Clayton and Luhrmann to remain 'faithful' to the so-called 'source' text, despite their fidelity-driven approach to plot and to recreation of its period detail, the films they produce 'colonize' the story. It becomes first and foremost a romance quest, its film adaptations preoccupied with style and seduced by the glamourous splendour that a cinematic realization of the Prohibition era of the Roaring Twenties affords it. And this is not necessarily a negative outcome. In the realms of cinema, romance is a populist, profitable genre and the star casting of Gatsby a means of maximizing financial return in what is an expensive cost-driven enterprise. Moreover, the viewer who has not read the novel has no preconceived notion of what Gatsby could or should be (a notion that is inevitably coloured by individual experience anyway). Redford's sophisticated Gatsby, for example, works within the parameters of the romance genre, as does star persona Leonardo DiCaprio's equally handsome yet more likeable Gatsby. Both films, with some minor additions and omissions, follow the narrative trajectory of Fitzgerald's novel: the 'what' of the 'story' remains the same but the 'how' (or 'discourse') is transformed when translated to cinematic space, resulting in a very different set of textual preoccupations and two very different films, despite each ones fidelity-driven approach to the canonical text.

As adapters of *The Great Gatsby*, Clayton and Luhrmann have more in common than their *desire* for fidelity. Both are renowned non-American auteurs who shoot the film in non-American locales, despite the novel's reputation as the quintessential American novel. Clayton shoots his film at Elstree Studios in London: Australian Luhrmann shoots in various Sydney locales. Gatsby's mansion is Manly's St Patrick's Seminary, and Sydney's Centennial Park functions as its grounds, while Balmain and Whitebay Power Station provide the backdrop for Luhrmann's valley of ashes. However, each director is at pains to maintain the illusion of its American landscape with its consumer driven culture, pre The Great Depression. Both films attracted a large production budget and achieved significant financial success. Luhrmann's *Gatsby*, made on a budget of 105 million US dollars has since earned 144 million at the American box office and 206 million in foreign returns, giving a worldwide return of 351 million US dollars (Mojo). Through astute, strategic decision-making, Luhrmann's production also benefitted from substantial funding from Screen Australia in the form of tax cuts; though an American story, financed and produced by American studio Warner Brothers, *Gatsby* qualifies as an Australian product since it was filmed in Australia by a mainly Australian crew, and starred numerous Australian actors (Joel Egerton, Isla Fisher). Whereas Clayton was concerned that the size of his production budget would ultimately classify it as a blockbuster style movie of the kind he abhorred (Clayton qtd in Rosen), Luhrmann courted blockbuster status as a means to realizing his costly 3D vision of the story. Similarly, where Clayton rejected the hard-sell branding and marketing of his film, Luhrmann embraced it.

Debates about the marketing and pre-release success of each film has become part of the critical discourse surrounding them, from a questioning of the validity of Australian funding for a film set in a specific period of American history and adapted from a work of the American literary canon, to debates about the renaissance of flapper fashions and art deco style in the wake of each film. January's 2012 edition of *Vogue* features an article on 'Gatsby Glamour', noting a proliferation of collections that take a lead from the film initially due for release in December of that year, and Carey Mulligan, Luhrmann's Daisy Buchanan, appears in Twenties garb on the cover of *Vogue* in May 2103, when the film is eventually released. Deals with Tiffany, the long-standing American gents' outfitter Brooks brothers (notably the outfitter favoured by Fitzgerald in the twenties), and collaboration between costume designer Catherine Martin and Prada's Miuccia Prada ensure the film's high-end fashion status. Its eclectic soundtrack, merging the traditional jazz of Fitzgerald's era with contemporary pop and hip hop and featuring a host of contemporary music stars is another successful marketing, money-spinning force behind the film. The involvement of Jay-Z as executive producer of the soundtrack adds credence to the film as a product that crosses over from its canonical high art origins to the populist mainstream in its reincarnation as a Luhrmann film. It shares with Clayton's *Gatsby* enviable commercial success but it also shares its negative critical reception. For *New York Times* reviewer A. O. Scott, Luhrmann's film is no more than a 'splashy, trashy opera, a wayward, lavishly theatrical celebration of the emotional and material extravagance that Fitzgerald surveyed with fascinating ambivalence'; for Lee Marshall, it is 'an Oscar Wilde tea party without the dripping sarcasm' (200).

The inference here is that, while Luhrmann captures Fitzgerald's vision of the Roaring Twenties as a time of 'emotional and material extravagance', his capacity to imbibe his film text with an equivalent sense of 'ambivalence' or with the kind of wit that Marshall refers to, is sorely lacking. From a slim novella, Luhrmann creates an 'epic melodrama', a 'fus[ion] of old-movie theatrics and subjective filmmaking' (Ebert): for some, that may still constitute an overblown soap-style 'bastardizaton' of Fitzgerald's tale, but for others – as its 2013 Oscar and BAFTA awards for costume design and set design attest – its visual and aural excesses are what make this film an intriguing and innovative adaptation. Since Clayton's adaptation also won awards for its stylish screen realization of Fitzgerald's Jazz Age (Best Costume Design and Best Musical Score), it is fair to assume that it is the glamourous appeal of the era that continues to attract directors and audiences alike. There is also an innate contradiction at the heart of reviewer disdain for the power and energy with which these adapters create such cinematic splendour: the hue and cry over their preoccupation with the material 'look' of the tale fails to register the fact that material over-indulgence is part of the fabric of Fitzgerald's thematic schema. We must see it, acknowledge its powerful allure, if we are to believe in it, and cinema as a medium is inordinately equipped to oblige. The lens of both Clayton and Luhrmann is directed to linger on images of material beauty: from Gatsby's now iconic yellow car, to the stunning art deco interiors, the extravagantly attired transitory nouveau riche of West Egg 'gatecrashers' and of East Egg's established 'old moneyed' class. However, like Fitzgerald, each director provides a glimpse into the other side of society through its depiction of the valley of ashes, though neither fully realizes its comparative power to undermine the glamour of high society life that dominates from the outset. The dilapidated Dr T. J. Eckleburg advertising billboard looms ominously over the contrastingly dark and shabby valley of ashes – and in Luhrmann's film, the almost replicated sign becomes a pointed visual homage to the 1974 film – but there is little attempt by Clayton or Luhrmann to engage in more than a passing allusion to this counterpart of East and West Egg existence, and in Luhrmann's film, his penchant for creating highly stylized, theatrical images turns the valley of ashes into yet another aesthetically appealing scene, its workers artistically silhouetted against the skyline.

To a certain extent Luhrmann's *The Great Gatsby* can be viewed as remake rather than adaptation. Like Clayton's *Gatsby* it focuses first and foremost on the novel's romance quest, and there are moments when the visual style of Clayton's film permeates Luhrmann's film text. The latter's marketing trailer, for instance, picks up on the same geometric design emblazoned on the possessions that adorn Gatsby's dresser in Clayton's opening scene, and Gatsby's ornate swimming pool is tiled with the same geometric 'J.G.' insignia, providing a constant allusion to the earlier film. More pointedly, there are fragmentary echoes of and allusions to Clayton's film scattered throughout the text: a midway unexpected cut to empty rooms of Gatsby's mansion is almost a copy of the opening sequence of Clayton's film where the camera roams deserted spaces, curtains billowing. The scene in which Luhrmann's Daisy is introduced echoes Clayton's treatment yet it is even more stage-managed: the colour palette is again a startling white and highly stylized but here the scene is more opulent, and the synchronized moves of servants in attendance at every doorway adds a choreographed precision that speaks of obscene wealth and over-indulgence. Some of Luhrmann's textual additions also build upon what Coppola and Clayton have added to the narrative mix. Both Gatsbys now display an obsession with the celebrity status of their Daisy whose image and story is captured in lovingly preserved newspaper clippings, to almost comedic effect in Luhrmann's film as the camera scans his leather-bound volumes of Daisy trivia. Intimate love scenes, taken to the point of sex scenes in the 2013 adaptation, are viewed by both directors as a much needed addition to this love story – a necessary prerequisite of romance for a contemporary audience.

However, to regard Clayton's film as anything more than an intertext to which Luhrmann is paying reverential homage is to underestimate the differences between these two cinematic adaptations of *The Great Gatsby*. The auteur signature these directors bring to the adaptive project ensures each is strikingly different. Much to his dismay, the marketing trailer for Clayton's film presents it as a romance, while the theatrical trailer for Luhrmann's *The Great Gatsby* presents it first and foremost as a Baz Luhrmann film. Luhrmann is 'the entrepreneur showman' who (like Fitzgerald's Gatsby) 'manages our experience' (Cook 34) and whose 'cinesonic style' continues to dismantle the boundaries between high and low culture (Coyle 23). Our sense of Luhrmann's auteur signature is indelibly linked to what he terms his Red Curtain Trilogy. If we consider his *Gatsby* in relation to the Red Curtain Trilogy – *Strictly Ballroom* (1992), *Romeo + Juliet* (1996), *Moulin Rouge* (2001) – we can trace the many stylistic, thematic and narrational parallels it shares with this body of film. It emerges as a fourth Red Curtain film. Luhrmann's Red Curtain films are governed by three basic rules: they consist of a simple story, based on an identifiable myth with a known outcome; they are set in a 'heightened creative world' that is at once distant yet familiar; and each employs a non-naturalistic storytelling device, from dance (*Strictly Ballroom*) to Shakespearean verse (*Romeo + Juliet*) to song (*Moulin Rouge*) (Luhrmann in Frank). *The Great Gatsby* explores the primary Alger myth of the American dream and of 'true love'. Moreover, its naïve protagonist engineers his own 'heightened world' that is 'at once familiar' and known to the audience as a specific moment in American history (the hedonistic Roaring Twenties), a distant time viewed with historical hindsight and yet presented as 'exotic' enough to be intriguing. In all but one of these love stories, their love is doomed: like Romeo and Juliet, Christian and Satine, Gatsby and Daisy cannot sustain their relationship as lovers. The marketing trailer for *The Great Gatsby* acknowledges the significance of its love story but it also serves as a showcase for Luhrmann's distinctive approach to cinematic storytelling. Luhrmann foregrounds the constructed nature of the 'reality' he presents, highlighting the processes at work in its visual and aural creation and making us constantly aware that we are watching a film rather than the kind of seamless continuity-edited realist cinema of mainstream Hollywood. The Red Curtain films are characterized by self-conscious, frenetic cinematography, fast edits, a saturated colour palette and a layering of screen images and words; *The Great Gatsby* employs all of these techniques alongside the added technological trickery of 3D imaging and Green Screen. Luhrmann wants his viewers to be constantly aware that they are watching a film.

A further marker of Luhrmann's auteur style is the emphasis on spectacle, an emphasis well-suited to certain aspects of Fitzgerald's novel. His Red Curtain films are all highly theatrical; built around theatrical motifs – the ballroom, the Verona Beach stage, the Moulin Rouge Club – they present a carnivalesque atmosphere of visual and musical mayhem. The party scenes in Luhrmann's Gatsby are similarly theatrical: Gatsby's West Egg mansion becomes the central theatrical motif, a stage overseen by Gatsby as a behind-the-scenes Zigleresque Master of Ceremonies. As in Clayton's 1974 film, the hedonistic parties become the film's central spectacle, but whilst each film's period detail is carefully researched and reproduced on screen, Luhrmann adds anachronistic flourishes that embellish the film text with pop culture references that seamlessly intertextualize his earlier films. The party scenes are visually chaotic and are reminiscent of those orchestrated by Harold Zigler in *Moulin Rouge* or of the Capulets' fancy dress ball in *Romeo + Juliet*. Luhrmman is also adept at constructing the deceptively spontaneous and far more raucous party scene at Myrtle's flat; with its edits to the trumpet playing jazz musician sitting out on the fire escape, it is as stylized and crafted as the grand Gatsby party scenes and handled with the same panache.

The choreography and the soundtrack of all three Red Curtain films fuse music and dance: they become part of each film's storytelling mode. Pam Cook claims Luhrmann's films are 'characterized by a global aesthetic that is culturally hybrid' (35): and part of their global currency is their capacity to bring together culturally incongruous elements – pop and hip hop, hip hop and jazz, dance moves of the Twenties and of the late twentieth and twenty-first centuries' dance culture. Luhrmann exploits the novel's nostalgic potentialities and the edginess of the Prohibition era by creating an unashamedly postmodern musical pastiche that melds traditional jazz with hip hop and the early strains of tin pan alley jazz, covers of songs by current artists and songs composed specifically for the movie. Whilst Clayton is at pains to reproduce the music of the twenties, Luhrmann seeks instead to reproduce the raw *edge* of that music as it would have been received back in the twenties, equating tin pan alley sounds and the crudities of hip hop with that period rather than the jazz of the era which has now become 'safe' fare. Luhrmann claims 'Fitzgerald put African American music in his book because he wanted it to be dangerous. I put African American street music into the film – it just happens to be hip hop because jazz is now quaint' (*Empire*). Similarly, whereas Clayton employs the populist 20s song 'What'll I do?' as form of romantic musical cue, Luhrmann uses a song composed and sung by contemporary artist Lana Del Ray to serve the same function. Music and dance also become part of Luhrmann's self-referential agenda: at one point in the film, as Gatsby and Carraway drive over the Queensborough Bridge, the film reprises a moment from both Fitzgerald's novel *and* Luhrmann's *Romeo + Juliet*. As they pass an open-topped car full of people gyrating to a hip hop beat, the viewer familiar with the arrival of Mercutio and company at the Capulet party is taken back to the sights and sounds of that equally extravagant, staged moment from *Romeo + Juliet*.

Luhrmann's Red Curtain films also present us with an equally extravagant, exaggerated cast of characters, from the stereo-typical figures of *Strictly Ballroom's* dancing circuit to *Romeo + Juliet's* outrageously camp Mercutio and the comedic Toulouse-Lautrec of *Moulin Rouge*. The complexity of characterization achieved by Fitzgerald seems at odds with such a treatment. However, in his adaptation of *The Great Gatsby*, Luhrmann's use of exaggerated character types is less overt. His depiction of the throng of party-goers is suitably exaggerated, and there are some visual nods to Fitzgerald's text – the girls dressed in yellow, for example, make a fleeting appearance, as do the various film industry types mentioned in the novel – and he exploits the comedic potential of characters like Klipspringer. Bombastic Tom Buchanan is at times exaggerated to comedic effect: he becomes the stereotypical villain of the piece. The scene at Myrtle's flat serves to illustrate this point. We open with an embarrassed Nick, subjected to the off-screen sound of Tom and Myrtle's sexual exploits, playfully choreographed to sync with the sounds of her dog as it feeds noisily; similarly, the scene ends with Tom punching Myrtle, but the violence of the moment is conveyed in cartoon-like slow-motion, distancing us from the horror of Tom's aggressive actions. Yet Luhrmann also adds more subtle visual flourishes that underscore the disturbing aspects of Tom's nature: in this adaptation his racist rants are accentuated by his actions, and the tension is heightened in a theatrical manner as he delivers his misceganist diatribe in the presence of a black servant to whom he callously gestures. And as in Clayton's film, Tom is shown inciting Wilson to avenge Myrtle's death by killing Gatsby, turning him into the story's villain.

Luhrmann's distanciation techniques, employed so effectively in his Red Curtain trilogy (dance, verse, song), are again reprised in *The Great Gatsby*; Nick Carraway's first person narration serves as a device designed to maintain our heightened and continuing awareness that what we are watching is a construct. We are always conscious of his purposely intrusive voiceover, guiding us from the edge of the cinematic frame. Carraway becomes more than the narrator of this one tale: like Christian in *Moulin Rouge*, he becomes a writer recording past events, and though we move back in time with him to these recollected plot points, we return throughout to the controlling device of Carraway as narrator/creator of story. Luhrmann plays with the notion that there are biographical connections between Fitzgerald and Carraway. The film begins with an addition to the narrative: now commencing in 1929, two days after Black Tuesday and the infamous stock exchange Crash that heralds the Great Depression, the story opens in the Perkins Sanatorium, where Carraway is being treated for 'morbid alcoholism'. The allusion to Fitzgerald's alcoholism in these opening moments, and the construction of Carraway (a fellow Ivy League man from the Mid-West) as author, writing down the story as part of his therapy serves to remind us of the constructed nature of this tale. In addition to the visual splendour of the film, Luhrmann injects a reverence to the canonical text, affording it an on-screen presence as Carraway's recollections become words on page and screen. We edit in the opening moments from Carraway's blank notebook and pen to the meticulously constructed image of workers in the valley of ashes, before cutting back to his writing, his words appearing left of screen and superimposed on his face. By making Carraway the author of the narrative, Luhrmann gives credence to the use of a voiceover that employs Fitzgerald's lyrical prose verbatim, whereas its usage by Clayton's Carraway remains stilted and at times out of place. Carraway becomes a pseudo Fitzgerald constructing characters and manipulating events to his narrative purpose. Luhrmann cleverly merges Fitzgerald the author and Carraway the narrator in the final moments of the film: as the camera focuses in close up on the front page of a book titled 'Gatsby', Carraway delivers Fitzgerald's closing lines and adds by hand the word 'Great', inferring that he is the author of the canonical text. The further inference is that Luhrmann, as adapter, is also authoring Fitzgerald's story anew.

Though a distancing device, Luhrmann's narrator is not the distanced, awkward voyeur of Clayton's film, for Luhrmann justifies Carrway's writerly voiceover and his presence by making the relationship between Gatsby and Carraway more central to the story. In this adaptation, despite his boyish portrayal, Nick acts as a foil to the naïve, vulnerable Gatsby. Through simple additions to the dialogue, Luhrmann constructs a more likeable Gatsby and a more credible sense of the growing friendship between the two. For example, Gatsby is amazed when Nick assures him that there really is no need to reward him for arranging the meeting between himself and Daisy; Gatsby's delight is endearing and the fact that he is so accustomed to having to buy favour highlights his emotional and cultural isolation. Gatsby's attempts to impress and Nick's endearing reassurances that he has no need to do so, flesh out the growing friendship between these two outsiders to East and West Egg. Similarly, Nick's presence during the very awkward reunion between Daisy and Gatsby has a dramatic relevance not attained in Clayton's film. The scene's exaggerated comedic treatment as Gatsby arrives with his entourage of servants, armed with an overload of hothouse flowers that dominate the interior of Nick's small cottage foregrounds his emotional vulnerability and reveals both the organically evolving relationship between Nick and Gatsby, as Nick prompts a very nervous Gatsby to stay, and the chinks in Gatsby's sophisticated exterior. Gatsby's clumsiness, as he knocks the clock from the mantel, may negate our sense of his mystery and poise but inclusion of this moment from Fitzgerald's novel serves to highlight Gatsby's anxiety, his insecurity, making him a more relatable and familiar figure whose shortcomings evoke audience empathy.

Luhrmann's emphasis on spectacle is, according to Coyle, designed to 'engage cinema audiences in universal themes in preference to complex characterization' (21): it is not a constructed 'spectacle' designed to simply attain awards for costume and set design nor is it an empty exercise in visual splendour of the kind criticized by film reviewers. The themes of doomed love, the unattainable American dream, and the emptiness of consumer-driven culture are central to both Fitzgerald's novel and Luhrmann's film adaptation. The enigmatic Gatsby remains in part unknown and unknowable, his staged presence visualized on screen in a highly stylized manner, but Luhrmann's attempts to add a touch of human fallibility and vulnerability to his hero's innate naivety result in a character study that surpasses that of Clayton's sophisticated leading man, and connects with some of the complexities of Fitzgerald's Gatsby. He *is* a pseudo Harold Zidler, a Master of Ceremonies extraordinaire, orchestrating parties and weaving his own version of events, but he is also the naïve lover, lacking in confidence despite his rise to millionaire status. Martin's set design amplifies the staged nature of Gatsby, the 'overreacher': the seminary chosen to represent Gatsby's West Egg mansion is a suitably ostentatious Neo-Gothic revival, that connotes gaudy excess and visually reinscribes the notion that Gatsby can never attain the social status of his refined East Egg neighbours, despite his material wealth. In this adaptation, we catch the odd glimpse of Gatsby, a solitary figure who watches from the sidelines. His dramatic entrance is delayed until twenty-eight minutes into the film, and his first on camera appearance sets him up as a Cary Grant-like movie star pin up, full of charisma, quietly confident. Placed against a reflected backdrop of exploding fireworks, he turns to camera and raises his glass of champagne, bestowing on his cinema audience as well as on Carraway 'one of those rare smiles with a quality of eternal reassurance in it, that you may come across four or five times in life (Fitzgerald 32)'.

He is, notes Ebert 'playing the man he wishes he were'. However, whilst Redford retains his sophisticated star persona throughout, our perception of DiCaprio's Gatsby develops in part due to his relationship with Carraway, leading us to an awareness of the 'real' Gatsby rather than this carefully manufactured star persona. Additions to the narrative in the form of flashbacks to Gatsby's time spent in the trenches during the First World War further add to the credibility of his character: he may carry around medals as 'proof' of his war time valour, but the potential fakery of his claims is undermined by the gritty reality of flashbacks to the harsh realities of war and Gatsby's anxious response to it as the film aligns us with him in the trenches, albeit momentarily. He is also a man of more substance and credibility than Clayton's Gatsby. Luhrmann does not ignore his gangster affiliations:

Wolfsheim is a more visible character within the narrative, and the addition of a scene in a hidden gambling club, presumably owned by Wolfsheim and Gatsby, gives credence to Gatsby's accumulated wealth without turning it into a gangster film of the kind envisaged in the 1949 adaptation. There are also flashbacks to the young Gatz' relationship with Cody that provide the backstory necessary for the plausibility of his evolution from Gatz to Gatsby, though Luhrmann chooses not to include reference to Gatz Sr, editing out his appearance at Gatsby's funeral. The reinvented Gatsby is presented as an isolated, defeated figure, mourned only by the narrator of his tale.

Similarly, flashbacks to the blossoming romance between Gatsby and Daisy give credence to their love and though this may work contrary to Fitzgerald's intent, Luhrmann's far more likeable Daisy works within the generic conventions of cinematic romance. To a certain extent DiCaprio is reprising his role as the doomed, love-struck Romeo of Luhrmann's *Romeo + Juliet*, playing his Gatsby as similarly naïve and romantic, and the nostalgic flashbacks to the youthful exuberance of his former relationship with Daisy construct her as a pseudo Juliet. Through his casting, Luhrmann lends his film the cultural weight of Shakespeare's time-honoured love story, setting up his Gatsby and Daisy as 'star-crossed lovers' whose relationship is doomed from the outset. It also serves as a reverential nod to his auteurial signature through its allusion to one his own Red Curtain films. Carey Mulligan's Daisy is a far more credible and likeable character in this adaptation. She is not Fitzgerald's Daisy with the 'impersonal eyes' (Fitzgerald 10), whose disdain of West Egg leads Gatsby to abandon his role as orchestrator of grand parties. The scene in which she becomes emotional when holding Gatsby's 'beautiful shirts' is notoriously awkward in Clayton's film, but Luhrmann constructs it as part of a fun-filled, alcohol-fuelled exploration of Gatsby's house, with Gatsby throwing his shirts in the air in a playful manner and Daisy overwhelmed by the moment. Here, Carraway's authorial voiceover provides a context for Daisy's bizarre response, noting that 'five years' of lost time 'struggled on Daisy's lips but all she could manage was "They're such beautiful shirts"' (59). However, as in Fitzgerald's novel, the love story becomes consumed by Gatsby's desire to control. This Daisy may be far more vulnerable and relatable, and her love for Gatsby more sincere, but the climactic Plaza Hotel scene foregrounds male ego rather than romance. Tom Buchanan and Gatsby engage in both a verbal and physical battle for ownership of Daisy, and in this sense Luhrmann's film is faithful to the canonical text's preoccupation with Gatsby's reinvention of himself as an upwardly mobile interloper whose possession of Daisy is integral to his identity quest rather than his romance quest. For DiCaprio, his Gatsby is on 'an endless journey' – a journey that 'no longer bec[omes] a love story but this great tragedy of a man who lost his sense of who he was' (Hogan).

Public perception of the 'classic' screen adaptations of *The Great Gatsby* considered in this section is mixed. Where Lean's 1946 *Great Expectations* and Clayton's *The Innocents* have acquired cinematic canonical status, an equally canonical adaptation of *The Great Gatsby* has yet to be realized on screen. Its cinematic treatment by Clayton and Luhrmann is memorable first and foremost for its visual splendour and for the on-screen depiction of a specific moment in history that is aligned with heritage cinema. For some, these films become an exercise in style over substance that negates the ideological preoccupations of the so-called source text, without introducing any further insights. Yet, regardless of negative critical reception, each film was a box office hit, and each film successfully exploited the visual and aural properties of the very different medium of cinema as an alternative means to exploring the myth of the American dream.

The Great Gatsby: Re-visioning the text (*Bodega Dreams* and *Great*)

As with other re-visionary adaptations studied thus far, adapters Ernesto Quiñonez and Sara Benincasa seek to redefine the source text's dominant discourse, but they do so in decidedly different ways. Benincasa undertakes a similar exploration of white affluence in the contemporary equivalent of East and West Egg (the Hamptons), but her focus shifts to her now female narrator and plays with themes of direct relevance to her twenty-first century, social networking teen audience. Quiñonez relocates the narrative to the very different cultural, socio-political space of a contemporary Spanish Harlem; like Benincasa, he creates a narrator who becomes much more than a storytelling device, though his narrative maps a very different communal quest for the elusive 'American dream'.

Quiñonez draws upon novels from the American literary canon, citing the influence of Fitgerald's *The Great Gatsby*, J. D. Salinger's *The Catcher in the Rye* and the works of his writing mentor Walter Mosley (Quiñonez qtd in Wiegand). At the level of narrative, *The Great Gatsby* serves as a literary scaffold for his *Bodega Dreams*, providing a familiar framework upon which to build his contemporary Latino version of the American dream. However, his engagement with Fitzgerald's novel goes beyond the practicalities of story: Quiñonez seeks to legitimize and reaffirm Latino literature by taking on a work from the American canon. He challenges the hierarchical definitions of what could and should be deemed canonical and foregrounds the significance of ethnic art, literature and experience:

> When rich people see Gatsby they think that he belongs to the rich, but Gatsby doesn't belong to the rich. Gatsby belongs to the poor. He was a hoodlum. (Quiñonez qtd in Wiegand)

By staking a claim in *The Great Gatsby*, Quinonez highlights its universal significance as the quintessential immigrant's tale. Like Jean Rhys and Peter Carey in their respective adaptations of *Jane Eyre* and *Great Expectations*, he inhabits the canonical text to his own ends, 'entering [the] old text from a new critical direction' (Rich 18), colonizing its narrative and its politics and transforming Gatsby into a Latino American dreamer who seeks social mobility not for himself but for the community he remains a part of. While Fitzgerald presents us with a 'canonically modernist' and culturally isolated figure for whom 'loss is irremediable and desire impossible to fulfil' (Porter 143), Quiñonez constructs a postmodern Gatsby whose identity is intrinsically linked to his past and to his cultural roots and for whom the personal becomes the political. His writing follows 'a "ghetto fiction" tradition', that 'celebrates ones ethnic roots, affiliations, and cultural practices' (Moiles115), creating a space for Latino self-invention that mirrors Gatsby's, yet embraces past and present cultural identity as an essential part thereof. 'Modern elitism' no longer prevails: the alienated heroes of a modernist text like *The Great Gatsby* have been replaced by 'ethnic heroes' like Willie Bodega, and 'ethnic authors' like Quiñonez are gradually entering the American canon (Dwyer 176).

Quiñonez draws parallels between the capitalist-driven twenties that serve as the backdrop to Fitzgerald's tale, and the 'finance capitalism of the 1990s' explored in *Bodega Dreams* (Moiles 119). Where Fitzgerald creates a vision of wealth, privilege and carefree over-indulgence in the East and West Eggs of the twenties, Quiñonez creates an urban 'pastoral' that is rooted in the harsh realities of contemporary Spanish Harlem, depicting the lives of Latinos who 'lived in the projects with pissed-up elevators, junkies on the stairs, posters of rapist of the month', where 'shoot-outs, hold-ups, babies falling out of windows were things you took as part of life' (Quiñonez 5). The focus shifts to a contemporary ethnic equivalent of Fitzgerald's valley of ashes and its working-class inhabitants, providing a very different social and cultural backdrop to the narrative, yet retaining the wider New York locale – a locale that provides a 'well-established literary site for politicized Puerto Rican immigrant writing about nationhood, identity and nostalgia' (Otero 174). Employing the tropes of Puerto Rican literature – 'themes of home, the journey, and resettlement' (174) – Quinonez foregrounds not the 'poetry of wealth and possessions' that characterizes *The Great Gatsby* (Gilliam and Stark 480) but the poetry of ethnic culture embedded in his Latino community in general and in the Puerto Rican community in particular. Building on the history and the literature of his Puerto Rican origins, Quinonez writes of the bodega and the barrio, of an East Harlem 'filled with broken promises of a better life, dating decades back to the day when many Puerto Ricans and Latinos gathered their bags and carried their dreams on their backs and arrived in America, God's country' (Quiñonez 162). Quinonez engages in the same kind of critique of the American dream achieved by Fitzgerald through his lyrical prose, but here the social commentary, filtered through the story's narrator, Chino, is more overtly critical and political. Chino points out that the newly arrived and hopelessly optimistic immigrants of ethnic origin 'would never see God's face' since 'like all slum landlords, God lived in the suburbs' (162). There is an almost Dickensian feel to Quiñonez' social commentary as he recounts the situation for the Latino immigrant: problems with housing, education, social welfare and opportunities in general come to the fore, and his representation of the Latino is far from romanticized. Inclusion of characters like Sapo and Negra ensures a realistic rather than an idealistic portrayal of the community Quiñonez brings into focus; but he also resists the stereotypical representation of urban gangs and their members and provides historical credence to the current position of his protagonist, Willie Bodega, as he strives to reinstate a sense of cultural pride and self-esteem in his fellow barrio inhabitants. Bodega emerges as an altruistic Gatsby who speaks of his 'Great Society' and his desire to 'take care of the community' (30–31); he becomes the just 'landlord', a Moses figure whose endeavours are designed to lead his people into the promised land of the American dream. This is not the individualistic dream of the Alger hero with whom Fitzgerald's Gatsby is synonymous: this is part of a communal dream in which Bodega 'creates a green light of hope' not for himself but for fellow Puerto Rican immigrants (14).

A major part of Bodega's socialist agenda involves the re-education of a people led by the system to believe they have 'no culture, no smart people…no Latino history' (7). The text is littered with self-conscious references to Puerto Rican artists and writers, from Puerto Rican writer Julia de Burgos after whom the school in the Latino quarter is named yet whose highly revered poetry is never discussed in lessons to the novel's title, taken from a collection by Nuyorican poet Miguel Piñero, or quotations employed at the start of each Book, from Piñero and fellow Nuyorican poet Pedro Pinari. Quiñonez foregrounds Nuyorican literature over and above that of the traditional American canon and the canonical text he consciously colonizes, and presents it, via Bodega, as a source of national pride and cultural identity. His hero is aligned with Nuyorican literary figures as well as with a fictional construct from a revered canonical text. Bodega is a patron of the arts: he supports El Museo del Barrio, the Salsa Museum – a 'symbol of past glory, of early migration to the US and the dreams that people brought over along with the music' (Quiñonez 105) – and sets up a gallery for painters from the neighbourhood, all of whom live in housing provided by him. But like Pinero and Pinari, he is also a former member of the Young Lords Puerto Rican Marxist Civil Rights movement from the sixties. By acknowledging this shared past and the political activism of an earlier, more hopeful, historically romanticized period, Quiñonez provides a rationale for the less idealistic and more capitalist driven approach Bodega and his partner, Nazario, now adopt as a means to securing their vision for a better future for the Latino community, through the acquisition of property rather than through armed protest. As with Gatsby, the name change from Young Lord William Irizary to crime boss Willie Bodega marks a shift in his social position. Such name changes are presented as part of the cultural territory within Spanish Harlem – they serve as a reaffirmation of cultural identity rather than an attempt to move away from it. Bodega reinvents himself through the mechanisms of social change; his pride in his national identity (and his migrant origins) is never compromised.

Bodega Dreams is divided into three books, containing a series of chapters, or 'rounds'; the story's climax comes in 'Round 12: Knockout' and is followed by a much shorter Book III ('A New Language Being Born') that serves as a eulogy. Quiñonez uses this boxing metaphor to create the sense of life as a constant battle for his Latino community – a fight that they will continue to engage in – and the uplifting eulogy of Book III provides a close that is very different to that of the canonical text Quiñonez has appropriated throughout. Like *The Great Gatsby* it is structured around events within a three month period and revisits past events as a means to providing back-story, but here forays into the past deal with not only the former life of the hero but of the Latino community in general and the novel's narrator, Chino, in particular, presenting us with a less elusive yet more rounded sense of the lives of those living in nineties Harlem. Quiñonez introduces numerous subplots and tensions that provide further details of life in El Barrio, such as relationships between Chino's sister-in-law Negra and her husband or between the youthful 'messiah' from Blanca's church and his green card girlfriend, while the tensions that exist between different immigrant groups within the Latino community – rivalries, for example, between Puerto Ricans and Cubans form part of the fabric of the text, Cuban detective DeJesus stating 'if it was up to me I'd send you all back to that monkey island of yours' (Quiñonez 177). There is no hint of a homosexual subtext in this novel but homosocial bonding is construed as part of Latino culture as evidenced by the long-standing relationship between Chino and Sapo, Bodega and Nene.

Quiñonez employs narrative hinge points from Fitzgerald's novel, ensuring the connections between *Gatsby* and *Bodega Dreams* are self-evident, but he focuses on the life of his narrator, Chino, to a much greater extent. Unlike Bodega, who embraces his past and advocates mobility within the construct of existing culture and community, Chino, shares with Gatsby an initial desire to move beyond the class and culture into which he is born. Both Chino and his wife, Blanca, see education as their pathway out of East Harlem, but in this text, Chino's journey towards a realization that 'no matter how much you learn … how many books you read … how many degrees you get, in the end you are from East Harlem' (Quiñonez 36) is as central to the narrative as Bodega's story. Where Carraway serves as a lone distanced observer, Chino is an active participant in the narrative and in his community: his marital strife, his continuing friendship with Sapo and recounts of his childhood growing up in East Harlem add another narrative layer to the myth of the American dream, lensed through immigrant experience. Narrative momentum continues to revolve around the doomed romance quest as Bodega, like Gatsby, seeks the help of a third party (Chino) to bring about a reunion with lost love Veronica who eventually betrays him, leaving him to take responsibility for her crime. The text is infused with a similar sense of the protagonist's naïve, nostalgic longing; however, Bodega's reunion with Veronica is not constructed as an essential part of his identity quest, and Bodega cannot be construed as the wealthy hero of American fairy tale romance. Quiñonez also deconstructs preconceived notions of the American dream as a tale of individual betterment. Bodega is not the traditional hero of the Alger myth. He is not the poor farm boy who seeks his fortune in 'the big city'; rather, he is an urban immigrant situated throughout within an urban landscape, and his rise from 'rags to riches' does not entail the accumulation of wealth or upward mobility of the kind that ensures personal re-invention. In this story, self 'reinvention' of the kind Gatsby undertakes is conveyed as a negative and it is the canonical text's Daisy figure who attains it: Veronica becomes Vera, who sheds her accent and her culture in a move to Miami, acquiring wealth and social mobility through marriage. She is a Latino trying to 'pass' for an 'Anglo woman' with 'a taste for shopping on Fifth Avenue' (119); she displays the same disdain as Daisy for those she now deems of a lower class than herself and is conveyed as equally shallow and manipulative.

Bodega's past is an integral part of who he is. His is not a personal identity quest: he is already a confident and self assured figure. His quest revolves around ways and means to instil self-esteem into the Latino community, through both spiritual and physical interventions, by means of supporting the arts and provision of housing. Dwyer sees Bodega's preoccupation with communal advancement as a 'peculiarly *postmodern*' stance that 'destabilizes the *modernist* image of the alienated striving hero' (170 my italics). He remains an elusive, enigmatic figure whose identity is shielded as a consequence of his criminal activities, but he is not a loner. In this narrative, he shares his vision with Nazario who functions as the legitimate public face of Bodega's altruism. Nazario's ultimate betrayal of Bodega and of their shared vision sets Bodega up as an even more tragic, self-effacing hero. In the final book, titled 'A New Language Being Born' and labelled as a 'Eulogy', Quinonez inverts the closing moments of Fitzgerald's novel. Though Gatsby and Bodega share a similar fate, the dreams of each 'dissolv[ing] like a wafer in water' (Quiñonez 205), as Gatsby awaits Daisy's call and Bodega's buildings are 'reclaimed by the city', their passing is marked in stark contrast. Unlike Gatsby, the lone tragic hero whose death and funeral become almost a postscript to the narrative, Bodega is mourned by 'the entire barrio'. His three day wake resembles that of 'a head of state' (172), his funeral procession, a 'pageant for a dying monarch' (207), as 'Rainbow Race Latinos … spla[sh] their multi-colored complexion at the edge of Central Park', and parade past US landmarks, from the iconic Gugenheim to El Museo del Barrio, ensuring the representation of sites of Latino significance as part of that New York landscape too. Carraway's closing reference to what 'flowered once for Dutch sailors' eyes – a fresh green breast of the new world' (115) is replaced by a Fifth Avenue transformed into a multi-coloured 'parrot' (207), as Bodega's Latino mourners stake out their claim on US soil. In the closing sequence of *Bodega Dreams*, Quiñonez engages in a meticulous re-vision of the final lines of the canonical text, writing into the literature of the American canon the story of its Latino immigrant communities: Gatsby's belief in 'the green light, the orgiastic future that year by year recedes before us' yet holds out the promise that 'tomorrow we will run faster, stretch out our arms farther ...' (Fitzgerald 115) is translated by Quinonez into 'a green light of hope for everyone' that empowers 'tomorrow['s] Spanish Harlem' to 'run faster, fly higher, stretch out its arms farther', so that 'one day those dreams [can] carry its people to new beginnings' (Quiñonez 213). Bodega, dressed as a Young Lord, appears to Chino in a dream with an optimistic prophecy of multicultural enlightenment that foresees the emergence of 'a beautiful new language' – 'Spanglish' – 'born out of the ashes of two cultures clashing with each other' (212). He legitimizes their native language and directs Chino to its lyrical beauty as they listen to a woman in the barrio whose standard English and Latino words merge, creating new rhythms, new cadences, a new shared language: 'Mira, Junito, go buy un mapo, un conten de leche, and tell el bodeguero yo le pago next Friday. And I don't want to see you in el rufo!' (212). Like other contemporary Latino writers such as Dominican-American Junot Diaz and Mexican-American John Rechy, Quiñonez intermittently employs Spanglish – 'a hybrid of street register', an increasingly popular 'underground vehicle of communication' (Stavans 555) – as a mode of expression that legitimizes his native language and ensures retention of his cultural heritage, identity and history, even as he engages in the adaptation of a canonical narrative written in standard English. In stark contrast to the silenced hero of *The Great Gatsby*, Bodega's dream continues to play out in contemporary Nuyorican literature.

Bodega becomes the community's saviour: presented in murals throughout the barrio as 'Christ with a halo' (Quiñonez 213), he becomes emblematic of the Latino community's capacity to attain an American dream that does not involve excision of immigrant culture. It is a more modest realization of the dream, fuelled not by the traditional desire for personal advancement but by a collective desire to attain a better life in a newly adopted land. For some, the uplifting, idealized optimism of *Bodega Dreams*' closing moments detracts from the more radical politics that have informed Quiñonez' adaptation thus far (Moiles 129). However, Quiñonez' aim as an adapter is to rewrite and revise the canon as a means to foregrounding both ethnic immigrant experience and the value of Nuyorican literature, and for many readers, *Bodega Dreams*, like *Wide Sargasso Sea* and *Jack Maggs* is a re-visionist text that fulfils its creator's political agenda. He successfully hijacks the canon, reclaiming the 'hoodlum' Gatsby as one of his own and transforming him into a vehicle for the exploration of the Latino American dream.

As a work of Young Adult fiction, Sara Benincasa's *Great* occupies a different narrative terrain to that of *Bodega Dreams* or *The Great Gatsby*, but like Quiñonez, Benincasa revises the Gatsby story within a different temporal and cultural landscape, exploring its universal themes in fresh ways of relevance to a specific contemporary audience. The novel is, notes its author 'a girly love drama' – a 'Gatsby-inspired tale of love and lust' with an LGBTQ (Lesbian/Gay/Bi-sexual/Transgendered/Queer) take on the narrative, 'rebooted with girls as the main characters' (Benincasa qtd in Winter). Instantly, we are entering a very different yet intriguing narrative space that places teen female experience centre-stage. This girl-centred re-visionist approach to modernizing the canon for a teen audience is becoming a trademark of writer-comedian Benincasa: her next novel, *Believers*, inspired by William Golding's *Lord of the Flies*, sees the canonical text's all male cast replaced by a teen Christian girls' show choir from Texas, obsessed with Jesus and Taylor Swift (Benincasa qtd in Winter). However, as an adapter, Benincasa's intent is not to present educators with ways to make works of the literary canon more palatable and accessible to the teens who are asked to engage with them as part of their English studies. Benincasa plays with the mythical, universal properties of these canonical texts, aiming to make them familiar and relevant to a contemporary teen–centred readership; her adaptations are far more than 'teacher-friendly' exercises. *Great*, voted by *Teen Vogue* as one of the fifteen most exciting YA novels of 2012, is a successful work of YA fiction in its own right, and for many of its teen readers, it is their *primary* experience of the narrative. It 'reboots' *The Great Gatsby*, and for readers who are familiar with that text, there are meaningful resonances between the two, but it functions within the genre of YA fiction as a stand-alone text that speaks to its teen audience without a hint of teacherly patronage.

Benincasa is an author who is interested in questions of the mind and, in particular, in those instabilities that haunt young women from teenage years to adulthood. Her memoir, *Agorafabulous! Dispatches from My Bedroom* (2012) focuses on her own mental health issues, and in *Great*, she engages with issues in our contemporary society that are problematic for her teen audience. YA author David Belbin claims teen fiction of this type provides its teen audience with 'a bridge to take them to the other side' (142), not to a greater appreciation of the canon as may be deemed an appropriate comment about one function of *Great*, but as an aid to transition, from reading of children's fiction to adult fiction. More importantly in Benincasa's novel, the 'bridge' provides a point of transition from teen-hood to adulthood, from self questioning to self-knowledge via shared experiences played out in the novel, and primarily through the filter of a first-person narrator. YA fiction is reflective of the societal norms of its era of production, yet it also explores the tensions between familiarity and novelty, providing effortless pleasure and immersion in the story-world while introducing new experiences for its reader – experiences through which they can gain knowledge of situations and emotions beyond the parameters of their known world. Its authors are, notes Belbin, acutely aware that 'they are writing for an audience that [they] want to disappear, to move on' (134). As with J. D. Salinger's teen narrator, Holden Caulfield from *The Catcher in the Rye*, *Great*'s narrator, Naomi Rye (after whom we can assume she is in part named), becomes a filter for shared teen experiences, expressing teenage angst in its many forms in response to the complex contemporary pressures teens have to deal with as they transition to adulthood. The current popularity of dystopian YA fiction is dependent upon its capacity to simplify life for its teen reader: despite some romantic tokenism, survival is all in narratives like *The Hunger Games* trilogy or *The Maze Runner*, and matters of life and death take precedence over navigation of day-to-day complexities of relationships within this social-networking age. Where *The Hunger Games* and *Maze Runner* negate the significance of consumerist ideology, Benincasa's *Great* mirrors Fitzgerald's critique of it. Her exploration of the darker side of self-reinvention and the class-bound limitations of the American dream within a contemporary Hamptons setting, presents a modern equivalent to affluent East and West Egg. Here, though, the cultural referents are consciously late twentieth, early twenty-first century pop culture references – *Clueless* (1995), *Legally Blond* (2001) and *Gossip Girl* (2007–2012), fashion blogs and Facebook, products such as Birkin handbags, Marc Jacobs designer dresses and Ferragamo shoes. They invest the text with familiarity for Benincasa's teen readers, allowing them to identify with its protagonist, and maintaining a connection to the consumer-driven critique that is central to *The Great Gatsby*. Its Hamptons setting provides not only an apt modern-day equivalent to Fitzgerald's Roaring Twenties, but a story-world that meets the teen girl's interest in the arenas of fashion, social networking and romance.

The novel's narrator, Naomi, provides the teen reader with access to the world of the Hamptons social set, signalling to her readers from the outset that it is a place inhabited by 'fakes and liars' who retain their class status 'through delicate subterfuge' (Benincasa). Like Chino in *Bodega Dreams* she takes a far more active role in the story than Nick Carraway, and employs the language of her social group rather than a more distanced literary voice. 'I was going to lose my copter V-card' (12), she tells us in the opening moments, and the many witty, frank conversations between Naomi and her best friend, Skags, establish a teen-specific point of reference adhered to throughout. Naomi opens her narrative with sage words of fatherly advice (1–2) similar to those imparted by Carraway, and the life lessons each narrator learns during this brief yet crucial three month period become an integral part of the story. However, *Great* is more *Naomi's* story than that of this novel's Gatsby figure, Jacinta Trimalchio, whose presence in the Hamptons during that particular summer shapes the narrative but whose experience is secondary to that of its narrator. Benincasa's gender switch, from male to female narrator, and from the normative heterosexual romance of Gatsby and Daisy to the same sex romance of Jacinta Trimalchio and Delilah Fairweather, constitutes a radical shift from the canonical text's original premise. However, its most telling re-vision is related to its structural redefinition as a bildungsroman or contemporary 'coming of age' story. Although, with the exception of its closing moments, the novel employs the narrative hinge points of Fitzgerald's canonical text, it becomes the story of Naomi's summer – a summer during which she embarks on an emotional journey of self discovery and from which she emerges – like Dorothy in *The Wizard of Oz* to whom she compares herself (13) – with the realization that there is no place like her Chicago home. She begins the narrative as a 'Chicagoan through and through' (46) but during her time in the Hamptons she undergoes significant changes before she returns to that starting point, a better informed and wiser individual. Skags, as level-headed observer and commentator on teen sexual behaviours and the pitfalls of the Hamptons mind-set Naomi is increasingly seduced by, becomes an important addition to the narrative. She provides a more distanced estimation of the story's events and functions as Naomi's conscience – an extra diegetic component – indicating once more the increased significance of this novel's first person narrator and of her journey towards self knowledge.

Benincasa establishes an intimate relationship between her narrator and the female teen reader: Naomi is the kind of likeable, morally grounded character that a teen reader can easily relate to and journey with. The narrative charts her shift from being a 'Chicagoan through and through' (Benincasa 46), to a girl who unwittingly becomes increasingly a part of the Hampton's social set she initially despises. She may never lose her 'Chicagoan' perspective entirely – Skags' narrative interjections ensure this – but as with Dickens' Pip, or Brontë's Jane Eyre, there are significant moments when the reader and the narrator can recognize that change in attitude. She notes initially, the small ways in which she begins to fit in:

> ' "So you don't usually *summer* in the Hamptons?" I said. It was the first time I'd ever used *summer* as a verb. Only rich people do that' (18).

Naomi becomes increasingly willing to participate, compromising her values until we reach a point in the narrative where she 'stop[s] thinking about home' (144). The many asides that detail how she feels as opposed to how she ought to feel according to the edicts of her politically correct best friend Skags cleverly illustrate the complex choices the teenage girl faces, torn between what she wants to do/feel and what she ought. She notes, for example that Skags would admonish her for being 'woefully complicit in [her] own subjugation' to 'conventional narrow-minded notions of femininity' when Delilah and Jacinta, her 'plastic friends' (142), treat her as their 'pet project' (145), undertaking her fashion transformation. But, like the average teenage girl, Naomi chooses to take part in her own Cinderella type make-over. This notion of the makeover is particularly relevant to Benincasa's contemporary teen audience: we begin with a rebellious Naomi dressed in a Cure T-shirt and Doc Martens but her readiness to comply with her mother's requests to change into Marc Jacobs designer dresses demonstrates not her acquiescence to her mother's desires but to her *own*, albeit temporarily. Similarly, when she fails to challenge Jeff on his increasingly non PC behaviours, she may note that Skags would be disappointed in her for not tackling his hetero-normative, rich boy stance, yet she is willing to compromise her values at this point in time since Jeff 'was the best shot [she] had at getting a beach boyfriend, something [she'd] always secretly wanted' (92). Skag's critical commentaries are brought seamlessly into the narrative without any foregrounding of didactic intent on the part of the author and without alienating the reader because they are filtered through Naomi's naïve, adolescent voice – a voice teen readers will more readily identify with. The relationship between Naomi and Skags facilitates this kind of commentary without recourse to moralistic preaching.

By the close of the narrative, Naomi returns to her Chicagoan roots and values, 'slipping back into [her] real skin instead of the plastic facsimile [she'd] been wearing all summer long' (Benincasa 247), but for the duration of the novel, she has undergone a valuable journey to a point of self-knowledge, a journey of the kind that helps Benincasa's teen audience to build bridges between the experiences of adolescence and adulthood. Though Naomi's astute comments on the shallow, morally redundant Hamptons set are well founded, what she – unlike Skags – fails to see, until the closing moments of the novel, is that she too is becoming part of that set. Hamptons socialite and blogger, Olivia, claims that Naomi is by choice one of 'the fabulous people' she claims to despise (170). Her relationship with her society obsessed mother forms part of Naomi's narrative journey: from an initial point of mother/daughter conflict of the kind so often explored in teen fiction, she begins to develop a grudging acceptance of her mother, only to experience its collapse in the closing moments when Anne Rye's immoral behaviour is exposed. Similarly, we witness Naomi's blossoming relationship with Jeff, from the moment of the first kiss (93) to the point where, post White Party, she can no longer ignore his moral shortcomings and rejects him. However, before she reaches this moment of recognition, the lure of having a boyfriend, of belonging, of having 'a girly girlfriend' like Delilah (93) seduces her to the point that she stops calling her father and Skags, 'stops thinking about home' (144). Despite her father's sound advice and the ongoing commentaries of Skags, Naomi reaches a dark point where she is willing to get into a car with a drunken Teddy Barrington, but after witnessing the aftermath of the car accident and the careless response of people like Teddy and Jeff, her final withdrawal begins, prompted here by her *own* conscience.

For Benincasa, 'it was a challenge to write a narrator who was on one level quite progressive and forward-thinking, but who held prejudices she didn't acknowledge'(Winter). However, by employing the structure of the bildungsroman and the extra-diegetic device of a second narrator, Benincasa draws a complex portrait of teen experience that explores the kind of difficult life choices faced by her readership. *Great* tackles head on the kinds of complexities that are excised from dystopian YA fiction and to a certain extent from other adaptations of *The Great Gatsby*. It functions as an LGBTQ (or GLBT – Gay, Lesbian, Bi-sexual, Transgendered) text; as with other novels written in this particular YA sub-genre, it is concerned with 'modeling how our culture has and should change in order to reflect our increasing sense of tolerance' (Hill 20). Christine Jenkins notes that gay characters are now becoming integrated into the narrative in ways that do not bring the storyline 'to a halt' in order to explicate 'gay identity' (Jenkins quoted in Hill 20); instead, gay characters form an integral part of the storyline and are no longer seen only in narratives preoccupied with 'coming out'. Assertive lesbian Skags functions in *Great* as a more distanced, insightful social commentator providing, from the edges of the story, other ways of interpreting events and actions of characters involved for both readers *and* first person narrator, Naomi. Her lesbian relationship with Jenny Carpenter is set up as a contrast to both the Jacinta/Delilah relationship (which only hints at such a possibility) and Naomi's 'normative' relationship with her first boyfriend, Jeff. Via commentaries from the sexually experienced Skags, Benincasa explores teen female sexuality in its many guises, presenting her reader with an array of sexual identities and emotional responses with which they can choose to identify their own experience and desire.

The romance quest forms part of *Great*'s narrative structure, but unlike romance-driven film adaptations, its exploration of 'romance' is tempered by the realization that 'love' can take many different forms, and it is intrinsically connected here to notions of selfhood – that of Jacinta and Naomi in particular. Instead of replacing the Daisy/Gatsby relationship with yet another heterosexual romance quest, Benincasa presents a same sex romance, 'a love story that [is] more about obsession and desire than about true love'. It is a 'Sapphic' relationship and Jacinta's obsession, like Gatsby's, is fuelled as much by a nostalgic yearning for some lost aspect of her past self, as by sexual desire. For Benincasa, the Gatsby/Daisy relationship brings to mind 'the way girls sometimes obsess over one another in middle school and high school'; they 'see things they want to embody and fall into a kind of love with one another that has very little to do with romance' *or* 'true love' and everything to do with teen female experience. She questions whether Jacinta and Delilah would 'self-identify' as lesbians and leaves her readers to interpret the nature of their relationship as they see fit (Benincasa qtd in Winter). It is ironic that female sexuality in general and homosexuality in particular is addressed so openly in this YA novel given that to engage with the canonical text's subtextual references to Nick and Jordan's homosexuality was deemed too risqué for cinema audiences in the seventies. Inclusion of such referencing in Truman Capote's screenplay for the 1974 film adaptation resulted in its rejection by the studio, and it is not until 2000 that Nick's latent homosexuality is revisited in Markowitz' TV movie. Despite the gatekeeping roles of publishers, educators, parents and so on, successful YA fiction does not shy away from what may be seen as difficult content of a sexual nature.

In addition to its exploration of teen sexual awareness, the novel examines other tropes readily associated with YA fiction: the depiction of relationships between parents and teens (often involving conflict), between friends and friendship groups forms part of the fabric of such literature. While the pursuit of the American dream is a central premise of *The Great Gatsby*, here it becomes one of the narrative's many parts, and it is explored through several characters. Naomi's mother, Anne Rye, formerly waitress Anne Gryzkowski and now successful entrepreneur and celebrity baker, 'Brand Name TM' (Benincasa 124), realizes her American dream. Misti and Goiovanni, children of immigrant bakers, do not. The rise and impending fall of the Bake like Anne Rye! empire forms a subplot within the novel that explores the relationship between Naomi and her mother, and culminates in Naomi's rejection of her, despite a softening of antagonisms between them during the course of the novel. It also exposes this American dream as something that is dependent on the deceit and exploitation of others. For Fitzgerald's Alger hero, the acquisition of wealth, by whatever means, is in and of itself a powerful driver; without wealth Gatsby's other dream of rekindling his relationship with upper-class Daisy is untenable, and without Daisy he remains incomplete. However, Benincasa's contemporary Gatsby dreamer has already experienced life as one of the privileged Hamptons set; for Jacinta, wealth becomes purely a transitory means to a desired end, and when introduced to the narrative, her status in society is attained not through wealth but through the cult of the celebrity – a celebrity that constructs a suitably modern riff on the canonical text's thematic preoccupation with self-reinvention. Her dream identity as fashion blogger, based on high school wunderkind fashion blogger Tavi Gevinson (Benincasa qtd in Winter), is one of a number of fairy tale tropes employed in the novel. It raises her to the status of a celebrity, again fuelled by rumours and built on fabricated truth, and ensures her acceptance into Hamptons society. Anne Rye notes 'her branding is fantastic. A mix of high-end and DIY. Aspirational yet accessible' (Benincasa 68) which again suggests that Jacinta, like Gatsby, is instrumental in her own reinvention. As blogger Olivia notes, Jacinta is never at the parties she blogs about: her blog is yet another fabrication, her self-reinvention just a pictorial chimera as she posts headless shots of herself, dressed in 'free' Vivien Westwood. She is still a loner by choice and cites the anonymity of blogging as one of its most attractive facets, but, where Gatsby struggles to gain any kind of acceptance, her constructed identity gives her not only a revered place within the teens social set of the Hamptons as they hang on her every fashion word but a means to accessing and impressing Delilah, her first love. She is, however, a Cinderella figure for whom the clock is ticking as her trust fund dwindles away and her investment in an impossible dream of an independent life with Delilah in the Bronx is perceived as pure fairy tale by everyone except Jacinta. Like the naïve Gatsby, she cannot see how inconceivable the union between her penniless self and the privileged Delilah really is.

Just as Benincasa has updated the consumerist elements of the canonical text, turning, for example, the iconic Dr T J Eckleberg advertising sign for spectacles into a sign advertising Dr Zazzle's plastic surgery, she uses Jacinta's demise to address another issue of relevance to contemporary teens. Presenting her death as an act of teen suicide brings to the fore the sense of hopelessness and isolation teens, who appear to have it all, can feel. Jacinta, 'always so full of hope – irrational, astonishing, sometimes even irritating hope' (Benincasa 2), is reduced to a wilful act of suicide. On the verge of being exposed as 'Adriana DeStefano' – whose last name was 'like a curse word' (210) in Hamptons society – she resumes her other identity as a working-class Miami girl who eats junk food and dresses in the kind of clothes that Naomi wears as part of her teen rebellion rather than as a signifier of class at the start of the novel. It is at this point in the narrative that Naomi takes on the more adult role that has thus far fallen to Skags as she cautions the ever-optimistic Jacinta against relying on Delilah to do the right thing and urges her to go to the police. It is one of the final steps in her bildungsroman journey; 'deleting' her mother is another. However, while Fitzgerald's Gatsby's death is unheeded, Jacinta's death becomes a global event of even greater proportions than that of Willie Bodega, though for less honourable reasons. Jacinta works her internet celebrity status from beyond the grave, leaving Naomi a Vimeo recording for upload onto her Facebook and Twitter account; predictably, the news of her version of events goes viral within seconds. Here, Benincasa exploits the social networking aspect of her narrative for her internet savvy teen audience and ends Jacinta's tale in a manner that will satisfy that audience's desire for justice. The last scene, however, returns us to the novel's narrator who in this story functions as its protagonist. We end with a return to the normalcy of her life in Chicago, to her long-standing relationship with Skags, in the company of a narrator who, in the spirit of all good bildungsroman narratives, has matured along the way.

The Great Gatsby: A radical rethink (*G* and *The Great Gatsby*, a graphic adaptation)

Classic adaptations signal their relationship with a precursor text, and *The Great Gatsby* film adaptations from Clayton and Luhrmann flag up their relationship with Fitzgerald's *The Great Gatsby* from the outset. They work to establish and to maintain their connection with the canonical text, even as they translate it into the very different medium of film. Re-visionist adaptations studied in this section redefine the source text's dominant discourse yet they too acknowledge on ongoing relationship with *The Great Gatsby* as a text that is synonymous with certain universal themes of continuing interest. However, there are inevitably instances where classification systems do not offer a clear indication of adaptive type. South Park's 'Pip', for example, is radical in its presentation, though 'faithful' in its adherence to the bare narrative bones of Dickens' *Great Expectations*; Lewton's *I Walked with a Zombie'* relocates elements of *Jane Eyre* and *Rebecca* to the most unexpected of cinematic genres, the zombie film, yet it remains close to certain thematic and narrative elements of both source texts; a film like *The Others* has a more tentative relationship with Henry James 'The Turn of the Screw'. Like Sandra Goldbacher (*The Governess*) and Alejandro Amenabar (*The Others*), the makers of G offer no definitive statement of adaptive intent, but here the parallels that can be drawn between the storyline of G and *The Great Gatsby* suggest overwhelmingly that it is a close reading of the canonical text, if only at the level of plot. Does this mean that it is a classic adaptation of Fitzgerald's novel, despite its very different treatment? Can it be a re-visionist adaptation without any declared adaptive intent or fully realized re-vision of its textual politics? Or does its soap opera take on *The Great Gatsby* signal a more radical digression? Similarly, Nicki Greenberg's graphic novel relocates the narrative within a very different medium and involves an even more radical re-imagining (from fictitious humans to surreal animal forms) than that realized in the *South Park* adaptation of *Great Expectations* whilst simultaneously retaining the narrative template, characterization and thematic concerns of the source text. In this instance the intent to adapt is never in question and Greenberg's lyrical prose is akin to that of Fitzgerald. In many ways, both G and Greenberg's graphic novel, *The Great Gatsby*, can be read as classic adaptations, leading us to question, as anticipated from the outset of this wide ranging study of adaptation as a process and a mode of textual analysis, that classification systems serve as a means to opening up discussion rather than as definitive statements of adaptive intent.

Like Ernesto Quiñonez, the makers of G have the potential to reclaim the 'hoodlum' Gatsby in what could have been an insightful exploration of the socio-political landscape of contemporary hip hop culture. The reconstruction of *The Great Gatsby's* rags to riches protagonist as a self-made hip hop mogul, residing not in twenties West Egg but in an equally affluent Hamptons of the late nineties offers an intriguing and credible extension of Fitzgerald's mythical tale for a media-saturated twenty-first-century audience preoccupied with pop culture and the cult of celebrity. Where Willie Bodega becomes emblematic of the Latino community's collective desire and potential to attain an American dream that does not involve excision of immigrant culture, in this adaptation the protagonist, Summer G, is constructed as a Gatsbyesque figure who is distanced from his urban ghetto roots, despite the fact that his credibility as a hip hop artist remains intrinsically linked to his cultural origins. It draws intriguing parallels between nineties hip hop stars who, by transcending their working-class origins through their music, have become synonymous with self-reinvention and the kind of extravagant affluence we readily associate with the mythical Gatsby, but while Fitzgerald's immigrant Alger hero is able to efface his former working-class status (and Bodega has no desire to), this is not a credible possibility for his hip hop counterpart. Herein lies one of the film's insurmountable flaws: to detach hip hop artists from the culture that informs their music is to negate their identity as hip hop artists. The film's title signals its adaptive relationship with *The Great Gatsby* and it employs many of the novel's narrative hinge points, but there is little engagement with Fitzgerald's ideological concerns and no reference to his novel in the film's credits. The universal themes of central importance in Fitzgerald's text are ripe for re-vision in this adaptation: matters of race, class, consumerism and pursuit of the American dream are of equal relevance, but here they are either consciously excised, side-lined or dealt with in a superficial manner. Instead of an equally telling critique of the American dream of the type realized in Quiñonez' *Bodega Dreams*, Cherot's film revises the canonical text into a soap opera version of that dream, diluting the politics of the story in favour of a narrative that reconfigures its characters as predictable stereotypes and foregrounds its romance quest to the exclusion of all else.

Within the industrial and financial constraints of cinema, adaptation to a commercially viable genre like romance is not necessarily a bad thing. Earlier and later film adaptations play the romance card to attain box office success. Yet this adaptation attains neither critical nor box office success: it is more B movie, or TV movie at best, and given its soap opera style would have been better suited to small screen adaptation. Collaborative work practices are also a given in the film industry, yet in this instance the collaboration results in a lack of adaptive direction and creative control. G is a film conceived and financed as a vanity project by Andrew Lauren (son of Ralph Lauren, whose own immigrant success story possibly informs this re-vision of the *Gatsby* narrative and whose costumes adorn males in Clayton's 1974 adaptation); he worked collaboratively with Charles E. Drew Jr on the idea and on production, and Drew Jr co-wrote the screenplay with director, Cherot. Though Clayton and Luhrmann work as part of a successful collaborative team on their film adaptations of *The Great Gatsby*, their directorial leadership shapes the decision-making process, and each film has a clear identity, a clear authorial/adaptive intent. However, by his own admission Cherot was employed as little more than a 'director for hire' on this project – a metteur en scene rather than an auteur of the status of Clayton or Luhrmann (Morales) and while this does not preclude the critical or commercial success or failure of *G*, it does highlight the absence of a clear adaptive agenda. Despite his directorial promise and his earlier success with the self-financed indie screwball rom-com, *Hav Plenty* (1997), Cherot's artistic investment in *G* was limited, and the end product, shot on a tight budget to a tight schedule, was altered considerably by Lauren in post production.

In *Hav Plenty*, Cherot seeks to transcend the black movie genre: his characters' 'blackness' is of no significance to the narrative. Cherot speaks of his desire to construct a different, non-stereotypical image of the black man and woman; his aim is to replace images of the 'black pimp' and the black 'buffoon' with 'images of the responsible black father and mother', making the 'literate black masculine on screen … not just the *exception* but the *norm*' (Cherot qtd in Bey). Such an approach is to a certain extent evident in *G*: its cast of predominantly black performers consists of a diverse range of Hamptonites, from the affluent nouveau riche Summer G brigade and numerous successful professionals to wealthy heir Chip Hightower and the less privileged social groups represented by his mistress and Sky's cousin Trey. But without the creative control to explore such aspects of racial transcendence, Cherot's attempts to move beyond tired stereotypes becomes tokenistic, and the characters (protagonist included) are ostensibly defined by their soap opera roles: the jilted lover, the unfaithful husband, the conflicted wife/lover, the comedic sidekicks, and so on. Despite the *desire* to transcend race, the production is unable to *transcend* its soap opera qualities on screen and its politics are lost in translation. It becomes a sanitized version of *The Great Gatsby* that still comes from a white middle to upper class perspective (that of Lauren) when it could have been an exploration of the American dream from the perspective of hip hop's Bronx neighbourhood African-Americans, speaking to and from that culture in the way that Quinonez' *Bodega Dreams* speaks to and from Latino culture.

Instead, we have Summer G, whose success is dependent on hip hop music, originating from a ghettoized urban scene that the film steadfastly refuses to acknowledge.

In pursuit of distribution deals, the film was first shown on the festival circuit in 2002 and secured only a limited domestic theatrical release in 2005, taking just over $3,000,000 in box office returns. While adaptations in 1974 and 2013, were afforded a big production budget that allowed them to translate the *Gatsby* narrative to screen in all of its visual and aural splendour, this revised *Gatsby* was restricted by its limited budget from the outset. Its Hamptons party scenes lack the required visual glamour and opulence, and though its affiliation with hip hop should dictate the importance of music in general and of hip hop music in particular, its musical identity is almost non-existent. With the exception of the odd moment of diegetic music on car radios and during party scenes, music is a hardly discernible feature in this film. Only one song – a ballad rather than a hip hop track – is performed in the film at Sky's funeral. Musical director, Bill Conti, is a white middle-aged male best known for his work on *Rocky* (1976) and its sequels, and the melodramatic orchestral score offers no point of connection with the musical rhythms of hip hop or its lyrics. Conti's score is more in tune with his work on TV soap opera *Dynasty* than with a film narrative based on the rise of a hip hop artist and the music industry. Though this is meant to be the story of a hip hop Gatsby there is far less hip hop vibe in *G* than in Luhrmann's 'faithful' 2013 adaptation. Its music is incidental and conservative rather than edgy and evocative of the contemporary hip hop scene, and it has none of the anticipated musical moments of other hip hop films like *Eight Mile* (2002) or *Hustle & Flow* (2005) in which music becomes a storytelling device and a means to attaining personal redemption.

G is, according to film critic Roger Ebert, a 'fictional recycling of the Sean Combs aka P Diddy story', at least at the level of 'lifestyle'; self-made hip hop millionaire Combs is synonymous with consumer culture of the kind Fitzgerald describes in his novel and his now famous annual Hamptons White Party is reprised in the film's closing party scene. The life stories of hip hop artists like Combs are intertextualized in this adaptation and in later films such as 50 Cents' semi-autobiographical *Get Rich or Die Tryin'* (2005) or *Notorious* (2009), which details the rags to riches story of rap artist B.I.G. But perhaps a closer referencing of the rags to riches rise of such hip hop artists would have yielded a more telling exploration of the myth of the American dream from an African-American perspective. It would certainly have entailed a more detailed engagement with the back-story that informs the transition from urban ghetto to Hamptons affluence than that which is afforded in *G*. It would also have prompted inclusion of narrative threads related to our contemporary obsession with celebrity culture. Instead, we have a scene that has the *potential* to parody our contemporary obsession with celebrity culture but becomes an exercise in comedic stereotyping. When rising hip hop artists Bo and Daisy approach an affluent Hamptons black man for directions to the nearest McDonald's, they are immediately assumed to be drug-taking reprobates, and it is his white partner who responds in an exaggerated show of celeb-struck enthusiasm. The story's representative of inherited wealth, Chip Hightower, is also a black man far removed from any connection to the urban roots of hip hop. This racial inversion of the canonical text's racist Tom Buchanan should provide an interesting point of comparison, but Chip's loaded soap opera name, his cosy relationship with his white neighbours, and the inclusion of crass moments such as the retrieval of his mistress's underwear from his coat pocket, undermine any sense of his credibility as other than a soap opera stereotype. Furthermore, in a patronizing twist, the only white character of any prominence – G's PA, who is played by Andrew Lauren – emerges as the voice of reason when G and his 'home boys', armed with baseball bats, foolishly plan to assault a love rival. Similarly, fellow hip hop artists under G's tutelage rarely transcend their stereotype, despite the fact that the film excises any reference to their former urban identity. Bo may claim that 'the old days of writing about the ghetto are over' as young black rappers now have social mobility, but without any reference to where hip hop music has come from or to what lives characters like Summer G have led prior to their 'rise', the significance of that rise and the journeying towards it is negated.

The life of James Gatz is known only in part, but his past is slowly revealed during the course of Carraway's narration. In this re-vision of the *Gatsby* narrative, there is no referencing of Summer G's childhood or to any gangster past: we return once only, to the point where he is a respectable business student living with his lover, Sky, and struggling to begin his record label. In an effort to assure 'racial transcendence', we are presented with a sanitized version of G – an altruistic entrepreneur whose only connection with his ghetto roots comes from a Hamptons party scene in which he plays host to disadvantaged kids from Harlem. By twenty minutes into the narrative, all of the limited back-story – of G, of his relationship with Sky – has been revealed. In true soap opera style, this narrative focuses instead on what happens during the course of the story as it plays out on screen rather than on what has led us to this point in time, and it is the romance at the centre of that story that dominates screen time. However, where Gatsby's romance quest has a grail-like quality, the reunion of G and Sky is constructed as a far more commonplace love story with which a soap audience can readily identify. There is no delayed entrance for hero G and the first reunion between former lovers G and Sky takes place in the opening stages of the film, establishing their relationship as its main narrative thread. Sky is initially the far more likable, conventional heroine of soap melodrama, and within a contemporary Hamptons scene, her alliance with rich Chip Hightower is its own kind of postfeminist rags to riches narrative. Pivotal plot points from the canonical text help to shape the narrative, but there are a number of detours, omissions and additions that serve to place the film in soap opera territory. Though the majority of the story revolves around a recount of the rekindled relationship between G and Sky to the point where she decides to remain with Chip, we open with a scene set in the future which, for viewers familiar with *The Great Gatsby* relays the end of the novel and Gatsby's demise, as a blood-covered G stumbles along the sea shore. We then cut to a funeral scene which again works on our assumption that Gatsby is dead but subverts expectation of the lone hero since the funeral is well attended. At this point we return to the story proper for the rest of the film's running time, and while the same limited time frame is adhered to, there is no attempt to employ the novel's first person narration. Tracy (aka Tre), a music journalist sent to interview Summer G, becomes just one of its many characters. Tre provides a conservative moral commentary of sorts but his role is not that of social observer: he functions as plot device rather than as a means to character development for either himself or G. Character development in general is sketchy, and the story is driven by events that when translated to this scenario appear shallow: Chip's affair, the rekindling of the love between Sky and G, the setting up of a 'love test' that G passes and yet still looses the girl and so on. Any additions to the plot, such as the arrival of a gun-toting Chip at G's house and Sky's similar gun-crazed moment when she threatens to shoot Chip or added love scenes between not only G and Sky but Sky and Chip, amplify its melodramatic potential. There are also story detours here as subplots introduce further melodramatic storylines. The parallel story of Nicole and Craig and their doomed love culminates in a violent showdown during the film's closing moments; at this point we learn that it is Sky whose funeral we have witnessed at the start – her blood, not G's, that covers his white suit as he shuffles along the sea shore – providing the audience with the kind of reveal we have come to anticipate in the genre of soap melodrama. The villainous Chip is also afforded a subplot that heightens the tension of the closing scene as police stake out G's house in the hope of apprehending him for an anticipated assault on Chip. It is interesting to note that G's Sky decides to stay with Chip, despite G's willingness to leave the music business for her and despite Chip's infidelities. The anticipated romantic close of the romance genre is sacrificed to the more salacious demands of melodrama but whether as a structural nod to *The Great Gatsby* or as a means to heightening the drama in true soap opera style is debatable.

In the final moments we return to the funeral scene and the farewell between G and Tre, as Tre delivers the film's syrup-laden tagline: 'Does hip hop have a heart?' Unlike the insightful portrayal of the myth of the Latino immigrant's American dream achieved by Quinonez in *Bodega Dreams*, adapters involved in the making of *G* construct the American dream as one already attained by the African-American. The potential to reconfigure the myth of the American dream from a credible African-American perspective is sacrificed in favour of its endeavours to re-vision the narrative as a tale of racial transcendence in which immigrant status and the journey towards the elusive dream is no longer of significance. This is ultimately a white man's take on racial ascendancy that serves to negate the blackness (and thus the authenticity) of hip hop culture in all of its richness and diversity. Sean Coombs (aka P Diddy) may see himself as a self-proclaimed Gatsby figure, but there is little sign of him asserting any affinity with Summer G and this melodramatic remix of *The Great Gatsby*, re-visioned as soap opera set in the Hamptons.

Adapter Nicki Greenberg foregrounds the connections between her graphic novel and the canonical work of literature she is adapting: she states on her opening page that what follows is 'based on the 1925 novel *The Great Gatsby* by F. Scott Fitzgerald', she retains its title, and she exploits the connections between this graphic text and its canonical counterpart in a way that is more readily associated with classic adaptation. And yet, like the *South Park* episode, 'Pip', and Lloyd Jones' novel, *Mr Pip*, (which similarly signal their relationship with Dickens' *Great Expectations* via their titles), it too works against our expectation of what a story thus named may involve. Greenberg realizes an even more radical re-imagining of her chosen canonical text than that realized in the cartoon series *South Park*, turning Fitzgerald's fictitious humans into surreal bestial forms while simultaneously retaining the narrative template, characterization and thematic concerns of *The Great Gatsby*. By adapting this quintessential American story into graphic novel form, Greenberg 'affect[s]' a 'decisive journey away from the informing source' (Sanders 26). The narrative is communicated in a medium that, due to its affiliation with the comic book, repositions this work of 'high art' within the realms of mainstream popular culture, and in this sense it challenges our perception of the canon.

Comic books and graphic novels have emerged as valid fields of scholarly debate in the last twenty years only (Dallacqua 365); fan sites and trade magazines continue to dominate discussion of such texts in print form and on the internet, while academic criticism remains 'emergent, oppositional and underground' (Freedman 28). However, there is a growing body of criticism that seeks to differentiate between the graphic novel and its comic book roots – roots that 'inscribe a series of assumptions about ambition, "seriousness" and quality' (30). Greenberg's decision to adapt a canonical text to graphic novel form demonstrates her faith in the medium's capacity to engage in ambitious and serious storytelling of a type that goes beyond our preconceived notions of the comic book. Her publisher, Allen & Unwin, seeks to distance the literary graphic novel from its comic book counterpart (Wagner qtd in Dunford) but remains resistant to some of the new alternative terminology – 'sequential art', graphic narrative[e]', 'paraliteracy' – and choose instead to apply the term 'graphic novel' to her fiction as 'a marketing buzzword' that 'promot[es] a new form that step[s] away from the restrictions on the comic book' (Wagner qtd in Dunford). However, there is no clear statement of such intent from Greenberg. She aligns the story content of her graphic novels with works of literature – she is currently working on a graphic novel adaptation of Shakespeare's *Hamlet* – but their pictorial and spatial design underscores their affinity with the comic book. Attempts to distance the graphic novel from its comic book origins are seen as counter-productive by some critics: it would, according to Charles Hatfield 'mak[e] no sense and indeed, would be bitterly ironic, to erect a "canon", an authoritative consensus that would reproduce within the comics field the same operations of domination and exclusion that have for so long been brought to bear against the field as a whole' (xiii). Should we begin to differentiate between the comic book and the graphic novel, particularly in an instance like this where, as an adaptation of a canonical text, it is directly related to a work of 'high art'? Or does such an exercise create hierarchical values based criteria of the kind that have plagued the study of adaptations for decades? The questions raised by the evaluative debates surrounding the comic book – its form, its content, its audience and its placement on the low art/high art continuum – present interesting lines of enquiry when one considers works that are adapted from the literary canon.

Greenberg's *The Great Gatsby* is not an abridged Classics illustrated of the kind that proved popular in the forties as a means of 'encourag[ing] wholesome reading habits' (Yang): she is not aiming to 'simplify' or to create an 'easy read' graphic novel of the kind educators continue to seize upon in order to create bridges to classic literature for reluctant students. As with Benincasa's *Great*, or Posy Simmonds' graphic novel, *Gemma Bovery*, there is no educative agenda here; instead, Greenberg and her publisher have pitched it as an adult read that exists beyond its identity as an adaptation of Fitzgerald's novel. Like the most successful graphic novels, it is the equal of print-based literature: it is 'complex, academically challenging, and rich with literary elements and devices' (Dallacqua 376). For Greenberg, adaptation is a 'creative process' during which 'the adapter's impulses must be guided by the meaning, tone and form of the original text': she advocates 'sensitive listening to the book' being adapted and urges restraint on the part of the adapter (Picturing Gatsby). *Gatsby* took her six years to complete, and her aim was to 'cradle' the precursor text, 'to turn it gently in [her] hands and allow different lights to play on it so that a reader might see new gleams of meaning flash across it' (Picturing Gatsby). In its treatment of the canonical text's thematic preoccupations, its story content, and even its lyrical prose, Greenberg's novel may again be deemed 'classic adaptation'; it is its re-imagining in graphic *form* that makes it a more radical reconstruction of the Gatsby narrative. Greenberg is interested in the way graphic novel's storytelling devices present us with other ways of receiving 'story'.

In the graphic novel 'meaning is generated by verbal language, iconographic language and the different modes of interplay between both' but its meaning is also communicated through the architectural sequencing of its frames (Adler 2278–2280). Furthermore, it is the silences (or spaces) between frames, commonly referred to in comic book terms as the 'gutters', that invite the reader/viewer 'to construct meaning within a sequence based on premises (of a textual or a visual kind)' (2279). Scott McCloud refers to such moments as 'a silent dance of the seen and the unseen', that 'several times on each page' releases the reader 'like a trapeze artist … into the open air of imagination' (McCloud qtd in Freedman 31–32). The 'rhetorical function of silence' within a sequence creates an 'ellipsis – of both imagery and text between frames, a space where the reader/observer is nonetheless called to reconstruct meaning' (Adler 2280). Our relationship with the adapted graphic novel becomes a much more proactive one; it engages us in the process of making meaning as we circumnavigate the textual silences and the purposeful placement of frames on the page. Rather than simplifying narrative, well conceived graphic novels construct narrative complexity through the way in which they organize 'story' on the page. Greenberg concurs, claiming that, while the visuals and the dialogue within the frame of each page are essential storytelling components, the atmosphere of that story is also relayed through its layout, its movements in space and time (and *at* the same time) and through its multiple-conversations. Even the black space around frames becomes part of the narrative in this medium; it can elongate time and thus hold the moment for further reader/viewer contemplation (Greenberg in Wheeler). Here, our processing of text is not dependent on readerly movements from left to right (or from right to left as in some reading cultures); instead, we move across the page using its visual and verbal cues, interpreting the spaces between each frame. Adler also notes that graphic novelists employ non-vocalized moments; in 'turn[ing] off the vocal channel' provided by a narrator, the author is again encouraging her reader/viewer to become an active participant in the process of making meaning, gaining understanding 'through observation and deduction' but also through 'decod[ing] the narrator's intentions' (2278–2279). Rather than solely relying on the narrator's interpretation of events, readers/viewers are allowed the space to process story on their own terms. For example, when Gatsby makes his first appearance, Greenberg follows this with two frames that cut from him, arms raised to the distant shore of East Egg, to firstly a star filled, moonlit sky and secondly, an image of the rising sun, before moving to a closing image of Gatsby in the same pose, as the narrator observes 'I could have sworn he was trembling.' There are several deductions that the reader/viewer can make here: namely that there has been an unspoken elongation of time as we have moved from a night time scene to sunrise; that Gatsby is so preoccupied that he has not changed his position throughout; *and* that our narrator has remained an onlooker for the duration. We may draw certain inferences about the nature of Gatsby's obsession with whatever lies across those waters and about the relationship between Gatsby and the narrator. It is not only the two frames of moonlit sky and sunrise that speak to the narrative but the black silence that surrounds them on the page.

There are numerous instances in which Greenberg isolates a particular character through the architecture of her page; the narrator, Nick Carraway, is often presented as a part of yet distanced from events unfolding around him, and though his feeling of isolation is achieved primarily through pictorial means – his facial expressions denoting his mood – his isolation is heightened by his positioning within the frame. In the aftermath of Tom Buchanan's violent altercation with Myrtle Wilson, Nick is held in a frame that depicts two windows, one of which contains a glum Nick looking out, the other a separate window that contains a bloodied Myrtle and her entourage; he shares with them the pictorial frame yet he is also isolated within it, placed in a separate 'framed' window; we then move across to an image from Nick's point of view as he looks out on the buildings that surround him; and finally, to a frame of the apartment block's windows, showing *all* of its inhabitants and depicting the various dramas taking place within (*Gatsby* 46–47). Our eyes must search for the image of Nick, embedded as it is within this larger pictorial image, suggesting as Fitzgerald does in his novel, that we are all but a tiny inconsequential part of the teeming mass of humanity. An equally telling illustration of the spatial dimension of Greenberg's storytelling occurs on page 170, when Daisy and Tom Buchanan are placed centre page in a dominant shared frame, surrounded by frames of drunken revellers: the Buchanans' facial expressions denote their dismay but the sense of their social distance from said revellers is enhanced by the architecture of the page and the silence that accompanies it. As we move across the images, we are made aware of the different positioning of the Buchanans, and here it is not only Daisy who is 'appalled by West Egg' and its 'raw vigour' (Fitzgerald 71) but Tom, suggesting a closer allegiance between the Buchanans than that communicated in Fitzgerald's novel at this stage in the narrative. As may be anticipated, Greenberg's Gatsby is similarly isolated at various points in the storyline and one of the most meaningful instances is depicted post Gatsby party, as he stands alone on the steps of his empty mansion bidding farewell to the revellers (*Gatsby* 74); Greenberg employs Fitzgerald's prose – '. . . a sudden emptiness seemed to flow from the windows and the great doors, endowing with complete isolation the figure of the host who stood on the porch, his hand up in a formal gesture of farewell' (Fitzgerald 37) – and the visual image replicates the prose, but it is the empty black space that surrounds the frame that carries the emotional energy of this poignant moment as, like McCloud's trapeze artist, we are 'thrust into the open air of the imagination' and then 'caught by the outstretched arms of the ever-present next panel' (McCloud qtd in Freedman 32). We are left to supply the missing details with 'an intense, emotional, intellectual and/or critical reaction to what is not articulated' (Adler 2279). The interpretive response of the reader/viewer who is already familiar with the precursor text, will be further complicated by prior knowledge of what transpires later.

The loaded silences characteristic of this graphic novel provide a meaningful storytelling device that cannot be replicated in prose. However, it is the graphic novel's association with visual storytelling that, above all else, provides the dominant mode of narration – a narration that in the best instances goes beyond the mechanics of depicting story events. Greenberg adopts a surreal style in this adaptation. In her depiction of the valley of ashes, she amplifies Fitzgerald's dark vision of a consumer-driven society by creating macabre images of a desolate landscape – 'a fantastic farm where ashes grow like wheat ridges and grotesque gardens' and where 'with a transcendent effort ... ash-grey men ... stir up an impenetrable cloud which screens their obscure operations from your sight', as the ever watchful eyes of the iconic Dr T J Eckleberg sign looms, god-like, over them (*Gatsby* 31–32). Greenberg introduces images of surreal complexity throughout the novel. For example, after the romantic reunion between Gatsby and Daisy, Greenberg depicts a radiant sunset fading on the waters from East to West Egg, onto which an insubstantial pencil outline of Daisy is super-imposed. We follow the images, as the hope-filled sunset onto which Daisy's form is projected, becomes one with Gatsby's nostalgia-fuelled green light, before being replaced in the closing frame by a rain-drenched scene, Daisy's image dissipating in the now grey expanse of water. Complementing the narrator's running commentary, the visuals add another dimension through which Greenberg infers from this much earlier stage in the narrative that the romance between Daisy and Gatsby is already doomed since she is unable to live up to his nostalgic reconstruction of her and of their romance.

Structurally, the novel takes its lead from the canonical text: it follows the same nine chapter format, and it employs parallel quests to drive narrative momentum. Where the comic book is synonymous with brevity and linearity, Greenberg's graphic novel mirrors the fragmented structure of the source text, reconstructing memories via a similar first person narratorial voice. Greenberg adopts a pictorial approach to the telling of the tale in more than a representational sense. Story content is foregrounded at the start of each chapter by a series of art deco framed portraits; a shot of Tom Buchanan and Myrtle Wilson, for example, introduces us to Chapter 2 and its recount of their affair. To mirror the kind of reflective thought processes of first person narration attained in prose is a challenge when one adapts to a visual medium, but Greenberg successfully employs her medium's visual affiliation to photography as a means of presenting the tale from narrator Nick Carraway's subjective, reflective point of view. Nick's construction of a photograph album becomes the novel's main storytelling device. The album is, states Greenberg, 'a way of looking at [Carraway's] thought processes, his narrative process' (Greenberg in Wheeler). It is a clever pictorial conceit that also heightens the nostalgic mood of the narrative, especially given the sepia tinted colour palette employed by Greenberg throughout. Carraway is seen from the outset sifting through photographs, searching for shards of memory that will help him to construct his narrative recount of events, and the focus of that narrative revolves around a torn image of Gatsby – an image we are led to assume the narrator is about to put back together. Instantly, Greenberg's visualization of Carraway as constructor of story cleverly infers the unreliability of his tale since it is so clearly put together from the selective memory of one individual. By foregrounding the mechanics of story construction, she invites us to become involved in that construction, questioning the image selection, looking in our minds for other possibilities, other stories left untold and so on. We are reminded of Carraway's role in the construction of story at several points in the novel (*Gatsby* 75, 76, 163), and in the closing moments we see him taping together a torn image of himself and Gatsby (299). The final frame on page 299 draws our attention to his hands as they piece it together, foregrounding once more his role in the construction of this narrative as he tries to reaffirm his allegiance to the now deceased Gatsby.

In her visualization of the narrative, Greenberg occasionally employs comic book tropes: when Tom hits Myrtle, the word 'CRACK!' (45) dominates the frame, as does the 'BLAM!BLAM!BLAM!' of gunshots during the depiction of the death of Rosie Rosenthal outside the Metropole (97), creating the same kind of distance from reality and softening of violence achieved in the pre-adult comic book. Her use of bestial forms to represent the various characters in *The Great Gatsby* is again in the comic book tradition – a tradition that employs animal stereotypes as an efficient visual shorthand. The brutish, uncivilized Tom Buchanan's representation as a colossal semi-naked beast speaks to his characterization rather than his class; Myrtle is represented in a similarly grotesque form as a one eyed creature with her cow-uddered breasts constantly on display. The working classes, whether serving the affluent or digging in the valley of ashes, share the same many-handed form – a form that denotes their function and that visually underscores the class issues at the heart of Fitzgerald's novel. Gatsby party revellers are presented as a wild array of types, captured most tellingly in a series of photo-booth type shots over which the eye is free to roam and to assess (58–59). It is interesting that the novel's 'criminal', Wolfsheim, is not depicted as wolf-like; he is a hairy, cuddly figure who, unlike semi-naked Tom, presents himself in a civilized fashion donning hat, collar and tie and cufflinks. Society women Daisy (a flighty bird) and Jordan (a slippery octopus) are constructed as pessimistic sophisticates who counter-balance Gatsby's optimism and Carraway's outsider realism. By choosing to represent Gatsby as a sea horse, Greenberg endows his character with a whimsical charm that offers a stark contrast to bestial Buchanan: he is a thing of rare beauty who, in accordance with a commonly held mythical misconception, mates with one life partner. Nick Carraway's lizard-like appearance is more notable for the antennae that adorn his head, suggesting that he is a receptive character – a good listener as is his human counterpart.

Here, as in Fitzgerald's novel, the romance quest forms a part of the narrative's momentum yet it is not, as is the case in the majority of screen adaptations, consumed by it nor is Greenberg tempted to glorify said quest. Her flighty, self-absorbed, and affectedly pessimistic Daisy is never going to be able to meet the nostalgia-fuelled expectations of this optimistic Gatsby's fantasies. The Alger-like journey from rags to riches that shapes the source text is explored in close detail, and Greenberg devotes narrative space and time to an unravelling of both Gatsby's rise and his reinvention of himself. We move from the exploits of the youthful Jay Gatz and his seemingly far-fetched ambitions – the latter recounted via depiction of a fantastical dreamscape – to the advent of his relationship with Cody, which is again recounted in pictorial detail (*Gatsby* 154–159). The images on pages 157–158 encapsulate the optimism of the young Jay Gatz as he rows into his sun-infused future as 'Jay Gatsby of West Egg, Long Island', a 'Platonic conception of himself', a 'son of God', wearing a crown and bearing a sceptre. Through both the reference to his '*Platonic* conception of himself' and Nick's reference to Cody as Gatsby's 'paramour' (159), Greenberg also echoes the canonical text's subtextual hints of a potentially homosexual relationship between Gatsby and Cody, configured here as the price a young Jay Gatz is prepared to pay to accomplish his American dream. Such a possibility also adds to the more grounded manner in which Greenberg handles her Gatsby. Where other adaptations tend to amplify his enigmatic qualities, Greenberg works to demystify him, even as she exploits the fantastical potentialities of her graphic retelling of his tale. His dreams and ambitions are realized on the page as youthful flights of fancy, grounded in the reality that there is a price to pay for advancement, namely taking Cody as his 'paramour' and later engaging in a life of crime. His criminal connections with Wolfshiem in particular are much more in evidence in this adaptation, and his image as distanced enigma is deconstructed here. Nick refers to him as the 'proprietor of an elaborate roadhouse next door' (83), and there are scenes in which they are depicted chatting in a neighbourly fashion over the backyard fence (120–122). His surreal visualization as a sea horse and the inevitable distance such a visualization creates between the reader/viewer and Gatsby is counteracted by the ordinary behaviours Greenberg affords her Gatsby. However, she leads us relentlessly on to the same downbeat ending, and the poignancy of the moment connects on another level because of this Gatsby's more relatable character traits – traits presented to us through the bias of Carraway as the maker of the narrative, but no matter how he reconstructs the shards of memory, Gatsby ends up dead and no-one but the narrator and his estranged father care to mourn his loss.

The literary graphic novel poses 'challenges to the border between high art and popular culture and between word and image' (Freedman 29). However, Greenberg is able to negotiate a pathway between the realms of high art and popular culture, creating a work that has currency in both and through exploiting rather than decrying its comic book allegiances. She marries the visual and spatial strengths of the comic book/graphic novel medium with the canonical text's wistful, nostalgic charm and the lyrical beauty of its prose whilst also addressing its troubling universal thematic concerns. It is an exemplary and in many ways 'radical' adaptation of *The Great Gatsby* and it sets up a meaningful dialogue with its precursor text. *G*, on the other hand, speaks only to the narrative template of Fitzgerald's novel, inadvertently translating it into a soap opera format that would be better suited to the televisual medium rather than the medium of film. Like *South Park's* cartoon adaptation of *Great Expectations* and Greenberg's graphic novel adaptation of *The Great Gatsby*, it is 'faithful' to the bare bones of the narrative, but has neither the former's satirical intent nor the latter's capacity to explore the ideological preoccupations of the source text. *G* fails to meet the criteria by which Hutcheon defines adaptation as 'repetition, but repetition without replication' (7); it 'replicates' without adding anything new to the narrative mix, despite its potential to 'enter an old text from a new critical direction' as a means of presenting the myth of the American dream through the 'fresh eyes' of African-American experience (Rich 18).

Contesting the boundaries of classification: Exercises related to *The Great Gatsby*, 'The Turn of the Screw', *Great Expectations, Jane Eyre* and adaptations of these canonical works

Adaptations and the 'auteur' (Part one)

Think back to one of the opening discussion points in Chapter 1 (An Introduction to Adaptation Studies: A Theoretical Overview) where we considered problematic notions of authorship, creative 'genius' and issues circulating the ownership of narratives, particularly in relation to works of the literary canon and adaptation.

Step one

Now think about how notions of 'authorship' operate in the collaborative fields of film, theatre and television, and ask yourself the following questions:

- How can we ascribe 'authorship' to one individual when working in a medium that involves the creative input of so many?
- Who is usually viewed as the 'author'/creative 'lead'? (e.g. script writer? director? set/costume designer(s)?)
- Is, for example, a stage production of *Hamlet* the creative work of its director or do we always view a production of *Hamlet* as a work by Shakespeare, no matter how radical and innovative the director's treatment of the source text?
- Should we, for example, see Hitchcock as 'author' of the film adaptation of *Rebecca* (1940) or is it a David O. Selznick film/part of his studio's brand? Or is its authorship retained by Daphne Du Maurier?
- Do we credit authorship of the 2006 BBC adaptation of *Jane Eyre* to director Susanna White, screenwriter Sandy Welch or to the canonical text's author?
- Why is producer Val Lewton, rather than director Jacques Tourneur, cited as creator of *I Walked with a Zombie*?

Step two

There are no easy answers, though within the post fifties world of cinema, notions of authorship are traditionally ascribed to a certain type of director, labelled an 'auteur'. Not all directors are afforded this label: film theorists distinguish between the director who crafts film in a workman-like manner (i.e. a 'metteur') and the director who is credited with the same kind of artistic signature as an author (an 'auteur').

The 'auteur' exhibits a distinctive style across a body of work and is credited with having a unique, creative vision. Regardless of the collaborative nature of the medium, it is usually the director who is afforded auteur status.

Though there are many practitioners and theorists who take issue with auteur theory* and the problematics of ownership in a collaborative medium like film, there are undeniably characteristic features to be found in the films of certain directors.

> *Auteur theory emerged in the fifties as a means to adding artistic credibility to the cinematic medium. You may wish to undertake further research into what the theory entails.

Which of the following screen adaptations studied through Chapters 2–5 would you see as the work of an auteur?

- 1940 *Rebecca*
- 1943 *I Walked with a Zombie*
- 1944 *Jane Eyre*
- 1946 *Great Expectations*
- 1961 *The Innocents*
- 1974 *The Great Gatsby*
- 1998 *Great Expectations*
- 1998 *The Governess*
- 2001 *The Others*
- 2002 *G*
- 2007 *The Orphanage*
- 2011 *Jane Eyre*
- 2013 *The Great Gatsby*

Now select one text that you feel is the work of an auteur, and one that you feel is the work of a metteur. Give specific reasons for your decision. How are your chosen directors (or other 'creatives') perceived within the film industry? What other films have they worked on? Can you see an emerging signature across a body of work?

Adaptations and the 'auteur' (Part two)

Director Baz Luhrmann is regarded as an auteur. His films have a distinctive style – a style that is readily associated with his work as a film director.

Step one

Take a look at the following mash-up of Luhrmann films collectively known as the Red Curtain Trilogy (*Strictly Ballroom/Romeo + Juliet/Moulin Rouge*): http://youtu.be/52PYW68VYJs

Now think of ways in which the style adopted in Luhrmann's Red Curtain Trilogy is also present in his 2013 adaptation of *The Great Gatsby*. Think about:

- use of colour
- soundtrack
- casting/performance
- cinematography
- costuming
- set design
- echoes across the various film texts
- e.g. treatment of party scenes
- e.g. treatment of romance

Step two

Can we/should we 'read' Luhrmann's *The Great Gatsby* as a fourth, belated film in his Red Curtain Trilogy?

Does this film adaptation support notions of the auteur in general, and of Luhrmann as auteur in particular? Why/why not?

Employing the bildungsroman story structure

Step one

A number of the canonical texts/adaptations we have studied are bildungsroman or 'coming of age' narratives, and all/most of them employ the following generic features:

- Story of one individual's growth (protagonist), from childhood/youth to point of adult knowledge/maturity
- An inciting incident sets the protagonist on her/his 'journey'
- Protagonist engages in self reflection/introspection during the course of her/his 'journey' to a final moment of self-knowledge
- Focuses on psychological/moral growth and 'education'
- Traditionally employs first person narration in medium of prose
- Traditionally focuses on questions of 'identity'
- Traditionally focuses on protagonist finding her/his place in society

Think about the story structure/content of *Jane Eyre*, *Great Expectations*, 'The Turn of the Screw' and *The Great Gatsby*:

- Which of these canonical texts does/does not employ the bildungsroman format? Justify your response.
- Which adaptations employ a similar bildungsroman format? Draw up a list of all adaptations that do so.
- Do all of them take their 'bildungsroman' lead from the canonical text or do some of them introduce that element?

Step two

When we explore adaptations of *Jane Eyre*, what happens to the bildungsroman structure?

- Does the focus shift from personal growth (child to adult) to preoccupation with its identity as gothic romance/the romantic couple rather than the protagonist?
- Why, for example, does the 2011 film adaptation begin with a distraught Jane Eyre's departure from Thornfield Hall?
- Does the focus shift solely to adult Jane/pseudo Jane?
- Why, for example, does *The Governess* excise all reference to the protagonist's formative years? Similarly, why does *Rebecca* (novel and film) or *I walked with a Zombie* begin with an adult protagonist?
- Does the focus shift to a different character/a different journey from childhood innocence to adult knowledge?
- Do we, for example, follow Rhys's protagonist, Antoinette, on her journey to the anticipated point of societal reintegration? Why? Why not?

Now apply the same thought processes to *Great Expectations* and its adaptations. Draw up your own list of questions, using the above as a role model but adding your own points of enquiry to the debate.

Step three

Texts like 'The Turn of the Screw' and *The Great Gatsby* do not present traditional coming of age stories. Draw up a list of reasons (for and against) as to why we should/should not view these two texts as bildungsroman narratives.

Now think about their various adaptations. Regardless of whether the canonical text does/does not employ the bildungsroman format, are there any adaptations of these texts that present their narratives as coming of age stories?

For example, can we read Harding's *Florence and Giles* as a bildungsroman that refocuses the narrative lens on Florence's journey? What are the strengths/limitations of viewing Florence as the protagonist of a bildungsroman? (Think about the trajectory of her journey, her capacity for self-reflection, her reintegration into society, and so on.)

Step four

Finally, think about Benincasa's adaptation, *Great*. Here, Benincasa translates Fitzgerald's novel into a teen coming of age story.

- How does she do this? Identify at least FIVE ways in which this narrative functions as bildungsroman.

Now think about ways to translate one of the other canonical texts into a successful Young Adult fiction narrative that follows the journey of a character other than its protagonist. You could choose from the following list:

- Estella
- Herbert Pocket
- Biddy
- Adele Varens
- Blanche Ingram
- Rochester
- Miles
- Miss Jessel

- Quint
- Daisy Buchanan
- Jordan

Think about:

- how this change of target audience will influence the ways in which you shape your adaptation;
- where to begin/end your narrative;
- where/when to set your narrative;
- thematic preoccupations you will choose to focus on/play down;
- character traits you will choose to focus on/play down; and
- relationships you will choose to foreground.

Step five

Finally, imagine you have been asked to pitch your idea for an adaptation of your chosen text to a YA fiction publisher. Write a compelling and brief three minute pitch devised to persuade the publisher to offer you a contract!

References

Adler, Silvia. 'Silence in the Graphic Novel'. *The Journal of Pragmatics* 43 (2011): 2278–2285. Print.

Atkins, Irene Kahn. 'In Search of the Greatest Gatsby'. *Literature Film Quarterly* 2.3 (1974): 216–228. Print.

Bahrenberg, Bruce. *Filming the Great Gatsby*. New York: Berkley Publishing, 1974. Print.

Belbin, David. 'What Is Young Adult Fiction?' *English in Education* 45.2 (2011): 132–143. Print.

Benincasa, Sara. *Great*. New York: HarperTeen, 2014. Print.

Bey, Amir. 'Christopher Scott Cherot, Director/Actor Revisited: Interview'. *The New Times Holler!* 2009. Web. 1 May 2013.

Canby, Vincent. 'A Lavish Gatsby Loses Book's Spirit: The Cast'. *The New York Times* 28 Mar. 1974: Movie Review. Print.

Cook, P. 'Transnational Utopias: Baz Luhrmann and Australian Cinema'. *Transnational Cinemas* 1.1 (2010): 23–26. Print.

Coyle, R. 'Love Is a Many Splendored Thing. Love Lifts Us Up Where We Belong. All You Need Is Love: Baz Luhrmann's Eclectic Musical Signature in the Red Curtain Trilogy'. *Screen Sound* 4 (2013): 9–30. Print.

Dallacqua, Ashley. 'Exploring Literary Devices in Graphic Novels'. *Language Arts* 89.6 (2012): 365–378. Print.

Dunford, George. 'The Written Image'. *Meanjin* 68.1 (2009): 20–28. Print.

Dwyer, June. 'When Willie Met Gatsby: The Critical Implications of Ernesto Quiñonez' *Bodega Dreams*'. *LIT: Literature Interpretation Theory* 14.2 (2003): 165–178. Print.

Ebert, Roger. '*The Great Gatsby*'. *RogerEbert.com*. 1 Jan. 1974. Web. 12 Jun. 2012.

Ebert, Roger. '*G*'. *RogerEbert.com*. 27 Oct. 2005. Web. 21 Jul. 2013.

Ebert, Roger. '*The Great Gatsby*'. *RogerEbert.com*. 8 May 2013. Web. 21 Jun. 2013.

Elliott, Kamilla. *Rethinking the Novel/Film Debate*. Cambridge: Cambridge University Press, 2003. Print.

Empire Magazine. 'Baz Luhrmann Interview: *The Great Gatsby*'. *YouTube*. YouTube, LCC, 4 Jun. 2103. Web. 3 Oct. 2013.

Fitzgerald, F. Scott. *The Great Gatsby*. Hertfordshire: Wordsworth Classics, 1993 [1925].

Frank, Jason. 'Baz Luhrmann Interview'. *GamesFirst!* 16 Apr. 2002. Web. 10 Jan. 2004.

Freedman, Ariela. 'Comics, Graphic Novels, Graphic Narrative: A Review'. *Literature Compass* 8.1 (2011): 28–46. Print.

Giannetti, Louis. 'The Gatsby Flap'. *Literature Film Quarterly* 3.1 (1975): 13–22. Print.

Giltrow, Janet and David Stouk. 'Style as Politics in *The Great Gatsby*'. *Studies in the Novel* 29.4 (1997): 476–489. Print.

Goldsmith, Meredith. 'White Skin, White Mask: Passing, Posing and Performing in *The Great Gatsby*'. *Modern Fiction Studies* 49.3 (2003): 443–468. Print.

Greenberg, Nicki. *The Great Gatsby*. Crows Nest NSW: Allen & Unwin. 2009 [2007].

Greenberg, Nicki. 'Nicki Greenberg Talks About Her Gatsby'. *The Wheeler Centre: Books Ideas, Writing*. YouTube, LCC, 24 Apr. 2010. Web. 10 May 2013.

Greenberg, Nicki. 'Picturing Gatsby'. *Readings*. 14 May 2013. Web. 4 Jul. 2013.

Hatfield, Charles. *Alternative Comics: An Emerging Literature*. Jackson: University of Mississippi. 1996. Print.

Hill, Rebecca A. 'GLBT Young Adult Fiction: Notes from the Field'. *School Library Monthly* 27.8 (2011): 20–21. Print.

Hogan, Mike. 'Baz Luhrmann, *Great Gatsby* Director, Explains the 3D, the Hip Hop, the Sanitarium and More'. *Huffington Post*. 13 May 2013. Web. 28 Jun. 2013.

Hutcheon, Linda. 'In Defence of Literary Adaptation as Cultural Production'. *M/C Journal* 10.2 (2007) n. pag. Web. 12 Jan. 2008.

Kerr, Frances. 'Feeling "Half Feminine": Modernism and the Politics of Emotion in *The Great Gatsby*'. *American Literature* 68.2 (1996): 405–431. Print.

Klein, Michael and Gillian Parker. *The English Novel and the Movies*. New York: Ungar, 1981. Print.

Marsh, Joss Lutz. 'Fitzgerald, Gatsby, and the Last Tycoon: The "American Dream" and the Hollywood Dream Factory'. *Literature Film Quarterly* 20.1 (1992): 3–13. Print.

Marsh, Joss Lutz. 'Fitzgerald, Gatsby, and the Last Tycoon: The "American Dream" and the Hollywood Dream Factory'. (Part 2). *Literature Film Quarterly* 20.1 (1992): 102–108. Print.

Marshall, Lee. 'GATSBY Forever'. *Queens Quarterly* 120.2 (2013): 194–204. Print.

McKee, Robert. *Story: Substance, Structure, Style, and the Principles of Screenwriting*. London: Methuen, 1999 [1998].

Moiles, Sean. 'The Politics of Gentrification in Ernesto Quiñonez's Novels'. *Critique: Studies in Contemporary Fiction* 52.1 (2010): 114–133. Print.

Mojo. 'Box Office: *The Great Gatsby* 2013'. Web. 9 Dec. 2013.

Morales, Wilson. 'The Return of *Hav Plenty's* Scott Cherot'. *Blackfilm.com*. 13 Mar. 2011. Web. 20 May 2014.

Needham, Alex. 'Gatz to Deliver Every Word of *The Great Gatsby* on West End Stage'. *The Guardian*. 9 Feb. 2012: Culture. Print.

Otero, Solimar. 'Barrio, Bodega, and Botanica Aesthetics'. *Atlantic Global Studies: Global Currents* 4.2 (2007): 173–194. Print.

Porter, Greg. 'Against Melancholia: Contemporary Mourning Theory, Fitzgerald's Great Gatsby and the Politics of Unfinished Grief'. *Differences: A Journal of Feminist Cultural Studies* 14.2 (2003): 134–170. Print.

Quiñonez, Ernesto. *Bodega Dreams*. New York: Vintage Books, 2000. Print.

Rich, Adrienne. 'When We Dead Awaken: Writing as Re-Vision'. *College English* 34.1 (1972) 18–30. Print.

Rosen, Marjorie. ' "I'm Proud of That Film": Jack Clayton Interview'. *Film Comment* 10.4 (1974): 49–51. Print.

Sanders, Julie. *Adaptation and Appropriation*. Abingdon: Routledge, 2006. Print.

Scott, A. O. 'Shimmying Off the Literary Mantle'. *The New York Times: Movie Review*. 11 May 2013. Web. 10 Jun. 2013.

Stavans, Ilán. 'Spanglish: Tickling the Tongue'. *World Literature Today* 74.3 (2000): 555–558. Print.

Wagner, Geoffrey. *The Novel and the Cinema*. Rutherford, NJ: Fairleigh Dickinson University Press, 1975. Print.

Wiegand, Scott. 'Ernesto Quiñonez: *Bodega Dreams*: Spanglish Stories'. *Spike Magazine: Books, Music, Art, Ideas*. 1 Feb. 2001. Web. 3 Mar. 2012.

Winter, Emily. 'Y A Author Sara Benincasa Revamps *The Great Gatsby* with a Same Sex Relationship: Interview'. *Sparknotes: Sparklife*. 8 Apr. 2014. Web. 10 Jun. 2014.

Yang, Gene Luen. 'Graphic Flair Beguiles the Mainstream'. *Australian Comics Journal.com*. 11 Mar. 2012. Web. 10 May 2013.

Filmography

G. Dir. Christopher Scott Cherot. 2002. DVD.
The Great Gatsby. Dir. Herbert Brenon. 1926. DVD.
The Great Gatsby. Dir. Elliot Nugent. 1949. DVD.
The Great Gatsby. Dir. Jack Clayton. 1974. DVD.
The Great Gatsby. Dir. Robert Markowitz. 2000. DVD.
The Great Gatsby. Dir. Baz Luhrmann. 2013. DVD.

Drawing Conclusions

Studying a body of adapted texts and the differing types of adaptations that are in dialogue with them presents new ways of exploring the nature of adaptation. What emerges, as our studies draw to a close, is an understanding of how, collectively, the stories we have been critiquing connect and evolve in relation to each other.

Though this study, like most studies that revolve around case studies, employs a specific classification system as a workable framework for discussion, the efficacy of such systems remains open to question. Boundaries between classifications are invariably breached: narratives are not easily contained nor constrained. Adaptation is not a neat painting by numbers exercise; it is instead a complex process that involves complex transitions, both cultural and ideological, in response to changing modes of storytelling and adaptive intent. What also becomes apparent is not only the rich and diverse range of adaptations that are generated but the ways in which all of these texts – whether canonical precursor or re-visionist reworking, screen adaptation or novel to novel adaptation – share a certain interconnectivity. Despite their very different cultural, temporal, spatial, medium-specific identities, the texts we have been exploring connect at some base level, each furthering in its own way an ongoing preoccupation that remains of significance across the adaptive divide, whatever that divide may be (whether related to genre, literary era, high/low art status, medium *or* adaptive 'type'). The stories seep into each other and across the artificial construct of classification divides and that is as it should be. Adaptations are as open to interpretation as the canonical texts they adapt.

When we consider the connections between all of the texts we have been studying, these collective preoccupations emerge: narratives revolving around notions of 'doomed love' and 'orphan' status abound. Lower class orphans Jane Eyre and Pip may ultimately realize romantic closure and social mobility, but the Rochesters live in self-imposed isolation at Ferndean rather than at Thornfield Hall, and the union of Pip and Estella is part of an imposed happy ending that undermines the anticipated narrative trajectory of Dickens' tale. Similarly, Jay Gatsby and James' governess harbour romantic fantasies of unattainable love of social superiors, as do Jacinta Trimalchio, Willie Bodega and the string of governesses that litter adaptations of 'The Turn of the Screw'. All such romantic fantasies end badly. Gatsby (and the various adaptive reincarnations of this figure) also courts a self-imposed orphan status that connects Fitzgerald's narrative with questions of fractured identity of the kind explored in *Jane Eyre*, *Great Expectations* and 'The Turn of the Screw'; and problematic matters related to identity are returned to again and again in adaptations as diverse as Carey's *Jack Maggs*, Rhys's *Wide Sargasso Sea*, Jones' *Mr Pip*, Harding's *Florence and Giles*, Goldbacher's *The Governess* and Bayona's *The Orphanage*. The adaptive tapestry is rich and complex when viewed as a body of intertextually connected work that shape-shifts in response to a whole host of contributory factors.

Thinking about theory

Taxonomies: Strengths and limitations

Taxonomies (or classification systems as they are often referred to) provide a framework for discussion of texts, but how effective are they, and what are their limitations?

Step one

Think about the canonical texts we have studied (across Chapters 2–5), and the various classification systems we have employed throughout as a means to grouping together different types of adaptations that connect with those canonical texts.

Now select a representative adaptation from each chapter, and decide where *you* would place those adaptations in relation to the classifications employed in our studies:

- The 'Classic' Treatment
- Re-visioning the Text
- A Radical Rethink

Ask yourself the following questions:

- How would you define what is meant by each of these classifications?
- Is your definition likely to be exactly the same as mine/your fellow students/general readers/viewers? Why? Why not?
- Does the language employed in each classification influence how we perceive the relationship between adaptation and canonical text?
- Could you place your selected adaptations into one of the *other* classifications? Justify your choices.

Step two

We have already considered the classification system proposed by Geoffrey Wagner back in the seventies (transposition/commentary/analogy, from *The Novel and the Cinema*, Fairleigh Dickinson University Press, 1975), but adaptations scholars continue to devise their own alternative taxonomies.

Now undertake some independent research into the various classification systems generated by at least two of the following theorists:

- Dudley Andrew: see 'Borrowing, Intersecting and Transforming'. *Concepts in Film Theory*. London: Oxford University Press, 1984. 98–102.
- Michael Klein and Gillian Parker: see Introduction to *The English Novel and the Movies*. New York: Ungar, 1981 for their classifications re fidelity, reinterpreting and source as raw material for an original work.
- Kamilla Elliott: see chapters on six classification types (psychic concept/ventriloquist concept/genetic concept/de(re)composing concept/incarnational concept/trumping concept) in *Rethinking the Novel/Film Debate*. Cambridge: Cambridge University Press, 2003.

Using your research and the knowledge you have acquired during our studies, sum up your response to the following questions in two to three sentences:

- How effective are those classification systems?
- Can we/should we apply such classifications to texts of differing media/content/audience/narrative treatment?
- Do such classifications imply any kind of value judgement/hierarchical placement?

Step three

After reflecting on the various taxonomies employed by adaptations theorists, devise your *own* classification system. It can be a three tier system like most of the above or one that breaks type down further as in Elliott's six tier system. You should consider carefully:

- The language you employ for your categories (i.e. what are the implications of your chosen vocabulary?)
- How you would define each category and the type of adaptation you would see fitting into it
- Your rationale for devising this kind of system

Now go back to adaptations chosen for Step one. Where would you place these adaptations within your own classification system and why?

Four models: Exploring relationships

Now that you have a pool of theoretical knowledge on which to draw, think about all of the adaptations we've studied thus far and about their relationship with the prose texts they adapt. We have considered several ways of classifying these adaptations according to type – for example, transposition, commentary, analogy and so on – but we have yet to consider (through application) the relationship between adaptation/adapted text in relation to the hierarchical debates that plague the study of adaptations – that is, notions of superiority and the inferred value judgements that are then attached to each according to their place in some kind of arbitrary 'pecking order'. (Think of the canonical, high art status of Shakespeare's plays, for example, and of how adaptations are invariably seen as secondary to these 'original' works, even though Shakespeare borrows and adapts his stories from a whole range of texts!)

Step one

Theorist Thomas Leitch identifies four models for the exploration of the relationship between adaptations and the texts they adapt (28–50).

Think about the adapted texts/adaptations we have been studying in relation to the following four models.

'Sunburst' model

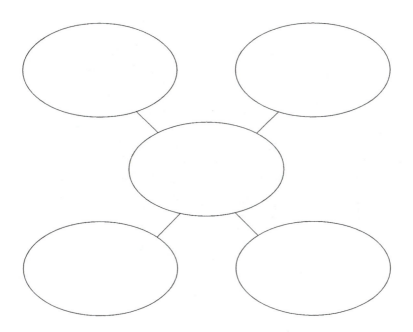

- Where would the text that is to be adapted be placed in this model and why?
- Where would adaptations that are connected to that text be placed in this model and why?
- What are the implications of the placement of adapted text/adaptations in this model?

Leitch has problems with this model because:

- it 'confirms the primacy of what is generally called its source text or its original and implies that adaptations borrow their value from the originals that spin off them'; and
- because of the 'difficulty of establishing a single hub in which all adaptations have their source' (28).

'Genealogical' model

- Where would the text that is to be adapted be placed in this model and why?
- Where would adaptations that are connected to that text be placed in this model and why?
- What are the implications of the placement of adapted text/adaptations in this model?

Leitch prefers this model because:

- it 'acknowledges not only the different relations that are possible among different generations but also the many different kinds of work they undertake' (31); and
- because, despite the implications of placing the adapted text at the top of the tree, there is room in this model for things to branch off and form other 'families'

'Daisy chain' model

- Where would the text that is to be adapted be placed in this model and why?
- Where would adaptations that are connected to that text be placed in this model and why?
- What are the implications of the placement of adapted text/adaptations in this model?

Leitch sees the strengths but also the weaknesses in such a model because:

- it avoids the primacy taint yet acknowledges connection (good!);

- with this model we have 'no beginning, no end, and no boundaries' (bad!) (37).

'Tracer' model

In this model the story or narrative is seen as a 'tracer text' – that is, a story with motifs/themes/images of archetypal and universal importance that address irresolvable cultural anxieties repeatedly. For example, we could identify doomed love as one such ongoing cultural anxiety that is pondered in stories across *different* times, locations, cultures, media, genre, and so on.

Consider the following example; it lists some of the adaptations we have studied, and it also notes other narratives that explore the notion of doomed love.

> Luhrmann's *Romeo & Juliet*
> *West Side Story*
> Zeffireli's *Romeo & Juliet*
> Shakespeare's *Romeo & Juliet*
> Fitzgerald's *The Great Gatsby*
> Clayton's *The Great Gatsby*
> Luhrmann's *The Great Gatsby*

Doomed love >

> G
> Chaucer's *Troilus and Criseyde*
> Shakespeare's *Troilus and Cressida*
> Benincasa's *Great*
> Quiñonez' *Bodega Dreams*
> Greenberg's *The Great Gatsby*
> Joe Wright's *Atonement*
> Ian McEwan's *Atonement*

- What happens to placement of texts in this model?
- What are the implications of the placement of adapted text/adaptations in this model?

Leitch likes this model because:

- it 'offers the possibility of avoiding' the kind of 'uncritical … privileging' inherent in the sunburst model;
- it avoids the unacknowledged patriarchalism of the genealogical model;

- it avoids the ungovernable intertextuality of the daisy chain model;
- it explores instead 'repeated dramatizations of irresolvable cultural anxieties' that connect a body of texts across disparate eras/cultures/ locations without giving primacy to any; and
- unlike the term 'original' (or source?), the term 'tracer' avoids the notion that there is ONE text 'at the centre of the textual universe' and implies instead that there are many (38–39).

Step two

Now go back to the list of texts related to doomed love.

- Could you add any of the other adapted texts/adaptations we have studied?
- Which of Leitch's four models do *you* feel is most effective and why?

Reference

Leitch, Thomas. 'Jekyll, Hyde, Jekyll, Hyde, Jekyll Hyde, Jekyll, Hyde: Four Models of Intertextuality'. *Victorian Literature & Film Adaptation*. Ed. Abigail Burnham Bloom and Mary Sanders Pollock. New York: Cambria, 2011. 28–50. Print.

Glossary

appropriation In the current context of adaptation studies this is a term (coined by Julie Sanders) applied to adapted texts that have a less definitive relationship with the source text.

archetype Serves as a prototype on which other similar things are modeled. In narratives, the archetype represents the typical character, narrative or action.

auteur Refers in the main to screen directors (though it can be a term applied to other creatives working on screen products) with a distinctive, identifiable style across a body of work; the auteur is seen as creative 'artist', taking us back to notions of 'authorship' which are especially problematic within the context of the collaborative film and television industries.

bildungsroman Also known as the 'coming of age' story, this refers to a story that plots the moral growth of the protagonist within a defined social context.

diegesis Refers to all that exists within the fictional on-screen world in which the story takes place.

diegetic sound Sounds that belong within/occur within the screen world (e.g. howling wind, music playing on radio, screeching seagull), though they can be added and/or amplified for dramatic effect post shoot.

distanciation The effect of purposely disrupting conventional spectator identification with the film world by forcing said spectator to reflect on the constructed nature of that film world. This is achieved by foregrounding the apparatus of filmmaking (using jump cuts, speaking to screen, non-continuity editing and so on).

everyman An archetypal character with whom the audience can readily identify and whose actions, within a film narrative, the audience is meant to follow.

fabula Refers to the chronological sequencing of events that make up a story.

film noir First and foremost a style of filmmaking rather than a genre, the term originates with films, first produced in the forties, that share certain cinematic/narrative conventions (shadowy low key lighting, urban setting, the femme fatale…).

genre Relates to the kind of story being told, and the anticipated conventions associated with a particular story type.

hypotext/hypertext Terms first employed by literary theorist Gerard

Genette to explore the relationship between adaptation and source text; 'hypotext' relates to the source text and 'hypertext' relates to the adaptation.

intertextuality Infers a complex, ongoing relationship/interdepencency between texts, through allusion, borrowing, citation, imitation, and so on (term first introduced by Julia Kristeva).

metafiction Relates to literature in which the writer self-consciously and systematically calls attention to the writing process, highlighting its constructed nature.

metteur-en-scène Refers in a literal sense to one who puts things into a scene (stage or screen) though it is now associated with screen directors who (unlike auteurs) are deemed technically able practitioners rather than creatives with a personal distinctive style across a body of work.

mise-en-scène Refers to everything within a given on-screen frame (props, costume, lighting, camera movement, shot type, sound, positioning of objects/performers), and provides a visual/aural mode of constructing meaning.

neologism Relates to a newly created word/phrase, often understood only by the creator and sometimes seen as symptomatic of psychological instability.

neo-Victorian A term that has recently emerged to describe contemporary creative works that consciously engage with the art, history and literature of the Victorian period.

non-diegetic sound Relates to sounds that do not form part of/occur within the screen world (musical score, voiceover, sound effects), and are added for dramatic effect post shoot.

postcolonialism A mode of cultural criticism that explores the relationship between colonized and colonizer mainly through analysis of the literature of countries/cultures formerly under the control of the European colonizer.

postfeminism Referring to that which comes after the politics of second wave feminism, it is a problematic term that infers a more popularized, individualistic mode of female 'politics'.

postmodernism A term that refers, in this context, to an artistic style that purposely references/reproduces/imitates fragments of existing objects/narratives/concepts.

sjuzhet Relates to the representation of story events (order of presentation, means of presentation).

the canon Traditionally refers to texts artistically defined and widely viewed as works of creative genius. In the context of adaptation studies the term can be applied to works of literature and screen.

the gaze Also referred to as 'the look', this term originates in film theory; grounded in psychoanalysis, it relates to the desires and pleasures of the spectator, and the way in which the object of the gaze (or look) is perceived.

Index